The Novels of Hermann Hesse

THE
NOVELS OF
HERMANN HESSE

A Study in
Theme and Structure

‣»)‣»

THEODORE ZIOLKOWSKI

PRINCETON UNIVERSITY PRESS · PRINCETON · N.J.

52177

Publication of this book has been aided by
the Ford Foundation Program to support publication,
through university presses, of works in
the humanities and social sciences.

Printed in the United States of America
by Princeton University Press, Princeton, New Jersey

For Hermann J. Weigand

"Der junge Schüler erlaubt sich,
dem Älteren Bruder seine
Aufwartung zu machen."
(*Das Glasperlenspiel*)

Preface

THIS BOOK has grown considerably in purpose and scope since its conception. I originally intended to attempt no more than a structural and technical analysis of Hesse's major novels. In a chapter on Hesse (in his *Kritische Essays zur europäischen Literatur*) Ernst Robert Curtius remarked that "thematic and technical analysis—this rarely practiced art—is the only adequate method for the interpretation of an author." It seemed to me that the vast library of Hesse scholarship revealed a conspicuous deficiency in studies of the technical aspects of his works—of "Hesse's Craftsmanship" (the title I contemplated at first). It gradually became apparent, however, that my individual interpretations suffered from a certain repetitiveness. Several themes came up constantly and had to be discussed anew in the context of each novel I treated. So I decided to deal with these main themes separately as an introduction to the structural analyses.

At the same time, I began to see more and more clearly a general pattern of development in the novels from *Demian* to *The Glass Bead Game*: Hesse's attempt to formulate his vision of the ideal, which grew from the vague image of a spiritual kingdom to the very specific conception of an aesthetic realm. This autonomous kingdom of art, called Castalia in the last novel, is ultimately rejected in favor of a new existential commitment to the world. I have tried to stress this development "to Castalia and beyond"—another rejected title—from chapter to chapter in Part Two.

Finally—and at this point I began to worry about shattering any form the book might have—I wanted very much to point out an aspect of Hesse's work that is generally overlooked or flatly denied: his close ties, thematically and structurally, with many of the major writers of the twentieth century. My attempt to "locate" Hesse in modern literature necessitated, in turn, a somewhat unorthodox treatment of his frequently mentioned "romanticism"—a discussion I purposely postponed to an epilogue for reasons that I hope will be persuasive.

Several of my critical evaluations—notably of *Narziss and Goldmund* and *The Glass Bead Game*—depart perceptibly from the general tenor of Hesse criticism. Since they are based in every case on structural analyses, I hope that they will be taken as evidence of more than merely personal predilection. It is probably superfluous to say that this book is a labor of love. Hesse's works have meant much to me for many years, and I have made no effort to temper the missionary zeal noted by several people who were kind enough to read my manuscript. At the same time, some of his novels, as *novels*, are less successful than others. I have tried to judge them according to the criterion upon which Hesse repeatedly insisted: their craft as fiction.

Because my approach is determined by problems of theme and structure, I have restricted myself, in the notes, to the most relevant secondary works; it would have been impossible to list the many books and articles that helped me in a more general way. If the specialist notes, here and there, that I have neglected to mention other interpretations, it is not because I regard my own as exclusive and restrictive (though I hope they are valid!), but rather because I was reluctant to interrupt the main line of argument in order to suggest perfectly plausible, but structurally irrelevant alternatives. In connection with Hesse and otherwise I am an advocate of critical perspectivism. The reader who wishes to go further into Hesse research would do well to consult two works that I have used often and gratefully: Joseph Mileck's critical bibliography, *Hermann*

Hesse and His Critics (Chapel Hill, N.C., 1957) and
Helmut Waibler's *Hermann Hesse: Eine Bibliographie*
(Bern und München, 1962).

Since I wrote with the general reader in mind—the
number of Hesse enthusiasts in America has been growing
slowly but with gratifying steadiness for several years—I
have supplied a certain amount of background information
regarding Hesse, some of the sources he used, and some of
the traditions within which he operated. All quotations
have been given in English, and in every case the translations are my own. There is no standard translation of
Hesse's works; the available ones are sometimes misleading
at crucial points; and most of the letters, essays, and
shorter pieces to which I refer constantly have never been
translated at all. (I have indicated a few important exceptions in the notes.) What my own translations may lack
in grace and felicity, I hope to have offset by precision and
a certain consistency of tone. The notes cite volume and
page of the standard six-volume edition published in 1952
by Suhrkamp (GD=*Gesammelte Dichtungen*); volume 7
was added in 1957 when the first edition was reprinted as
Gesammelte Schriften (=GS).

Much of the groundwork for the book was accomplished
during a Fulbright Research Grant to Germany in 1958-59.
I am also grateful to the American Philosophical Society
for a grant that made it possible for me, that same year,
to spend time in the Hesse archives of the Schiller-Nationalmuseum in Marbach. I should like to express my thanks
to the staff of the Schiller-Nationalmuseum, who were most
helpful and cooperative; and to Erich Weiss, who assembled the Westdeutsches Hermann-Hesse-Archiv that now
constitutes the core of the collection in Marbach.

My colleagues Inge Halpert and George Nordmeyer

were good enough to read the manuscript when I first completed it and to give me the encouragement necessary at that stage. I am especially indebted to Victor Lange and Ralph Freedman for their generous, frank, and knowledgeable suggestions; it was largely due to their comments —though perhaps not fully in their sense—that I decided to write a separate epilogue on Hesse "between romanticism and existentialism."

Long before the book was finished, Princeton University Press indicated a gratifying interest in my topic. I want to thank Miss R. Miriam Brokaw for her efforts on my behalf and Mrs. Gail M. Filion for her sensitive and sensible job of editing.

Two chapters have already appeared separately: chapter 3 in *Monatshefte für deutschen Unterricht*, 53 (1961), and chapter 9 in *Modern Language Quarterly*, 19 (1958). They are reprinted here in substantially revised and expanded form with the permission of the editors. Harcourt, Brace & World, Inc., has allowed me to quote two passages from T. S. Eliot's "Four Quartets" that appeared in *The Complete Poems and Plays, 1909-1950* (New York, 1952).

My final thanks go to my wife Yetta, who has always been my fiercest critic and patient typist. Her enthusiasm helped me through those dreadful moments when one's best ideas seem suddenly to be hopelessly trivial and scarcely worth putting on paper. She joins me in the sincere friendship and admiration expressed in the dedication.

Theodore Ziolkowski

Hastings-on-Hudson, New York
June 1964

Contents

PART I. THE THEMES

"Just imagine some professor, a hundred years from now, preaching to his students: Klingsor, born in 1877, and his contemporary Louis, called The Glutton; innovaters of painting, liberation from the naturalism of color; on closer scrutiny this pair of artists falls into three clearly distinguishable periods! I'd rather die under the wheels of a locomotive today."

"It would be better if the professors would fall under the wheels."

"They don't make such big locomotives. You know how petty our technology is."

(Hesse, *Klingsor's Last Summer*)

Years of Crisis

IN 1919 the novel *Demian* appeared in Germany under the name of Emil Sinclair. The immediate and enthusiastic response that the work elicited from the younger generation; the excited speculations regarding its author that were aroused among critics and admirers such as Thomas Mann; the intensification of public curiosity when the publishers returned the coveted Fontane Prize for first novels, announcing that the author was not a novice just breaking into print; and finally, several months later, the astonishing disclosure that Hermann Hesse was the author of this angry-young-man's book—all of these facts belong to Hesse's biography and to literary history in general, but they tend to obscure the heart of the affair. It was no desire for literary sensationalism that prompted Hesse to adopt a pseudonym; he was in fact no longer the same writer that the public knew so well, but a totally different man, entitled to a new name and a fresh reputation.

Like the hero of Max Frisch's novel *Stiller*, who returns to Switzerland with a different name and defiantly protests "I'm not Stiller," Hesse was rebelling against the identity into which he had, not unwillingly, allowed himself to be thrust for over ten years by an admiring public. Ever since the success of *Peter Camenzind* (1904) Hesse had enjoyed the reputation of a gifted, entertaining writer. His fiction and poetry were of sufficiently high merit to win the acclaim of contemporaries such as Thomas Mann, Stefan

Zweig, Rilke, and many others; at the same time he was one of the most commercially successful authors of the enterprising S. Fischer publishing house. His works were tinged with the bittersweet melancholy that is a frequent key of literature in the years preceding World War I—the products of a talented writer who suffered from the sobering realization that his own poetry would not match his cherished ideals of the past—Goethe, Mörike, Hölderlin, Novalis—and who exploited this sense of epigonalism in poignantly elegiac poems such as "In the Fog," "Melancholy," and "Resignation." The titles of his various collections of stories and poems from these years—*In this World* (1907), *Neighbors* (1908), *On the Road* (1911), *By-ways* (1912)—hint at the "other-directedness" and eschewal of serious problematics in most of these pleasant fictions.

It is true, of course, that the later Hesse is prefigured to a certain extent in these early works. However, source-seeking of this sort is an *a posteriori* pastime of readers looking back from the vantage point of later works. I frankly doubt whether Hesse, had his production ended with the outbreak of World War I, would be remembered as more than a talented exponent of pleasing tales after the fashion of acknowledged models such as Novalis, E. T. A. Hoffmann, and Gottfried Keller or neo-romantic poems in the manner of Mörike and Eichendorff. In the years before 1914 he certainly wrote nothing like Rilke's *New Poems* and *Malte Laurids Brigge* or Thomas Mann's *Buddenbrooks*, *Tonio Kröger*, and *Death in Venice*— works that assured their authors a place in the first rank regardless of what might come later. Some critics have ascribed prophetic significance to the last major work of this period, the novel *Rosshalde* (1914), suggesting that it foreshadows the inner turmoil in Hesse's own life as well as the outbreak of the war. To these well-meaning devotees one can only reply that there is not the least anticipation of external events in the sense that *The Steppenwolf* painted the conflict of World War II on the wall. The inner turmoil in the life of the painter Veraguth remains on a private level that reflects, to be sure, Hesse's own confused marital situation, but affords not the slightest hint of the almost archetypal self-seeking so characteristic of the later works. As a matter of fact, to the extent that Hesse can be identified with his hero, his own attitude toward his work on the very eve of the war is mirrored in the thoughts of Veraguth, who wished his paintings to be no more than "a perfect piece of craftsmanship": no deep problems, no profound comments on society and the world, no penetrating analyses of the individual psyche—just solid, respectable artistic workmanship.

This is not to belittle Hesse's early works. Conscientious craftsmanship has never been a quality to be disparaged, and *Peter Camenzind* is still an experience, like Thomas Wolfe's novels, that readers of a certain age and temperament should not miss. Yet there is a distinct and undeniable difference in temper and quality between these works and those of the major period. We must agree with Hesse, a shrewd and uncompromising judge of himself, when he characterizes his pre-war works as those of a talented popular author (*Unterhaltungsschriftsteller* or, worse yet, *Literat*). "I was considered a nice poet and lived at peace with the world."[1] In 1921, while writing the preface to a selected edition of his works, he became aware for the first time of the highly derivative nature of his early books. "From my childhood on I had loved and read those splendid masters of narrative, and out of this love there had arisen an imitation of which I was initially totally un-

---

[1] "Kurzgefasster Lebenslauf"; GD, IV, 475.

conscious and of which I later became only unclearly aware."[2] Because of this realization and because a wall of new experiences cut him off from the products of his youth, Hesse refused at that time to go through with the edition.

At times in his life, wrote Hesse in the essay *Mysteries* (1947), the writer feels a compelling urge to brush past the facile and accepted generalizations about life and to look the world in the face. The unmasking of reality can be precipitated by any sudden jolt in our lives—war, illness, misfortune—but when it happens, the shock of perception is severe enough "to render questionable all order, all comfort, all security, all faith, all knowledge."[3] It was a crisis of this sort that transformed Hesse from simply another best-selling writer of the decade 1904-1914 into the exciting, probing author of *Demian*, whose hitherto unquestioned reality had suddenly revealed itself as a perilous, seething turmoil. Like Rilke's Malte Laurids Brigge, Hesse found himself to be a "beginner in his own circumstances." In his letters he speaks of a "new note"[4] to be detected in his works from the time of *Demian* on.

Much of the literature and art of the twentieth century is predicated on the assumption that traditional standards of value have collapsed. To some writers, such as Hugo von Hofmannsthal, this revelation came quite early; many others became aware of the inner disintegration of nineteenth-century standards only after the war had completed the process externally, rendering it symbolically visible. Yet it seems safe to say that modern writers, in contrast to those who happened merely by an accident of birth to be living in the twentieth century—Stephen Spender speaks of

[2] "Vorrede eines Dichters zu seinen ausgewählten Werken"; GS, VII, 251.

[3] "Geheimnisse"; GS, VII, 789.   [4] GS, VII, 514.

"moderns" and "contemporaries"—distinguish themselves by this awareness that the former order has dissolved into chaos and by their attempts to come to terms with the new face of reality. In Hesse's case the crisis was precipitated by a series of blows during the years 1914-1917 that, hammerlike, reduced his former way of life, the comfortable reality of a successful *belletriste*, to a shambles.

In his "Conjectural Biography" (1925)[5] Hesse wrote that the First World War brought about the second major turning point in his life. (The first had been his decision, at the age of thirteen, to become a writer.) As a result of the war he came into conflict with the world with which he had previously lived in harmony. "Through this experience I crossed, for the first time, over the threshold of initiation into life." Until 1914 Hesse had not been strongly committed to any cause. As a founder and editor of the periodical *März* he had taken potshots at Wilhelm II, but this sort of criticism, directed more against the person of the Kaiser himself than his government or policies, was one of the accepted literary sports of the day. Hesse was in no sense politically *engagé*.

The outbreak of the war altered that. Although Hesse had been living in Switzerland since 1912, he still considered himself a German (and did not, in fact, become a Swiss citizen until 1923). He had assumed that there existed a sense of understanding and solidarity between himself and his readers, but the violent public reaction to his pacifistic essays in 1914 and 1915 showed how mistaken that assumption was. Subscriptions were canceled, book dealers refused to handle his works, he was branded

[5] "Kurzgefasster Lebenslauf"; GD, IV, 469-489. Translated by Denver Lindley in *Modern Writing no. 2* (New York, 1954), pp. 55-72.

as a traitor by the German press, poison-pen letters began flowing across the border, and even old "friends" in Germany terminated their relations with the "viper that they had nurtured at their breast." Previously uncommitted, a happy wanderer in his own private world of make-believe and sweet elegies, Hesse now began to look around and, for the first time, seriously to examine the world of reality. In one of the "objectionable" essays (which led to his friendship with the similarly minded Romain Rolland) he discerned signs of "a pernicious confusion in thinking."[6] Beginning in his own sacrosanct world of the spirit, he noted alarming symptoms. German patents were being disregarded in Russia, German music boycotted in France, and foreign books ceased to be translated or reviewed in Germany. Worst of all, the very individuals who should have stemmed this tide of unreasonable hatred—writers, professors, journalists—were eagerly volunteering their services to stir up the floods of calumny. For Hesse this was the supreme *trahison des clercs*, the most degrading form of blasphemy against the spirit, and it led to his "political awakening."[7]

Despite his rejection by official German spokesmen, Hesse tried to do his part for the country he still considered his home. Opposed though he was to the nationalistic fervor of the German war effort, Hesse was still a patriot. "I am a German," he wrote in that same essay of 1914, "and my sympathies and wishes belong to Germany." But he now realized that it was impossible to remain totally without commitment. He continued, in a series of articles in newspapers and periodicals, to plead for understanding and love among men. He put himself at the disposal of the German Consulate in Bern, where he had been living

[6] "O Freunde, nicht diese Töne!"; GS, VII, 44-50.
[7] Letter of Nov. 5, 1945; GS, VII, 647.

since 1912, and was engaged for the duration of the war in the care of prisoners of war interned in Switzerland and elsewhere. Impervious to the network of espionage and political intrigue that surrounded him, Hesse visited internment camps, edited a bi-weekly literary supplement (*Sonntagsbote für die deutschen Kriegsgefangenen*), contributed to another newspaper for prisoners of war (*Deutsche Internierten-Zeitung*), and helped to edit a series of literary pamphlets for soldiers. This frenzy of selfless activity probably did more than anything else to preserve Hesse's sanity, but in 1916 a succession of personal shocks shattered this enforced composure. First his father died. His youngest son, Martin, became seriously ill for more than a year just at the time when his wife's mental derangement made it imperative for her to be committed, for a time, to an institution. These calamities, coupled with the effects of the war, brought Hesse so close to a nervous breakdown that his physician urged psychiatric treatment. This period, which he later called "the hellish journey through myself,"[8] was the crucial turning point in Hesse's life and career.

During 1916 and 1917, in the sanitarium Sonnmatt near Lucerne, Hesse underwent some seventy-two psychiatric sessions with Joseph B. Lang, a disciple of C. G. Jung. (Lang became a personal friend and, in the next few years, appeared sporadically in Hesse's writings under the pseudonyms "Longus" and "Pistorius.") This treatment, which Hesse describes symbolically in *Demian* through the friendship of Sinclair and Pistorius, led Hesse to a total reexamination of his life and beliefs. Scrutinizing his previous ideals, he found them to be hollow. Dismayed at first by the disparity between his Romantic notions and the reality of the war, he subsequently realized that the disorder

[8] GS, IV, 481.

was not only in the world but in himself. When he looked beyond the tidy little existence that he had constructed for himself into his own soul, he saw that there was just as much conflict there as in the outside world—conflict that he had formerly been unwilling to acknowledge, sublimating it instead into the inchoate longing for an elegiac past. Now he had no right to throw stones at others, to point accusing fingers at the world. He shared in a common guilt, for his was no isolated case, but rather an almost archetypal model for suffering humanity as a whole.

Psychoanalysis altered Hesse's life and works. It enabled him to understand himself more fully than ever before, to look deep into his heart and acknowledge his own guilt in the evil that had befallen him and the world. And it was reflected both directly and indirectly in the books that he wrote from this time on. It would be a mistake, however, to interpret Hesse's later works one-sidedly from the psychological standpoint,[9] for even during the period of his greatest fascination with psychoanalysis—1916 to 1922—Hesse's interest was tempered by a certain skepticism. To be sure, he was deeply impressed in 1916 when he read Jung's epoch-making study on *The Transformations and Symbols of the Libido* (*Wandlungen und Symbole der Libido*, 1912), a work that contributed to the shaping of symbols in the novel *Demian*. That same year, through Dr. Lang, Hesse met Jung. Later he read selections from his works to Jung's psychoanalytic association in Zürich, and around 1921 Hesse had a few analytic sessions with the master himself. "Then too I got a nice impression of him, but I began to realize at that time

[9] For a discussion of the complicated problem of Hesse and psychology as well as a critique of the relevant bibliography see Joseph Mileck, *Hermann Hesse and His Critics* (Chapel Hill, N.C., 1958), pp. 158-166.

that, for analysts, a genuine relationship to art is unattainable; they lack the organ for it."[10] (Precisely this attitude characterizes Sinclair's criticism of Pistorius in *Demian*.) For this reason Jung's claim, years later, that he directly influenced the writing of *Demian*, *Siddhartha*, and *The Steppenwolf* must be taken with a grain of salt.[11] Hesse, by his own acknowledgment, profited from the stimulation of Jung and Lang, but he also makes it clear that his goals lay beyond psychoanalysis. He exploited his experience of psychoanalysis whenever it was relevant within the framework of his novels (e.g. *Demian*), but, in conception, his art transcends the scientific goals of psychology.

As early as 1918 Hesse had formulated these views in the essay "Artists and Psychoanalysis."[12] He states first that he studied, besides Jung, the writings of Freud, Stekel, and other prominent psychologists of his generation. These studies did not supply him with anything new, he maintains, but merely provided him with the scientific confirmation of psychological insights that he had already gleaned from such poets and writers as Jean Paul and Nietzsche.[13] Secondly, Hesse insists that the new methods of psychoanalysis can be of value to the artist only if the analysis is "not merely an intellectual affair, but a real experience." In other words, through his own contact with analysis Hesse was now in a position to apply the theories

[10] Benjamin Nelson, "Hesse and Jung. Two Newly Recovered Letters," *The Psychoanalytic Review*, 50 (1963), 11-16. The letters from Jung and Hesse to Emanuel Maier were written in 1950, in response to a specific inquiry regarding their relationship.

[11] *Ibid.*, p. 15.

[12] "Künstler und Psychoanalyse"; GS, VII, 137-143.

[13] This is, by the way, an attitude not unlike Joyce's, who once remarked: "I don't believe in any science, but my imagination grows when I read Vico as it doesn't when I read Freud or Jung." Quoted by Richard Ellmann, *James Joyce* (New York, 1959), p. 706.

with more justification than most salon psychiatrists. Analysis, he continues, "teaches us to see, to acknowledge, to investigate and to take seriously those things which we had most successfully suppressed within ourselves, which generations had suppressed under constant pressure." Finally, he emphasizes that the poet cannot stop at the limits beyond which the analyst hesitates to advance.

"What analysis recognized and formulated scientifically had always been known by the poets—yes, the poet revealed himself as the representative of a special kind of thinking that actually ran counter to analytical-psychological thought. He was the dreamer; the analyst was the interpreter of his dreams. Was any course left for the poet, despite all his interest in the new psychology, but to dream on and to follow the summons of his unconscious?"

The writer's responsibility leads him beyond psychology into other realms of experience and expression—the realms of the new fictional world that Hesse was about to create.[14]

External changes, related in more detail in the story *Klein and Wagner* (1919), paralleled the inner transformations.[15] Separated from his wife, his children in the care of friends, Hesse left Bern in 1919 and moved to Montagnola near Lugano in lush southern Switzerland. Here he began writing books of a new, disturbing nature, heralded by *Demian*, the first product of his revaluation. It was his secret hope that the feelings of guilt and responsibility that he had conceived in his own inner self could be awakened in many hearts. Renewed innocence—for the

[14] Oscar Seidlin, "Hermann Hesse: The Exorcism of the Demon," *Symposium*, 4 (1950), 325-348, is the most outspoken opponent of the narrow psychological interpretation of Hesse's works, which Seidlin regards, rather, as existential and mythic.

[15] For an analysis see Heinz W. Puppe, "Psychologie und Mystik in *Klein und Wagner* von Hermann Hesse," *PMLA*, 78 (1963), 128-135.

individual as well as humanity as a whole—is possible only
if one acknowledges one's sufferings and guilt, enduring it
to the end instead of seeking the guilt in others. In "Zarathustra's Return" (1919) he stated the problem bluntly.
Answering the young men who felt that it was selfish of
the individual to devote himself to his own problems when
the welfare of his country is at stake, Zarathustra remarks:
"Don't you believe that, ultimately, a fatherland is health-
ier and thrives better if every invalid is not reading his own
ailments into it, if every sufferer is not trying to cure it?"[16]
Instead of the melancholy tales of his early period, dealing
with the vague subjective yearnings of dissatisfied artists,
Hesse now wrote problematic, searching novels that pierced
mythically to the heart of human existence. In sharp contrast to the "other-directed" titles of his earlier works, the
first fruits of the new period—*Siddhartha, Klein and
Wagner*, and *Klingsor*—were republished in 1931 under a
collective title borrowed from Novalis: *The Inward Way*.[17]
These uncomfortable works drove off many of his former
readers, who had been glad to participate vicariously in
the romantic yearnings of his early heroes but were unwilling to incur any guilt by association with these radical
new protagonists—the unruly outsiders who people Hesse's
books from 1917 on.

Two of the most characteristic essays from the productive year of 1919 are "Zarathustra's Return" and "Self-
Reliance."[18] In the latter (published originally under the
pseudonym Emil Sinclair), Hesse advances the idea, so

[16] "Zarathustras Wiederkehr"; GS, VII, 210.
[17] The actual phraseology in the sixteenth of Novalis's *Blüten-
staub* fragments is: "Nach Innen geht der geheimnisvolle Weg."
[18] "Eigensinn"; GS, VII, 194-200. The title means literally something like "self-will" or even "obstinacy"; but the definition that
emerges in the course of the essay justifies, I believe, the more
meaningful translation.

important to him from this time on, that the individual must have moral courage enough to live according to his own inner dictates. This self-reliance, however, necessarily entails a feeling of alienation and loneliness. In "Zarathustra's Return," which is patterned after Nietzsche's style, there is a special section "On Loneliness." Loneliness, Zarathustra says, "is the road by which destiny strives to lead man to himself." In order to become a man, one must break all ties with the past and venture alone into the future. It is a road that most people never follow to the end, for even though many men may leave father and mother, they seek new security in love and companionship. "Living without a mother is wretched, my friends; living is wretched without home, without fatherland, without a people, and without fame, and without all the amenities of society." Yet anyone who wishes to discover his own true nature must be willing to sacrifice all these things, as Hesse was forced to do, and to live "self-reliantly."

Hesse has referred to this as a time of daily leave-taking. He had left his wife and family, his home, his comfortable existence, his popular reputation, his whole stock of facile ideals—and his name. For the name of Hermann Hesse was associated with all the old values that his new commitments had forced him to discard. To be absolutely consistent he must have a new name for the new man. He chose Emil Sinclair, the name that appeared on the title page of *Demian* when it was published in 1919. Hesse used it as the pseudonym for several important essays that he wrote between 1917 and 1920. Out of the spiritual vacuum created by his years of crisis and revaluation new values and ideals had to emerge. The creation of values out of chaos was to be the work of the years to come.

2

Totality: Magical Thinking

IN MAY 1922, T. S. Eliot visited Hesse in Montagnola. Two months earlier he had written to explain the reason for his interest: "During a recent trip to Switzerland I became acquainted with your book, *Blick ins Chaos*, for which I have formed a great admiration. I find in your book a concern with serious problems that has not yet penetrated to England, and I should like to spread its reputation. . . ."[1] It is a fact of literary history that Eliot attempted to do just that by calling attention to the little volume of essays in his notes to *The Waste Land*, which appeared that same year. (In the same volume of *Criterion* he published an essay by Hesse on "Recent German Poetry."[2]

What was the quality of Hesse's essays that appealed to Eliot and many other writers and thinkers of his gen-

[1] Quoted in *Hermann Hesse. Eine Chronik in Bildern*, ed. Bernard Zeller (Frankfurt am Main, 1960), p. 109. The letter, which is in French, was written on March 13, 1922: ". . . Pendant un voyage récent dans la Suisse j'ai fait la connaissance de votre 'Blick ins Chaos', pour lequel j'ai conçu une grande admiration. Je trouve votre 'Blick ins Chaos' d'un sérieux qui n'est pas encore arrivé en Angleterre, et je voudrais en répandre la réputation. . . ."

[2] *Criterion* (October 1922), pp. 89-93. For further information on the contact between Hesse and Eliot, see the letter from Eliot quoted by G. W. Field, "Hermann Hesse as Critic of English and American Literature," *Monatshefte für deutschen Unterricht*, 53 (April-May 1961), p. 158, n. 7. Eliot's attention was drawn to Hesse by Sydney Schiff, who gave him a copy of *Blick ins Chaos* to read and later (1923), under the pen-name Stephen Hudson, translated the two central essays into English. Eliot's memories of the visit are rather vague.

eration? The answer lies in the intellectual climate of
Europe at the beginning of the twentieth century. One of
the most striking phenomena of the age, if not the most
striking as Erich Kahler has maintained in an important
study,[3] was the breakdown of traditional views of reality.
Not only in physics, where Planck and Einstein had shattered classical conceptions of matter, time, and space—in
every area of intellectual activity the old categories were
falling apart. Nineteenth-century theology had reduced
Christ to a purely historical or mythical figure (David
Friedrich Strauss and Ernest Renan) or saw in God no
more than a projection of man's own image (Ludwig Feuerbach). In psychology Freud and Jung were tearing down
the comfortable concepts of deterministic behavior and
forging a vastly more complicated image of man than had
been hitherto assumed; while the emergence of nationalistic
minorities and the growth of new social classes played
havoc with customary theories of politics and economics.
The budding fields of anthropology and sociology insisted
upon the relativity of standards of ethics and morality,
thus undermining the already shaky foundations of Vic-
torian and Wilhelmine society. Developments of this sort,
through which science destroyed the totality of the past
without being able to replace it with a new unity, led to
the anti-intellectualism heralded, in France, by Brunetière's
outcry against the "bankruptcy of science"[4] and to the
attempt of poets and novelists to construct new visions
of totality to replace the disorder created by the break-

[3] "Untergang und Übergang der epischen Kunstform," *Die
neue Rundschau*, 64 (1953), 1-44. This topic has, of course, received much attention in recent years. Another imaginative study
is offered by R. M. Alberes, *L'Aventure intellectuelle du XXe
siècle* (Paris, 1950).

[4] In his famous essay "Après une visite au Vatican," *Revue des
deux mondes* (January 1895), 97-118.

down of traditional reality. Science had revealed a world that, from the atom to politics, was no longer a homogeneous whole, but rather a chaos of discrete and often conflicting parts. The order of the past, no matter how false and superficial it may have been, had given way to a meaningless present in which the individual was constantly confronted with apparently hostile forces at work against each other.

Much of the writing of our century represents the attempt of artists to come to terms with this chaos by giving it a new form: Joyce's *Ulysses*, Gide's *The Counterfeiters*, Broch's *Sleepwalkers*—the examples could be multiplied indefinitely. In his standard work on *Painting in the Twentieth Century* Werner Haftmann specifically mentions the quantum theory and relativity as factors that set off the artistic revolution of the first decade of the century, and he is able to document the impact of the scientific destruction of totality—e.g. the splitting of the atom—on artists such as Marc and Kandinsky.[5] The same factors —relativity and the loss of a common center to which everything can be related—are reflected in the development of the twelve-tone system in music just before 1920, as Hans von Dettelbach has argued.[6]

Like so many others, Hesse was preoccupied with the dilemma, and his most incisive analysis is expressed in the essays of the volume *In Sight of Chaos* (1920), which Eliot admired.[7] Particularly the first two, written in 1919,

---

[5] *Malerei im 20. Jahrhundert*; esp. *Textband* (3rd ed., München, 1963), p. 210, and *Tafelband* (München, 1955), pp. 9-31.

[6] *Breviarium Musicae. Probleme, Werke, Gestalten* (Darmstadt, 1958), pp. 365-366.

[7] I quote from "Die Brüder Karamasoff oder Der Untergang Europas" (GS, VII, 161-178) and "Gedanken zu Dostojewskijs *Idiot*" (GS, VII, 178-186). Stephen Hudson's translation (Zürich, 1923) contains only these two essays. The first essay also appeared separately in *Dial*, 72 (1922), 607-618; more recently it

are of importance here. (The third, Hesse's thoughts on certain developments in modern poetry, has no relation to the first two and was not included later in the definitive edition of his works.) They begin as analyses of Dostoevsky's *The Brothers Karamazov* and *The Idiot*, but proceed to develop a personal interpretation of the course of European civilization. Hesse's ideas, in many respects, parallel those of Oswald Spengler, whose *Decline of the West* was appearing in the same years (1918 to 1922). But Hesse read Spengler only after completion of his own essays,[8] and, in any case, his ideas emerge so organically from the whole pattern of his thought that there can be no question of influence. We have here another case of independent expression of a theme common to the times. (It has been noted often enough that Spengler and Toynbee owe the popularity of their theories to the fact that their works responded to a general public mood.)

Hesse's essays, as is frequently the case when writers discuss the works of their peers, are a truer reflection of his own thought than of Dostoevsky's. Hermann Bahr, the Protean dramatist and critic, whose early radicalism had simmered down to a slow-boiling conservatism by the 1920's, attacked the interpretation when it appeared,[9] and there is certainly justification for some of the criticism. One should really read the studies as one reads, for instance, Hermann Broch's essays on Joyce or Hofmannsthal, or Thomas Mann's essay on Goethe: as splendid expressions of the author's own views and sympathies and hence

---

was translated by Harvey Gross in *Western Review*, 17 (1953), 185-195.

[8] Joseph Mileck, *Hermann Hesse and His Critics: The Criticism of Half a Century* (Chapel Hill, N.C., 1958), pp. 55-56.

[9] *Kritik der Gegenwart* (1922), pp. 92-98.

as invaluable documents for the development of the writer himself.

The essay on *The Brothers Karamazov* bears the subtitle "The Decline of Europe," for Hesse feels that a new spirit, the ideal of the Karamazovs, is beginning to take over the mind of Europe, destroying all traditional beliefs. This Karamazovian ideal is, in brief, "the departure from all established ethics and morality in favor of an attempt to understand everything, to accept everything," and Hesse finds this ideal perfectly represented in the figures of Alyosha, Ivan, and other central figures of the Russian classic. Their actions are characterized by an amorality that does not make rigid distinctions between "good" and "bad" but is capable, rather, of determining what is divine or sacred even in the most profane aspects of reality. As this spirit transgresses upon Europe, the traditional boundaries between right and wrong are effaced, and the decline of Graeco-Roman, Judaeo-Christian Europe becomes imminent. In this Russian Man, good and bad, God and Satan, are one and the same. He worships a god who is at the same time the devil and who resides in a (Nietzschean) realm beyond good and evil.

If we pause to locate Hesse's theory in the context of the breakdown of reality, we see that his Russian Man accepts and condones all conflicting discrete elements as part of a greater whole, whereas European Men, in the face of a disintegrating reality, have arbitrarily formalized a certain set of rules into an ethical code because they are unwilling to face the consequences of a total relativization of all things. Confronted with the statement that A and B are equally valid, and unwilling to make a free choice, they codify their behavior: A is good and B is bad. They believe in a God who praises A and rejects B, or what

Hesse, in "Zarathustra's Return," called "this wretched old faith in the sacred opposites." This type of European Man occurs frequently in literature at the turn of the century—as in Hermann Sudermann's naturalistic tragedy *Honor*—but it is exemplified best perhaps by many characters in the novels of the late nineteenth-century realist Theodor Fontane, who insist upon upholding for the sake of society standards that they secretly realize to be obsolete (e.g., *Effi Briest*).

In his study of *The Sacred and the Profane*, Mircea Eliade found that one characteristic of tradition-bound societies is the dichotomy between the realm that they inhabit and the unknown and undetermined space that surrounds it.

"Their area is the 'world,' the cosmos. The other is no longer a cosmos, but a sort of 'other world,' a strange chaotic space in which ghosts, demons and 'strangers' dwell. . . . Every inhabited area is a 'cosmos' only because it has been previously consecrated, because it is the work of the gods or is in relation to the world of the gods."[10]

Eliade has determined anthropologically precisely the same relationship between chaos, cosmos, and religion that Hesse assumes in his essay. But for Hesse the whole relationship is internalized, as it were: chaos and cosmos exist within man, not in the world outside; and the selection (or creation) of an adequate deity is based upon man's reaction to those inner impulses.

The Karamazovs yearn for a deity who acknowledges and represents both A and B—for whom polarities have ceased to exist, because he views life from a perspective that transcends these opposites, embracing them all. From

[10] *Das Heilige und das Profane. Vom Wesen des Religiösen* (Hamburg, 1957; Rowohlts deutsche Enzyklopädie 31), p. 18.

the absolute standpoint of tradition, this revolt against accepted standards may seem criminal, but actually it is the same attitude exemplified by *The Rebel*, of whom Camus wrote: "In every rebellion is to be found the metaphysical demand for unity, the impossibility of capturing it, and the construction of a substitute universe." Hesse stresses the fact that his Russian Man is not a willful criminal. Generally he is satisfied merely "to think of crime, to dream of it, to be acquainted with its very possibility." For the criminal act, the *acte gratuit* in Gide's sense, is an extreme case, almost an existential *Grenzsituation*. Normally it suffices merely to think "criminally," that is, to acknowledge the validity of all things, the potentiality of all deeds. In one of his pamphlets (*L'Existentialisme est un humanisme*, 1946), Sartre defined the starting point of existentialism as the moment when Dostoevsky said that everything would be possible if God did not exist. This is precisely the situation of Hesse's Russian Man, for he must live without recourse to a facile ethical code. If the deity is conceived as a being that embraces both God and Satan, then Hesse's Russian Man is *de facto* in the same position as Sartre's existentialist, although the latter acknowledges no deity whatsoever. Both types are similar in that they have taken upon themselves the burden of freedom and the responsibility of choice in the face of collapsing values. (This is, of course, a characteristic modern attitude. In his theory of "Humane Politics" Hermann Broch outlined a similar code of ethics.)

Russian Man, Hesse continues, is a person who acknowledges the unconscious urges and impulses within himself. European culture has traditionally striven to reject, repress, and ignore these creatural impulses, to deny their very existence. The Karamazovs—and here Hesse is talking the language of Freud and Jung—peer into the chaos within their breasts and are healed by this act of self-recognition. The whole decline of Europe is nothing more than the act of coming to grips with the subconscious. It will thus be no violent political upheaval, but an internalized revolution. "It is possible that the whole 'decline of Europe' will take place 'only' inwardly, only in the souls of a generation, only in the reinterpretation of worn-out symbols, only in the transvaluation of spiritual values."

It is obvious that Hesse has a great deal in common with Nietzsche, Freud, Jung, and Spengler; yet his formulation of the problem is unique and represents Hesse's own answer to the disintegration of reality into chaos: instead of institutionalizing an arbitrary set of discrete elements, let us accept *all* of them as a manifestation of our natural reality. In his "Thoughts on Dostoevsky's *Idiot*," Hesse explains his conception more elaborately. The first essay defined the difference between European Man and Russian Man; the second explains by what means the acceptance of chaos is possible.

Myshkin, the hero of Dostoevsky's novel, is misunderstood, hated, and even feared by his fellows because his way of thinking is so completely different from theirs. It is not that he thinks less logically or more childishly-associatively than they: he simply denies the entire life, thought, and perception of the others. For him, reality is something wholly different, while their reality is like a shadow in his eyes. To be sure, Myshkin recognizes material values even though he has little use for them. His ideal is not an ascetic one that advocates denial of the world of apparent reality for the sake of the world of the spirit. He agrees completely to the mutual rights of nature and spirit and to the necessity of their interaction. Yet for the others this coexistence and justification of the two worlds is simply an intellectual conception, whereas for Myshkin it is life itself. He has actually stood on the magical boundary where everything is affirmed (during his epileptic seizures!), where every thought is true as well as its opposite. He realizes that no law and no formulation exists which is true and right except as seen from one pole, and every pole has its opposite. The person who even for an instant accepts the interchangeability of nature and spirit, of good and evil, is the worst enemy of all order, for at that point chaos begins. The greatest reality, in the sense of traditional human culture, is the dichotomy of the world in light and dark, good and evil, *fas* and *nefas*. But for Myshkin highest reality is the magical experience of the reversibility of all concepts, of the equally justified existence of both poles. *The Idiot*, thought to its logical conclusion, introduces a "matriarchy of the unconscious" and annihilates all culture. The future is uncertain, but the way which is shown is unambiguous: it is spiritual reevaluation. Leading beyond Myshkin, it demands "magical thinking," the acceptance of chaos, the return to the unordered, to the unconscious, to the formless, the animal and still farther back to all beginnings. Then men can be reborn.

Hesse's implications are clear. The inward way into the chaos of one's own nature leads man to the realization that he is the seat of a polarity between the opposite forces of spirit and nature. Man must accept this polarity positively, and the process of spiritual reevaluation through which this takes place is "magical thinking" (*magisches Denken*)—the search for a new totality through the acceptance of chaos. By way of elucidation it might be helpful to quote a contemporary view that accepts essentially the same process of reasoning. In *Science and Criticism* Herbert J. Muller writes:

"Emerson remarked that it is a good thing, now and then, to take a look at the landscape from between one's legs. Although this stunt might seem pointless when things are already topsy-turvy, it can be the more helpful then. One may say that what this chaotic world needs first of all is more *dis*sociation; by breaking up factitious alliances and oppositions, one may get at the deep uniformities."[11]

From the vantage point of these essays one can now understand what Hesse had in mind when he wrote in his "Conjectural Biography" (1925): "The magical view of life has always meant a lot to me."[12] An even more revealing indication can be found in a slightly earlier autobiographical sketch entitled "Childhood of the Magician."[13] Throughout this piercing self-analysis the theme of "magic" and "charm" recurs constantly. In the title Hesse considers himself as the "magician" since he is portraying the childhood of the magician. At the outset he writes: "I also knew how to make magic—an ability that I unfortunately lost at an early age and had to learn all over again when I was much older." The following passage explains what Hesse meant. As a child he felt dissatisfied with the common conception of "reality," which seemed to him to be nothing more than a foolish and arbitrary agreement on the part of adults. He was accustomed to reject this adult "reality" and it was his burning desire to transform it magically, to raise it, as it were, to a higher plane. While he was yet a child, this urge for transformation took on childish forms. In adult life the magic has simply been internalized: it is no longer the external world that he desires to transform, but his own inner world. In the tale

---

[11] Quoted in Walker Gibson, *The Limits of Language*. American Century Series (New York, 1962), p. 30.
[12] GD, IV, 485.
[13] "Kindheit des Zauberers"; GD, IV, 449-468.

"Within and Without" (1920)[14] Hesse defines magic as the ability to exchange inner and outer reality. This belief is confirmed again in the long essay *At the Spa*[15] (which appeared originally in 1924 under the title *Psychologia Balnearia*), where Hesse states that he believes in nothing so deeply as the essential unity of all things. All suffering and all evil stem from the fact that men as individuals no longer feel themselves to be inseparable parts of a great totality.

From passages such as these it is possible to deduce a system to Hesse's ideas on totality. The world, the macroanthropos, just like man, the microcosmos, is a unity comprising the forces of nature and spirit, night and day, inside and outside, and all other conceivable polar extremes. Ideally these forces are in perfect harmony, and the world is a stable unity of all opposites. Yet more often one pole has ascendancy over the other, and this condition is the basis of all human notions concerning good and evil. Good and evil are totally relative terms, depending for their validity upon the pole from which the subject views the object. Magical thinking is the capacity of the individual to see beyond the apparent disharmony of the polar opposites and to perceive the essential unity and totality of all things, within the individual as within the world.

The implications of "magical thinking" for Hesse's fiction cannot be overestimated, for only it can explain the visionary passages at the end of novels like *Siddhartha* and *Demian* or the "Magic Theater" in *The Steppenwolf*, which is no more than a symbolical exercise in magical thinking. In that section of the novel Harry Haller learns that his previous way of life, the arbitrary rejection of

[14] "Innen und Aussen"; GD, II, 836-850.
[15] *Kurgast. Aufzeichnungen von einer Badener Kur*; GD, IV, 7-115.

many aspects of reality, was false. He sees that he is actually capable of doing precisely the opposite in every case, whether it involves his attitudes toward sex or toward war. He finds in the Magic Theater that his polar conception of reality can easily give way to a view that embraces all manifestations of life. The first step is merely to acknowledge the chaos in our souls and in the world; the second step is to transcend the chaos by realizing that it is all a natural part of life.

Magical thinking reveals itself structurally in an important way, for it is responsible for many of the symbols and images that occur in Hesse's writings. The writer's task is not to philosophize, but to render ideas in a plausible form. The view that all polarities cease, that all opposites are resolved, expresses itself visually in the technique of delimitation, so characteristic of much poetry, painting, and music of the twentieth century. One thinks, for instance, of the poetry of Georg Trakl and Rilke, in which the borders between objects disappear and things flow one into the other; or of paintings by Marc Chagall or Kandinsky, in which objects, losing their normal contours, become part of a greater whole; or of twelve-tone compositions in which the individual notes, liberated from their prison of traditional chords and progressions, are allowed to associate freely with all other notes under the signature of a new unity.

Hesse's works are filled with symbols of unity and totality. Most of them, of course, can be fully comprehended only within the context of the work itself, but by way of anticipation let us mention briefly a few of the more outstanding symbols. In *Demian* Hesse employs the god Abraxas, who represents in Gnostic mysticism the unification of God and Satan; and in the same novel he makes use of the egg, traditionally a symbol of totality.

The Magic Theater in *The Steppenwolf*, as a projection of Harry Haller's inner nature into the outside world, is an externalization of the multifarious poles of his existence that, as he discovers, are by no means mutually exclusive. Here also, as in *Demian*, totality and delimitation are symbolized by the hermaphroditic nature of the women loved by the heroes (Frau Eva—Demian, and Hermann—Hermine). The Glass Bead Game, in the novel of that title, is an abstraction of all values of human culture that are invoked simultaneously in the game itself. Finally music, for Hesse just as for Hermann Broch, represents in almost every instance the symbolic manifestation of totality because in the counterpoint and harmony of music the most disparate elements can be brought together in a harmonious whole. It is not an exaggeration to say that every important symbol in Hesse's works is basically a representation of totality. This is certainly the case with fire, which is used symbolically in *Demian*, but which Hesse has described in its significance for himself as an individual in autobiographical documents like the idyll *Hours in the Garden* (1936). In fire, as in music or the Glass Bead Game, all elements are united and the boundaries between things disappear.

The symbol of metamorphosis plays a greater role in the stories, perhaps, than in the novels, although the Magic Theater of *The Steppenwolf* is a hymn to transformation of the Self. In *Pictor's Metamorphoses*,[16] a tale written in 1922, the whole plot revolves around the transformation of the hero, by means of a magical stone, into a tree. In such stories that partake of the fairy tale it is possible to render the theme of totality by means of the symbolic repre-

---

[16] *Piktors Verwandlungen* (Chemnitz, 1925). Not published in the collected works, but available in a facsimile edition by Suhrkamp Verlag (1954).

sentation of metamorphosis: one not only *thinks* of the totality of being, of the disappearance of boundaries between things; one literally *becomes* other things. Hesse took great delight in painting these transformations in the aquarelles included in the original manuscript edition.

In the novels, however, which have a more realistic basis, the symbol of fluidity is central. It is the final image in *Siddhartha*, when the hero finds unity and totality of being beside the river, and his very face begins to express the fluidity that he perceives there. The death of Klein in the story *Klein and Wagner* can likewise be interpreted only from the point of view of symbolic reunification with totality. In the other novels, in which the symbol of water is not so conspicuous as the river in *Siddhartha*, fluidity colors the language and imagery. In *The Steppenwolf*, for instance, at the peak of the action, Haller writes: "All the women of this feverish night had melted together and become one, who blossomed in my arms." At the end of *The Journey to the East*, when H. H. realizes that he and Leo are not actually opposites, as he had assumed, but complementary parts: ". . . I saw that my image was on the point of yielding itself more and more to Leo, and of flowing away, to nourish and strengthen him. In time, it seemed, all substance would flow from the one image into the other, and only a single one would be left: Leo."

Thus, like every major artist of his generation, Hesse faced the central problem of the early twentieth century: the breakdown of traditional reality in every area of life. The solution he found is explicitly a "magical" or mystical one that manifests itself in magical symbols and motifs in his works. To this extent Hesse represents one of the strong currents in modern literature, for the resolution of conflict on a super-rational level is a central theme of the reaction against positivism.

Many writers of the twentieth century might be called, as Hugo von Hofmannsthal styled himself, "mystics without mysticism"—writers keenly sensitive to the discongruities of life, who longed for a resolution of conflict here on earth and not in a transcendent realm of the future or the beyond. They are mystics inasmuch as they wish to pierce through the veil of apparent conflict; but without mysticism inasmuch as their resolution is immanent, not transcendent. Thus, Julius Langbehn, the partly absurd and partly serious disciple of Nietzsche who called himself "the philosopher with the egg," is significant in German intellectual history not so much because of any inherent importance of his book *Rembrandt als Erzieher* (1890; *Rembrandt as an Educator*), as because his work is so characteristic of the longing that was now beginning to be expressed in many quarters for a new totality, even if it must be on the plane of mysticism.[17]

The poet Rilke was fascinated with these "pure contradictions" of reality that, on the surface, seem irreconcilable. In his later poetry the rose emerged as the perfect symbol of resolution because the chaos of its petals stems ultimately from one common source of unity. He expressed the paradox most succinctly in one of his French poems:

> Ton innombrable état te fait-il connaître
> dans un mélange où tout se confond,
> cet ineffable accord du néant et de l'être
> que nous ignorons?

In the works of Thomas Mann, from early studies of the conflict between the artist and society (e.g. *Tonio Kröger*) to the later novels, resolution of conflict is a

---

[17] See in this connection H. Stuart Hughes, *Consciousness and Society. The Reconstruction of European Social Thought, 1890-1930*. Vintage Edition (New York, 1961), pp. 43ff.: and Fritz Stern, *The Politics of Cultural Despair* (Berkeley, Cal., 1961).

central theme. In *The Magic Mountain* Hans Castorp
achieves his sense of harmony in a mystical vision during
a snowstorm. Up to this point (the chapter "Snow")
Hans has been torn back and forth by the heated debates
of his spiritual mentors, Naphta and Settembrini, who
represent a chaotic variety of antithetical intellectual positions. Hans has pendulated from one extreme to the
other, but now, in a brilliant burst of clarity, he pierces
through the contradictions to the essential unity underlying them. "Death or Life," he reflects, "Disease, Health
—Spirit and Nature. Are these contradictions? I ask:
Are these legitimate questions? No, they are not questions."
He concludes that "Man is the Lord of Opposites. They
exist because of him, and therefore he is nobler than
they are." Since these apparent polarities have their
seat in his mind and heart, man as "Lord of Opposites"
has it in his power to reconcile them through an act of
will—or, as Hans Castorp puts it, through freedom and
reverence.

Hermann Broch was likewise plagued by the chaotic
pluralism that arose from what he called "the disintegration of values" in the modern world. His novels constitute
an attempt to uncover the harmony that underlies these
superficial contradictions. The finest symbolic expression
of this resolution comes at the end of *The Death of Vergil*.
At the hour of his death Vergil has succeeded in coming to
terms with the many aspects of reality for which he had
found no place in his work because they offended his
sense of beauty: disease, poverty, death, suffering, evil.
At the end, however, he perceives that these belong to
truth and beauty as much as health, wealth, life, happiness,
and good. The spiritual harmony that he achieves is
rendered symbolically in the extended lyrical conclusion

that describes his death. The poet is carried back—with images drawn from the Biblical creation experienced in reverse—through the stages of Paradise; through animal, plant, and mineral life; back through the separation of light and darkness; until ultimately he is reunited with the principle of Being that lies behind all creation and reality. Turning around, he surveys the universe and perceives, from this vantage point, that all the apparent opposites in life are illusory since they all proceed ultimately from the same divine source.

It should be stressed that all these visions represent what should be called an immanent rather than a transcendent mysticism. Man creates these apparent contradictions of reality within himself, and he can wipe them out again by an act of mind. The Lord of Opposites may reach this insight only through a vision (Mann), at the hour of death (Broch), or in a symbol (Rilke); but it is within his power to overcome the apparent contradictions. This brings us to a second important implication. The belief in an ontological unity of nature and spirit underlies all of these visions. But ontological questions are secondary. It is not an exaggeration to say that ontological monism is an accepted fact of twentieth-century thinking. (Einstein's search for a Unified Field Theory certainly implies this belief.) No, what interests these writers is the *ethical* problem. Ontological unity is an abstract question that hardly affects man's day-to-day existence. But questions of good and evil, right and wrong, confront us daily.

Most people, Hesse knows, will continue to judge good and evil by conventional standards; but he can wipe out these false standards by magical thinking and establish for himself a new ethical system that suits the exigencies of the times. Hans Castorp knows that Naphta and Settembrini will carry on their disputes; but in his flash of intuition he has perceived that their entire debate is based on the assumption of false polarities. Vergil knows that death and evil will not vanish from the face of the earth; but by an act of the mind one can destroy their threat and horror. In every case it is an ethical decision.

For the projection of their visions of unity both Broch and Hesse use ontological symbols: in fire, water, or through transformation the disparate elements of being are figuratively reunited. But these are symbols of an ethical revaluation, not of mystical sublimation of reality. This fact is worth stressing because the symbols that Hesse employs may lead the reader to forget that the magical thinking they represent is an ethical act through which the individual reexamines his life in order to cast off inherited prejudices and to affirm the totality of the world. The immanent quality of magical thinking is underscored when Hesse points out that the decline of Europe will take place "only" internally and that it is only his own inner world that he wishes to transform. This is "mysticism without mysticism," for the transformation is immanent and not transcendent, ethical and not ontological. Unless we understand this fully, we may misinterpret the symbols of physical transformation that occur in *Siddhartha, The Journey to the East,* or *Pictor's Metamorphoses.* They are Romantic symbols for an existential problem.

In his "Conjectural Biography," Hesse mentions a further implication of his magical thinking. "Because so-called reality does not play a very great role for me—because the past often fills me like the present and the present seems infinitely remote—for that reason I am also unable to separate the future so sharply from the present as people generally do. I live very much in the future." In his autobiographical sketch Hesse uses this passage as a transition to an imaginative projection of his life into the future. We can use it as a bridge from our consideration of simultaneity on the horizontal plane as totality to a discussion of simultaneity on the vertical plane as time-lessness.

3

Timelessness: The Chiliastic Vision

ONE OF mankind's most persistent beliefs is the consoling conviction that the present is no more than a stepping-stone to a glorious future in which the turmoil and frustration of existence will be resolved. Whether this belief manifests itself as the myth of the eternal return in its most primitive form of annual regeneration; as the Golden Age of Hesiod or its equivalent among the Chinese, Indians, and Hebrews; as the Christian millennium or the medieval idea of a world imperium; as Lessing's hope for an enlightened "age of the new eternal gospel" or Novalis's "new golden age" and "eternal Romantic assembly"; or as Nietzsche's impassioned cry for a realm "beyond good and evil"—we are dealing in each case with precisely the same mode of thought, although its goal, *mutatis mutandis*, may be aesthetic, religious, political, philosophic, or moral. This structure of thought, which results from a spiritual need that had been defined as the "longing for the Third Kingdom,"[1] remains constant despite the almost unlimited possibilities for variation in object and scope: it typically involves a triadic rhythm of the sort ideally represented by the Christian conception

---

[1] Julius Petersen, *Die Sehnsucht nach dem Dritten Reich in deutscher Sage und Dichtung* (Stuttgart, 1934). Petersen analyzes the symbol of the Third Reich with reference to Eduard Spranger's six "Lebensformen." The seventh possibility proposed by Petersen, the National Socialist People's Reich, can be dismissed as the most naïve and unadulterated propaganda; but the historical study that precedes it is objective, informative, and persuasive.

of an original state of grace followed first by the fall into sin and despair and, finally, the ultimate redemption. From the standpoint of a humanity enmeshed in the despair of the second stage, the millennium represents the chiliastic dream of ultimate redemption.

This chiliastic vision is an integral part of Hesse's thought and works. As a matter of fact, until Nazism corrupted the ancient term, Hesse used the technical expression "Third Kingdom" (*Drittes Reich*) to designate his chiliastic vision, but after 1933 he preferred terms such as "the Kingdom of the Spirit," "the Thousand-years," and other verbal surrogates. Appearing as a motif in the earliest prose and poems, it becomes the central theme in *Demian* and *The Steppenwolf*. No reader can fully understand the implications of *The Journey to the East* or *The Glass Bead Game* if he is unaware of the precise connotation that the belief has for the author.

Hesse's novels, if we disregard the tentative gropings in his early fiction, reveal three stages in the development of his chiliastic vision. The first stage, around the time of *Demian* (which was written in 1917 but published in 1919), adheres most closely to the traditional mode. At this point Hesse still believed in the possibility of a spiritual rebirth of humanity as a whole; humanity at the moment was conceived to be still toiling in the mires of despair, but within sight on the horizon lay hope. A letter to Romain Rolland (August 4, 1917) expresses this conviction most succinctly: "I believe not in Europe, but only in humanity: in a kingdom of the soul on earth in which all peoples participate and for whose most noble expression we are indebted to Asia."[2] As yet the ideal

[2] Hermann Hesse / Romain Rolland, *Briefe* (Zürich, 1954), p. 28. This correspondence is not included among the collected letters in GS, VII.

is not clearly defined: it is "a subterranean, timeless world of values and of the spirit,"[3] and "an international world of thought, of inner freedom, of intellectual conscience."[4] The characters of *Demian* are motivated by the vision of a new world in which traditional concepts of good and evil will have been renounced, and they often speak of it in almost religious terms: "I wanted most of all to become a priest in the new religion of which we have so many premonitions." Or more enigmatically: "For us humanity was a distant future toward which we were all on the way; whose image no one knew, whose laws were nowhere written." Demian and his friends regard the outbreak of the war as a harbinger of this rebirth: "The New is beginning, and for those who cling to the Old, the New will be terrible." The war itself is only a distracting epiphenomenon than conceals the vast transformation taking place beneath the surface: "Far below something was growing. Something like a new humanity." The traditional nature of this chiliasm is patent: along with the rest of humanity and still enmeshed in a world of despair, Demian and his friends look forward to a rebirth of humanity that is, to be sure, portrayed as imminent, but which they have thus far experienced only in their dreams.

The second stage, concentrated around the novel *The Steppenwolf* (1927), is characterized by three advances beyond the position expressed in *Demian*. In the first place, years of disillusionment—first with the postwar depression and then especially with the tawdry superficiality of the prosperous twenties—served to dull Hesse's enthusiasm and his belief in the impending spiritual rebirth of the world. He begins to concern himself less and less with humanity

---

[3] From the essay "Besuch aus Indien" (1922); GD, III, 857.
[4] From the essay "O Freunde, nicht diese Töne!" (1914); GS, VII, 48.

as a whole, believing that any general rebirth will be possible only as the sum total of individual rebirths. Secondly, the goal of the Third Kingdom is more clearly defined. In *Demian* Hesse had operated with the vague concept of "soul." Now he clearly and repeatedly postulates his belief in a realm where the conflict between the polar extremes of "nature" and "spirit" in man will be resolved. Finally, this chiliastic realm is not a future state that lies beyond the horizon, but rather an eternal realm in which the individual actually can participate through momentary visions and dreams. All of this is clearly expressed in *The Steppenwolf*:

"All people like us, who make greater claims on life; people with this longing, with the extra dimension—we couldn't even live if there were not, apart from the air of this world, another air for us to breathe; if there were no eternity outside of time. . . . In eternity there is no posterity, only a perpetual present. . . . It is the realm beyond time and beyond appearances. That's where we belong: there is our home, in that direction our hearts strive, Steppenwolf, and for that reason we long for our death. There you will find your Goethe again and your Novalis and your Mozart."

In these passages the Third Kingdom is quite lucidly defined. It is an eternal realm of spiritual values that exists independently of the everyday world, a realm that occupies modally the same position as the Christian millennium: that is, it represents a return to grace after the fall from innocence. Instead of being a third stage in the future, it exists simultaneously with the second stage of despair, but on a totally different level of being. In other words, the chiliastic world has been internalized, and it can thus exist in the present. In that realm Goethe and Novalis and

Mozart—symbols of permanent spiritual value—still live, and by projecting himself into that other sphere Harry Haller can also enjoy the bliss of the spiritual millennium. Total identification with the realm of the Immortals is possible only through death. Yet it is possible for the individual to have fleeting and provocative glimpses of that realm even in life. This happens at two points in the novel: once when Haller, in a drunken dream, has an interview with Goethe; and again when he encounters Mozart during an opium fantasy. At the end of the novel Haller still lives on the level of everyday reality at which we find him at the beginning of the book, but a development has taken place. Through his brief contact with the Immortals he has gained an awareness of the eternal realm of the spirit and has drawn consolation from its existence.

The third stage in the development of Hesse's chiliastic belief reveals two further steps: a final valid definition of the Third Kingdom, and a capacity for almost eidetic vision through which it becomes possible for him actually to enter the Third Kingdom. In 1930, Hesse stated in a letter that his beliefs with regard to the present would scarcely be altered; he does not believe in our science, in our politics, in our ways of thinking, believing and amusing ourselves, nor does he share a single one of the ideals of our times.

"But that does not mean that I am without faith. I believe in laws of humanity that are thousands of years old, and I believe that they will easily outlast the whole turmoil of our time. . . . During my entire life I have attempted many ways by which one can overcome time and live in the timeless."[5]

[5] GS, VII, 501.

From this point on, his conception of the Third Kingdom is more realistically formulated; it is no longer masked
in apocalyptic visions as in *Demian*, nor in narcotic dreams
as in *The Steppenwolf*, but is stated outright. The ideal
is now unquestionably a realm of the "spirit" (*Geist*), and
Hesse elaborates upon this concept in another letter from
the same period:

"Perhaps by 'spirit' you mean intelligence or something
similar. I—that is, my poem—call spirit 'divine' and
'eternal'; the poem implies by 'spirit' precisely what all
spiritual systems of thought have understood for three
thousand years: the divine substance. It is divine, but it
is not god—although there are religions that take it that
way, too."[6]

In still another letter explaining the poem "Reflection"
(*"Besinnung"*), Hesse makes it clear that his conception
of the Third Kingdom has shifted from that of a realm in
which nature and spirit are resolved, to a sphere of pure
spirit: "The need to formulate all this arose from the
acute strife regarding 'biocentric' or 'logocentric' views of
life, and I wanted to take my stand clearly on the side of
'logocentric.' "[7] The definition of "spirit" as the divine
substance implies for Hesse the essence of the best thought
and spirit of all time, the eternal *logos*. It can be observed
now to what extent Hesse's chiliastic vision has changed
since *Demian*. There the envisaged future was a hazy community of the future characterized best by the word "soul"
with all its vague associations. In *The Steppenwolf* (and
likewise in *Narziss and Goldmund*) Hesse is engaged in
the attempt to reconcile nature and spirit, whereby both
poles are felt to be equally desirable. Now, however,

[6] GS, VII, 572.   [7] GS, VII, 589.

"spirit" alone is the object of man's striving. There is no
negative connotation whatsoever attached to the concept
of nature; it is simply man's destiny to transcend nature and
attain the spirit as the ultimate goal, as the poem *"Besinnung"* affirms.

Hesse's first attempt to depict a sustained vision of the
chiliastic world was *The Journey to the East* (1932), in
which man's adventures in the realm of the mind are
projected into physical reality. The fiction of the book
portrays a League assembled for the purpose of a pilgrimage to the East, and the time is specified as the period immediately following the Great War. The story is ostensibly
limited both geographically and temporally. But H. H.,
the narrator, soon realizes that it is actually much more:
in a higher sense this pilgrimage is only one wave in the
eternal stream of souls striving homeward "to the home
of light." He rapidly perceives, moreover, that:

"we were not wandering merely through space, but likewise through time. We were journeying to the Orient, but
we were also going into the Middle Ages or into the Golden
Age; we passed through Italy or Switzerland, but we also
sometimes spent the night in the tenth century and dwelled
among the patriarchs or among fairies. . . . Our East was
not only a land and something geographic; it was Everywhere and Nowhere, the unification of all times."

In this realm of utopism and uchronism H. H. encounters
childhood friends and figures of world literature (Parzival,
Goldmund, and Sancho Panza) all on the same level of
reality. He sees the writer E. T. A. Hoffmann and his
creation, the Archivarius Lindhorst; he conjures up figures
from his own works: Hermann Lauscher, Klingsor, Pablo;
and he strolls through the gardens with friends who were
still alive and close to him (Hesse) in 1932. The meaning

of this phantasmagoria is perfectly clear if it is considered as a vivid representation of Hesse's conception of the Third Kingdom. There, in the realm of the spirit, all things exist together and forever: ". . . thus we summoned the past, the future, the imaginary creatively into the present moment." *The Journey to the East* is an intensification of the fiction employed in *The Steppenwolf*. Harry Haller encountered the Immortals only in his dreams and entered the Third Kingdom only vicariously. Here the reader is asked to accept the various figures of the fiction as pure reality on the plane of actual life and, like the figure of the narrator, "never to be confused by rational reasons, always to know that faith is stronger than so-called reality." (This is a delimitation of the boundaries of time and space, reality and imagination, of precisely the sort that one finds in so much modern poetry—for instance, Georg Trakl, Gottfried Benn, or Günter Eich.) This point is the stumbling block for H. H. He loses faith, and, after the opening chapters, the bulk of the story is concerned not with the representation of the Third Kingdom, but with H. H.'s attempt to regain his faith. Yet the entire book is a profession of Hesse's own belief in the existence of the spiritual chiliad and the potential capacity of the individual to share in it.

Hesse's last great novel, *The Glass Bead Game* (1943), may be interpreted as another attempt, on a grand scale, to project the ideal into reality. In the Latin motto to the novel (ascribed to a certain Albertus Secundus, but actually a fictitious motto of Hesse's own creation) it is said:

". . . for even though in certain respects and for frivolous people non-existent things can be portrayed in words more easily and with less responsibility than existing things; for the pious and conscientious writer of history it is just the opposite: nothing is more remote from representation by means of words, and yet nothing needs more to be placed before the eyes of men than certain things whose existence is neither provable nor probable, but which, simply by the fact that pious and conscientious men treat them, as it were, as existent things, are brought one step closer to existence and to the possibility of being born."

The "Glass Bead Game," as is explained in the fictional introduction to the book, is a product of the same spiritual need that produced, in the "feuilletonistic age," the Magic Theater; and the Magic Theater in *The Steppenwolf* is, among other things, one of the means by which Harry Haller came into direct contact with the Immortals and the realm of the spirit. The whole work, moreover, is dedicated to the "Eastern Wayfarers," and the fictitious chronicler tells us that this League was one of the few strongholds of the spirit during a period when true spiritual culture was apparently in a steep decline. The Eastern Wayfarers contributed substantially to the development of the Glass Bead Game "through their capacity, based upon old secret exercises, of magically entering remote times and cultural circumstances." This function of the League was most closely related to Hesse's concept of the Third Kingdom as the "unification of all times." These introductory remarks immediately cause us to sense that the very essence of the Glass Bead Game is directly connected with the chiliastic realm of the spirit.

The Glass Bead Game is the focal point of the panorama that Hesse unfolds in his novel, and as such it gives the work its title. The author emphasizes at the outset that he is unable to give a full history and theory of the institution; it is a task that exceeds the capacities of his age. Thus a concise image of the game never emerges, and the reader is left only with a few indications as to the nature and scope of this concept. But they suffice to demonstrate that here again, as in *The Journey to the East*, Hesse is attempting to present in concrete form a plastic representation of his chiliastic vision. If the central passages are singled out, the following pattern emerges:

"The Glass Bead Game is a game involving all the contents and values of our culture. . . . What humanity, in its creative periods, has produced in the way of knowledge, lofty thoughts and works of art; what the succeeding periods of learned contemplation have conceptualized and made our intellectual property—this entire vast material of spiritual values is played by the Glass Bead player like an organ by the organist . . . theoretically the entire spiritual substance of the world could be produced in the game by means of this instrument."

What was originally simply an intellectual game or exercise has developed into "the essence of everything spiritual and museal, a sublime cult, an *unio mystica* of all disparate elements of the Universitas Litterarum." It is "a lining up, ordering, grouping and opposing of consecrated concepts from many areas of thought and beauty . . . a rapid recapitulation of supratemporal values and forms, a virtuoso flight through the realms of the spirit," coupled with the meditation and reverent contemplation necessary to prevent it from becoming pure intellectual pyrotechnics.

The pattern should be familiar from *The Steppenwolf* and *The Journey to the East*. There the values were personified almost allegorically by the Immortals and actual figures from the realm of the spirit; here, on the other hand, in the realistic (though futuristic) setting of Castalia, such tangible personifications are inadmissible. Instead, one deals with the abstracted spiritual values themselves. The

Glass Bead Game does not lead the individual mystically into the Third Kingdom; instead, it brings all the elements of the Third Kingdom to the individual. It is an abstraction of the world of values that constantly lies within the reach of the individual, allowing him to exist, as it were, in the spiritual millennium.

The cited instances are all drawn from the fictitious introduction to the novel, which the reader is asked to assume to have been written around the year 2400 by a student of Castalia who lived sometime after Joseph Knecht. It is interesting, in contrast, to see what the Glass Bead Game means to Hesse himself as an individual of our own time. The introduction was written and appeared as early as 1934: two years later, in the idyllic poem *Hours in the Garden* (1936),[8] Hesse wrote the following lines:

> Und nun beginnt im Gemüt mir
> Ein Gedankenspiel, dessen ich mich schon seit Jahren
>   befleisse,
> Glasperlenspiel genannt, eine hübsche Erfindung,
> Deren Gerüst die Musik und deren Grund Meditation
>   ist.
> Joseph Knecht ist der Meister, dem ich das Wissen
>   um diese
> Schöne Imagination verdanke. In Zeiten der Freude
> Ist sie mir Spiel und Glück, in Zeiten des Leids und
>   der Wirren
> Ist sie mir Trost und Besinnung, und hier am Feuer,
>   beim Siebe,
> Spiel ich es oft, das Glasperlenspiel, wenn auch längst
>   noch wie Knecht nicht.
> Während der Kegel sich türmt und vom Siebe das
>   Erdmehl herabrinnt,

---

[8] *Stunden im Garten;* GD, v, 348-349.

. . . .
Hör ich Musik und sehe vergangene und künftige
     Menschen,
Sehe Weise und Dichter und Forscher und Künstler
     einmütig
Bauen—am hunderttorigen Dom des Geistes—ich will
     es
Einmal später berichten, noch ist der Tag nicht
     gekommen.

(And now there begins within me/a game of thoughts
that I have been practicing for years,/ called Glass
Bead Game, a nice invention,/ whose framework is
music and whose basis is meditation./ Joseph Knecht
is the master to whom I owe my knowledge of this/
lovely exercise of the imagination. In times of joy/
it is a game and pleasure, in times of sorrow and dis-
tress/ it is consolation and reflection for me, and here
at the fire, with my sieve/ I often play it, the Glass
Bead Game, though by far not so well as Knecht./
While the heap of ashes piles up and the soil filters
down from the sieve/ I hear music and see men of
the past and the future;/ I see wise men and poets and
scholars and artists harmoniously/ building—the
hundred-gated cathedral of the spirit—I intend/ to
tell about it sometime, but the day still has not come.)

This passage proves that the Glass Bead Game is identical with what we have been calling Hesse's chiliastic
vision of a Third Kingdom. Whereas in the novel the
various elements of Spirit are raised consistently to abstract
symbols, the game as Hesse plays it in his garden, in its
simplest form, is actually a mystical and eidetic conjura-
tion of the eternal realm of the spirit and of the very men
who have contributed to its imposing structure. Hesse,

the man, requires more flesh and blood, more imagery, than the hyperintellectual mandarins of Castalia, who avoid whenever possible the personal and tangible, choosing rather to deal with disembodied abstractions. We have here the difference between conceptualized or cognitive thinking and the eidetic vision of the poet.

The theme of simultaneity is one of the central concerns of modern literature in general, and there are a number of parallels to Hesse's conception of a timeless realm of the spirit. This is conspicuously the case in one of the earliest "modern" novels, Rilke's *Notebooks of Malte Laurids Brigge* (1910). Malte's grandfather, Count Brahe, is described in the following way:

"Sequences of time played no role for him. Death was an insignificant incident which he completely ignored. Persons whom he had once taken up in his memory existed, and their death could not alter that fact in the least. A number of years later, after the death of the old gentleman, it was told that he also felt the future to be present with the same obstinacy."

This particular passage, which comes toward the beginning, prefigures the structure of the entire novel, for in Malte's mind, as he makes his journal entries, time plays no role: his own childhood, the historical past, the immediate present and even the future all merge into one spiritual whole that exists eternally and simultaneously. The fiction of the two books differs, of course. Yet the chiliastic vision is remarkably similar.

Probably no other modern novelist has made such a systematic attempt to incorporate the principle of simultaneity into his works as Hermann Broch. The theme is conspicuous in all of his novels, but his artistic programme is stated most explicitly in his essay on James Joyce:

"It is always a question of simultaneity, the simultaneity of the infinite, multifaceted potentialities of the symbolic. Everywhere one senses the attempt to apprehend the infinity of the incomprehensible element in which the world rests and which is its reality, and to hedge in the infinite with chains of symbols that are to be expressed as simultaneously as possible. . . . The demand for simultaneity remains the true goal of all epic, yes, of all poetry: to force the sequence of impressions and experience into a unity . . . in a word: to produce the supratemporality of the work of art within the concept of indivisible unity."[9]

In the last analysis, the striving for simultaneity accounts for many of the characteristics of modern literature. What is Proust's technique of association other than a means of revealing the permanent, timeless core of experience? Joyce's epiphanies, by his own definition in *Stephen Hero*, represent an attempt to encounter the timeless essence of things beneath their temporal appearance. The technique of typological prefiguration or mythical archetypes—in Joyce's *Ulysses*, Thomas Mann's *Joseph* tetralogy or *Doctor Faustus*, as well as in Hesse's *Demian* and *Siddhartha*—is ultimately motivated by the desire to show an "eternal recurrence" of events: in other words, to overcome time by exposing the timeless essence of a higher reality. To this extent Hesse's chiliastic vision of simultaneity reflects a common feature of the modern novel.[10]

To determine that the striving for simultaneity exists in an entire literary generation is only one step. The second,

[9] "James Joyce und die Gegenwart," in: Hermann Broch, *Dichten und Erkennen* (Essays Bd. 1), ed. Hannah Arendt (Zürich, 1955), pp. 192-193.

[10] Oscar Seidlin, "Hermann Hesse: The Exorcism of the Devil," *Symposium*, 4 (1950), p. 340: "In this attempt to conquer time, Hesse's heroes are the true companions of Proust's, Joyce's, Thomas Mann's protagonists."

more interesting step must be to ask *why* this is the case.
In his critical study, *The Picaresque Saint*, R. W. B. Lewis
observed that "the best way to distinguish the two or
three literary generations of our century is in their manner
of responding to the fact of death—that is, their manner
of somehow getting beyond it."[11] Lewis devotes much of
his book to the discussion of attitudes toward death in
the generation immediately following Hesse (Moravia,
Silone, Camus, Malraux, Greene, Faulkner). Now if we
consider Rilke, Hesse, Thomas Mann, Broch, Joyce, and
Proust of a generation—as surely they are—then we can
ascertain that they unanimously react to death by striving
to create an aesthetic realm of simultaneity or timelessness
in which the threat of death is annulled.

In a perceptive study Hans Meyerhoff has analyzed
the philosophical basis of this preoccupation of writers with
the theme of timelessness and simultaneity. "The significance of a timeless dimension in experience, the self,
the work of art, or beyond experience can be fully ap-
preciated only when it is placed within the context of the
melancholy, gloomy reflections ensuing from the direction
of time toward death and nothingness."[12] Broch once remarked that the only proper subject for the novel, now
that science has completely appropriated the sphere of life,
is death. In Professor Meyerhoff's terms Broch's attitude
toward death would explain his concern for simultaneity
in the novel, and *The Death of Vergil* actually does co-
ordinate the two themes in just this fashion. Likewise,
one of the principal themes in Rilke's novel, obvious even
in the brief passage quoted above, is death, which is
overcome ultimately by a sense of timelessness. In Hesse's
works, as in the novels of Thomas Mann or Proust, death

[11] Keystone Edition (Philadelphia and New York, 1961), p. 19.
[12] *Time and Literature* (Berkeley and Los Angeles, 1955), p. 74.

is constantly in evidence as a counterpoint to the timelessness of the Third Kingdom or simultaneity.

In all of the novels from *Demian* to *The Glass Bead Game*, except for *The Journey to the East*, death and speculations about death play a central role. The fact to be observed, however, is that the power of death over men—the threat of death—is sublimated to the extent that it becomes unimportant. Demian's death is balanced symbolically by the dying kiss through which he implants in Emil Sinclair his spirit and faith in the kingdom of the soul toward which they both aspire. The same symbolism occurs in the next novel, in which Siddhartha comes to resemble Vasudeva so completely that, after the latter's death, it is scarcely apparent that a different ferryman now transports travelers across the river. In the last novels, in which the heroes no longer merely aspire toward but actually live in the timeless realm of *The Journey to the East* or Castalia, death has lost all of its abrasive qualities. The old Magister Musicae in *The Glass Bead Game* does not really die; he gradually dematerializes until his spiritual element is subsumed, as it were, in the abstract realm of spirit.

The most explicit association of timelessness and death occurs in *Klein and Wagner*,[13] which Hesse wrote in the spring of 1919, during the composition of *Siddhartha*. At the end of the novella Friedrich Klein, in a moment of almost existential nausea, nearly murders his mistress Teresina. Appalled at his own wretchedness and determined to put an end to his life of anguish, Klein rows out onto the lake and lets himself sink into the water. Then a revelation comes to him. After the instant when he freely decided to drown himself, his death no longer has any meaning. In the flood of images and thoughts that rush

[13] *Klein und Wagner*; both quotations in GD, III, 553.

through his mind in those last moments, released as he is from the exigencies of existence, he realizes "that there is no such thing as time!" With this perception he would be able to live, now, in peace and harmony since life on earth would be tolerable if one knew that there is a realm of timelessness apart from the inexorable corporality of daily life. Yet once Klein realizes that there is no time, then existence also has no further meaning, and he willingly lets himself sink into the realm of simultaneity:

"One of the inventions of the human mind was time. A fine invention, a sophisticated instrument for tormenting oneself even more fervently and making the world complex and difficult. Man was separated from everything he desired only by time, this crazy invention. It was one of the supports, the crutches that one had to let go if one wanted to be free."

In *Klein and Wagner* death and the tyranny of time are subsumed in the realm of simultaneity in exemplary form. In Hesse's other works death is always more or less explicitly the antithesis of the timeless Third Kingdom.

Hesse's novels from *Demian* on represent the search for a realm of timeless values that he ultimately defines most perfectly in the ideal vision of Castalia in the introduction to *The Glass Bead Game*. In this sense, his works after the years of crisis are a journey to Castalia, the aesthetic realm in which all values are reunited in an all-embracing totality and in which the threat of death is canceled out. To this extent Hesse's work is representative of his generation—the writers who, like him, sought the answers to life in an absolute world of art. In his last novel, however, Hesse both reached and transcended this ideal. The introduction to *The Glass Bead Game* postulates a utopian vision of the timeless realm; but the Joseph

Knecht who dies on the last page of the novel is much more of a picaresque saint than a mandarin of autonomous art in a timeless spiritual realm. The last novel, as we shall see, leads beyond Castalia to a renewed commitment to life—and to death.

❖〔❖

4

The Triadic Rhythm of Humanization

THE SIMULTANEITY of the chiliastic vision and the totality of magical thinking are not achieved goals, but simply ideals to be realized. The development of the individual toward these goals follows according to an inevitable triadic pattern. This triadic rhythm in the development of the individual, as a conception, is no more unique, of course, than the chiliastic vision: only the qualities with which Hesse invests the basic structure are novel. Traditionally the sequence, as implied in the myth of a Golden Age or in the dream of a Christian millennium, applies to humanity as a whole. Beginning with the Enlightenment, however, a certain shift in perspective can be detected. The development of the individual parallels that of humanity, proceeding according to a triadic rhythm like that of the chiliastic dream. At the end of *The Education of the Human Race* (*Die Erziehung des Menschengeschlechts*; 1780), after discussing the triadic course of humanity as a whole, which he equates with the Father, the Son, and the Holy Ghost of the Bible, Lessing concludes (§ 93): "The very same course by which the race arrives at its perfection must first have been followed by every single individual—some sooner, some later." In the twenty-fifth of his *Letters on the Aesthetic Education of Man* (*Briefe über die ästhetische Erziehung des Menschen*; 1793) Schiller likewise, in a note, implies that the structure of development outlined for humanity as a whole also applies to the path of the individual: "These three moments that I mentioned at the beginning of the twenty-fourth letter are thus, taken as a whole, three different epochs for the development of all humanity and for the total development of each individual." For Lessing and Schiller, the development of humanity as a whole is still the central issue; but with Hölderlin, Kleist, and the generation of the Romanticists the emphasis shifts. In his novel *Hyperion*, for instance, Hölderlin clearly regards the development of the individual as triadic in structure, beginning with the child's union with nature, proceeding to the alienation of the adult from the whole, and culminating in the serene harmony of the "Blissful." Kleist's famous essay *On the Puppet Theater* (*Über das Marionetten-theater*; 1810) invests the same rhythm with new qualities: at one end of the scale he sees the total lack of self-consciousness of the child or the animal and at the other end the total self-awareness of God. In the middle, at various levels of self-knowledge, he sees man, who suffers because he has lost his innocence but not yet attained full knowledge.

This triadic view of individual growth is not limited, of course, to pre-twentieth-century thinkers; it can also be found in the recent work of a contemporary American philosopher. In "The Uses of Thinking" (*Saturday Review*, March 2, 1963) James K. Feibleman outlines a view of human development that reflects the traditional triad adapted to contemporary circumstances. "From infancy to maturity man goes through two well-recognized stages: innocence and innocence lost." On the second level adults have lost the gift of questioning; they are absorbed with the "small business of everyday" and satisfied with the ritual or formalized code of answers supplied by society. "A few, a very few, however, take a third step to innocence regained. They are more sensitive than the rest, or more stubborn, I do not know which. . . . From this tiny group come all the productive and original people among us, the artists and philosophers who through their efforts make up the social world in which we live."

Hesse is perfectly well aware that he is operating within a traditional thought structure, and in the essay "A Bit of Theology" (1932) he has outlined his position quite programmatically.[1] There he sketches at length a "developmental history of the soul" which he regards as a sacred truth. "The course of humanization," he writes, "begins with innocence (paradise, childhood, a pre-stage without a sense of responsibility). From there it leads into guilt, into the knowledge of good and evil, into the behests of culture, morality, religion, human ideals." But the realization that these various ideals are unattainable in reality plunges the individual into despair. "This despair, now, leads either to a downfall, or, on the other hand, to the Third Kingdom of the Spirit, to the experience of a condition beyond morality and law, an advance to grace and redemption, to a new and higher kind of irresponsibility, or in short: to faith." Hesse concedes that the process of development as he has outlined it here is European and almost Christian; but, he continues, the same pattern can be found among all peoples and all religions. Taking Buddhism as an example, he equates yoga with the second stage and nirvana with the third. For Lao Tse the road likewise leads from a life of vain striving to fulfillment in Tao. The important fact for Hesse is: despair leads either to downfall or to salvation—not back, behind morality and culture, to a child's paradise, but over and

---

[1] "Ein Stückchen Theologie"; GS, VII, 388-402. Note, in the quotation below, the *terminus technicus* "Third Reich" (*drittes Reich*), used here in the time-honored, pre-Nazi sense.

beyond it into a realm where one can live according to one's own beliefs.

This triadic rhythm is, of course, an idealized scheme. He goes on to say:

"Most people never become men; they remain in the primal state, in the childish state this side of conflicts and development; most people perhaps never even find the second stage, but remain in the irresponsible animal world of their impulses and infantile dreams; and the legend of a condition beyond their twilight, of good and evil, of a rise from despair into the light of grace—all this seems ridiculous to them."

They might be compared to the dancing master Knaak in Thomas Mann's *Tonio Kröger*, whose eyes "do not look into things to the point where they become complicated and sad," while Tonio and artists like himself begin to perceive contradictions in the world "even at an age when they should reasonably still be living in peace and harmony with God and world." For Thomas Mann the bourgeois Knaak and the artist Tonio clearly represent types equivalent to Hesse's first and second levels of humanization.

Not all of those, by far, who undergo the process reach the third stage; and again, many who fleetingly enter the realm of redemption fall back to the second level and are again subject to its laws and unfulfillable exigencies. This is the process of individuation as Hesse knows it:

"I know it from my own experience and from the documents of many other souls. Always, at all times in history and in all religions and forms of life, we find the same typical experiences, always in the same progression and succession: loss of innocence, striving for justice under the law, the consequent despair in the futile struggle to overcome guilt by deeds or by knowledge, and finally the emergence from hell into a transformed world and into a new kind of innocence."

There is an important corollary to this conception of triadic development. In Hesse's terminology the process of humanization (*Menschwerdung*) involves progressive individuation, a term that Hesse has consciously borrowed from Schopenhauer by way of Nietzsche and Jung. The *principium individuationis* to which he refers in *The Steppenwolf* and elsewhere is understood in a quite Schopenhauerian sense: that is, by asserting ourselves as individuals we at the same time cut ourselves off from the totality of the first stage. Individuation is thus a mixed blessing: positive in that it is a necessary step toward the development of the individual personality, but negative to the extent that it is ultimately responsible for our despair. The third stage of individuation, however, turns back upon itself, for it implies reunification with totality on a higher level. Since the third step of individuation leads beyond the individual and back to the community, at this level no particular premium is placed upon individuality. One is absorbed, almost fluidly, into the whole again. Ethically, therefore, the insistence upon individuality that is the earmark of man on the second level gives way to another ethos: on the third level it is service to the whole and subjugation of the individual desire that counts. As a result, the ideal of service is a characteristic of those among Hesse's characters who have reached the third level: the old Siddhartha, who spends his last days as a ferryman; Leo in *The Journey to the East*, who is the leader of the League and at the same time its most humble servant; Joseph Knecht, who as Master of the Order must renounce all individuality in order better to serve it. In other words, the emphasis upon pronounced individuality or "personalism" (the "Self-Reliance" of Hesse's earlier essay) on the second level of individuation, manifested in the obstinate self-seeking of Harry Haller, Emil Sinclair, young Siddhartha, or Goldmund, is in no way in conflict with the avowed ideal of service in other parts of Hesse's works. Rather, extreme individualism and service to the community on the ethical level correspond to individuation and reunification with the whole on the metaphysical level. Implicit in the many essays and letters in which Hesse has admonished others to be true only to themselves, is the understanding that consummate self-knowledge will ultimately bring the individual back into the community on the third level of humanization. This attitude may be clarified by reference to a farfetched parallel, yet one that is compelling in its primitive simplicity: namely, John Steinbeck's doctrine of the "oversoul" in *Grapes of Wrath*, which attributes the suffering of mankind to the excessive "personalism" that has alienated him from the universal soul: "Maybe all men got one big soul and evr'body's a part of it."[2]

The importance of these ideas for Hesse's novels cannot be overemphasized. Their connection with the visions of simultaneity and totality should be perfectly apparent: the man who has achieved the timelessness of the chiliastic vision and the totality of magical thinking is on the third and final level of humanization. In actuality, however, it is the second stage that interests Hesse, for it is on the level of conflicts with reality that novelistic action can take place—either externally or "only" internally, as Hesse stated in his essay on *The Brothers Karamazov*. As a novelist Hesse is interested in conflict and development,

---

[2] See the analysis by R. W. B. Lewis in *The Picaresque Saint*, pp. 184-185.

and only on the second level are these possible: stages one
and three are essentially static and idyllic states, while the
second level is progressive and dynamic. In some novels—
Demian, Siddhartha, Narziss and Goldmund, as well as
The Glass Bead Game—all three stages of development
are portrayed. But the innocence of childhood is depicted
not for its own sake, but only as a quality to be lost in
antithesis to the turmoil that follows; this is most conspicuous in the early chapters of *Demian.* In itself the first stage
is of little interest because it involves no conflicts and,
once having been transcended, can never be attained again.
Likewise, all of the novels depict, in one way or another,
the third stage, but only in *Siddhartha* is the level of simultaneity and totality actually maintained at the end. Otherwise, as is best shown in *The Steppenwolf,* the individual
constantly slips back into the world of despair after brief,
tantalizing glimpses of the third realm, which exists as a
source of hope and despair in one. As a result, all of
Hesse's novels have a characteristic underlying pattern:
the triadic rhythm of humanization, which each hero follows according to the dictates of his nature.

Hesse is concerned primarily with man in his despair
and freedom. His heroes are typically individuals who,
living in the second stage, are confronted with the necessity to make free choices and judgments; they are unable
to fall back upon the comfortable codes of conformity.
And they despair because they are aware of the higher
reality of the chiliastic vision without being able to attain or
sustain it constantly. To this extent Hesse's range as a
novelist is narrow. His focus does not embrace the many
who, living in the first stage of innocence, are unaware of
any conflict in life or of the challenge of freedom. He
similarly ignores those who, having reached the second
stage, take recourse in the facile formulations of accepted

ethical codes rather than face the consequences of freedom in the absence of any established laws. But within the
area that he has staked out as his own fictional domain,
he explores characters of the greatest variety and under
the most varied circumstances: Sinclair, the adolescent
hero of *Demian* who, in his questioning of established
values, had the same hold upon the youth of the twenties
as J. D. Salinger's Holden Caulfield upon the teenagers
of today; Siddhartha, the son of a Brahman priest living
at the time of Buddha; Harry Haller, the weary and
cynical intellectual of interbellum Europe; Narziss and
Goldmund, representatives of the sacred and profane in
medieval Europe; H. H., the lost, alienated man of the
thirties, a "stranger" in Camus's sense of the word: and
Joseph Knecht, the symbolic leader of a spiritual monastic
order projected into a future five hundred years hence.
Over and over again the same triadic rhythm, but clothed
each time in a different garb, reaching three thousand years
across European civilization. The sense of continuity thus
achieved, if one regards Hesse's novels as a whole, is
in itself a manifestation of the Goethean *Dauer im Wechsel*
of simultaneity, a tribute to the eternal quality of mankind.

Although "A Bit of Theology" was not written until
1932, it represents with fair accuracy Hesse's views from
Demian (1917) on. Nowhere, perhaps, is the theme stated
more programmatically than in the interpolated essay of
the novel *The Steppenwolf*. In this theoretical discourse
we learn that the Steppenwolf, the lone wolf, is a type
which, by virtue of its high degree of individuation, has
transcended the realm of the bourgeoisie; he has reached
what Hesse would call the second level. The author of
the tract tells us further that most intellectuals and artists
belong to this class. "Only the strongest of them force
their way through the atmosphere of the bourgeois world

and arrive in the cosmos; all others resign themselves and make compromises." These individuals are neither intense and stubborn enough to be destroyed nor powerful enough to reach the third level permanently. Their strength suffices merely to bring them into conflict with traditional reality and thus to make them miserable. Harry Haller, the Steppenwolf, belongs to these unhappy existences. The tract suggests, within the framework of the fiction, that three escape hatches are open to him: "Either he will obtain one of our little mirrors, or he will encounter the Immortals, or perhaps will find in one of our Magic Theaters whatever he needs for the liberation of his ravaged soul." All three of these images symbolize the themes we have discussed. The magic mirror signifies a look into the chaos of one's own soul. The Immortals inhabit the chiliastic realm of simultaneity. The Magic Theater embraces the full span of potentialities in the totality of the present moment. All three are doorways from the second level of individuation to the third. For those who fail, however, for those who are doomed to fall back constantly from the third level to the second; for those whose existence necessitates a constant confrontation of higher reality with the reality of the everyday world, the tract proposes a fourth solution: humor.

❖)❖

5

Perspectives of Reality: Humor

IN HIS ESSAY *On Naïve and Sentimental Poetry* (1795) Schiller created a useful heuristic tool for the analysis of dualistic conceptions of the world. Schiller was concerned specifically with the problem of the "sentimentive" poet who, alienated from the integral world of "naïve" writers, senses a disparity between the real and the ideal. Regardless of the nature of the ideal, however, his pattern of analysis can be applied to any personality which finds everyday reality in conflict with an envisioned ideal. It is relevant to Hesse as well as Schiller, or, in our own times, to Heinrich Böll as well as Albert Camus.[1] It is valid for any man who, in Hesse's scale of individuation, lives on the second level of awareness. According to Schiller, the sense of disparity can lead to three modes of literature. If the vision of the ideal is strong enough to force reality into the background, the resulting mode is elegiac. If, on the other hand, reality obtrudes forcefully upon the ideal, all but obscuring it, the tone of satire prevails. When, finally, the real and the ideal coalesce into a whole, the literary product is the idyll.[2]

[1] In a study of "Albert Camus and Heinrich Böll" (*Modern Language Notes*, 77, 1962, 282-291) I have applied Schiller's categories to two contemporary writers in an attempt to illustrate some of their basic similarities.

[2] A lucid analysis of Schiller's essay in Hermann J. Weigand's "Illustrations to Highlight Some Points in Schiller's Essay on Poetry," *Monatshefte für deutschen Unterricht*, 46 (1954) 161-169.

Hesse, as we have seen, believes in an ideal which, for him, is a higher type of reality. Repeatedly he speaks in his fiction, essays, and letters of reality and "reality"—indicating by quotation marks the so-called reality of everyday life, which for him has nothing in common with the true and eternal reality of the human spirit. "No matter how lively life may be in the universities and shops, in the stock markets and entertainment halls of the 'real' world, we are still no closer to the life that matters than we are when we spend an hour or two every day on the wise men and poets of the past."[3] It is stylistically characteristic of this attitude that Hesse is forced to use comparative forms that are not usually employed. If we must compare two realities, then one must be more or less real than the other—a stylistic dilemma that Rilke also exploited consistently in his poetry, as in the fourth of his *Sonnets to Orpheus*:

> O ihr Seligen, o ihr Heilen,
> die ihr der Anfang der Herzen scheint.
> Bogen der Pfeile und Ziele von Pfeilen,
> ewiger glänzt euer Lächeln verweint.

The word "eternally" does not, of course, normally admit a comparative form in German, English, or any other language; yet in order to render the poignant intensity of his vision, Rilke constructs the form "more eternally." Such uncommon comparatives in Hesse's prose are absolutely consistent with the theme that he is hoping to express:

". . . it is becoming apparent that the so-called "reality" of the technologists, the generals, and the bank directors, is growing constantly less real, less substantial, less prob-

---

[3] "Eine Bibliothek der Weltliteratur" (1929); GS, VII, 341.

able. Even war, ever since its insistence upon totality, has lost almost all its attraction and majesty: the forces that fight one another in these material battles are gigantic ghosts and chimeras—while, on the other hand, all spiritual reality, all truth, all beauty, all longing for these things, appears today to be more and more substantial than ever."[4]

Schiller's dialectical pattern of analysis can be applied instructively to Hesse's conception of two realities, for the elegy, satire, and the idyll represent the principal tones of Hesse's works. When the writer loses himself in recollections of an age at which the disparity between reality and his vision has not yet become apparent to him, the tone is primarily elegiac, as is the case in most of his childhood reminiscences and in many of the poems. When he is obsessed, on the other hand, with the false values of the present, as in *The Steppenwolf* and many of the critical essays, his tone is satiric. And on the rare occasions —at the end of *Siddhartha*, in certain scenes of *The Steppenwolf*, *The Journey to the East*, and much of *The Glass Bead Game*—when the conflicts have been resolved, when "reality" and higher reality are one and the same whole, the mood changes yet again and becomes idyllic in Schiller's sense.

This corresponds generally to Hesse's conception of the triadic rhythm of humanization, for the individual's awareness of the dichotomy between the chiliastic dream and everyday "reality" proceeds in three separate stages: innocence, despair, resolution. From the writer's point of view the period of childhood innocence is elegiac: its subject is primarily the ideal, but an ideal totality that is irrevocably lost in the past. The gaping disparity between

[4] Letter of February 7, 1940; GS, VII, 623.

reality and ideal during the long middle period of despair supplies the perfect object for satire. And the fulfilled chiliastic vision or magical thinking must be related in idyllic terms since it lies in a still unrealized future (or potential present). In his fiction Hesse is concerned above all with the period of despair. There are, to be sure, occasional glimpses of innocence and resolution, often in one and the same work (e.g. *Siddhartha*). Principally, however, the story worth telling is the period of man's despair. Thus most of his writing falls into the category that Schiller would call satire.

Satire, in turn, can be of two kinds, depending on the author's feelings and intentions. It can be either jocular and scornful (*scherzend, spottend*) or rebuking and tinged with pathos (*strafend, pathetisch*). Now there are frequent passages of bitter satire in Hesse's works, especially during the period between *Siddhartha* and *The Steppenwolf*. His anger and indignation is often reminiscent of the tenth *Duino Elegy*, which Rilke was writing in these same years; according to one witness, the veins on Rilke's temple swelled with rage as he recited the lines depicting the gilded horror of accepted "reality":

> . . . der vergoldete Lärm, das platzende Denkmal.
> O, wie spurlos zerträte ein Engel ihnen den Trost-
> markt. . . .

Similarly, in narratives such as *At the Spa* (1924) and *The Nuremberg Journey* (1927), Hesse is capable of an almost Old Testament wrath because the disparity between the two realities is so glaringly great. Yet despite passages of this sort, no one would call Hesse (or Rilke) a satirist of Swiftian or Voltairian temper. In general he tends toward a milder form of satire—that is, toward irony and humor, both of which are lacking in the elegy and the idyll.

It is precisely this quality of irony and humor that has attracted Hesse's most sophisticated readers. In his introduction to the French translation of *The Journey to the East*, André Gide wrote that Hesse's style is tempered "by a certain indefinable latent irony, of which so few Germans seem capable and the total absence of which often ruins so many works of so many of their authors, who take themselves frightfully seriously."[5] Likewise Thomas Mann, the "Ironic German" par excellence (in Erich Heller's well-known phrase), was captivated by the same quality in *The Glass Bead Game*: "While reading it I felt very strongly how helpful the parodistic element is—the fiction and persiflage of a biography working with learned conjectures—in keeping a late-work like this, which runs the danger of progressive intellectualization, within manageable limits, in preserving its sense of play [*Spielfähigkeit*]."[6] It goes without saying that readers who completely missed this ironic or parodistic element totally misconstrued the meaning of these novels.

This humor emerges most strongly during the years following *Siddhartha*. *Demian* and *Siddhartha* are works almost devoid of humor: Hesse was far too greatly preoccupied with the construction of an ideal as an escape from his emotional crisis of the war years. As long as he was able to pursue his ideal in the near isolation of his retreat at Montagnola, he was able to avoid the problem. But when lecture tours in the twenties brought him and his ideal into a direct and brutal confrontation with the

[5] André Gide, *Préfaces* (Neuchâtel et Paris, 1948), p. 184. The translation by Jean Lambert (*Voyage en Orient*) was published in 1947.

[6] "Hermann Hesse zum siebzigsten Geburtstag," in Thomas Mann, *Gesammelte Werke* (S. Fischer, 1960), x, 518.

"reality" that he had fled, he had to reconcile the two or admit defeat—that is, to give way to despair. It was one thing to sit in the serene peace of the Swiss Alps and write about the Brahman's son who attained beatitude; but quite another thing to journey, like Zarathustra, down into the plains and to display his views in the market place. *The Nuremberg Journey* records this process of acclimatization. As he stood each evening before his audience, manuscript in hand, the conflict revealed itself to Hesse "in concentrated form." If this were an abstract situation, Hesse wrote, if it were an "ideal" poet standing before an "ideal" audience, then the situation would lead to a tragic catastrophe: it could end only with the self-destruction of the poet or in his being stoned by the audience, for neither side would be willing to concede the slightest margin of its own reality. "In the world of experience, however, everything is slightly different. Here there is room for little distortions; here, most of all, there is room for that ancient mediator between reality and the ideal: humor."[7] Through humor it is possible to avoid the head-on collision that would lead inevitably to the poet's defeat. "On evenings like that I use up a lot of humor—humor of every sort, especially gallows humor."

At times, of course, Hesse rebelled indignantly against his own acquiescence, assuring himself that he was completely in the right with his protest against "reality." But ultimately the new sense asserted itself: "Again I felt the tremor between pole and antipole, and above the abyss between reality and the ideal, between reality and beauty, I felt the sway of the airy bridge: humor." *The Nuremberg Journey* might well have had the subtitle "My Journey to a Sense of Humor," for this emerges as the central theme of the narrative and represents, as such, a turning point

[7] *Die Nürnberger Reise*; GD, IV, 117-181.

in Hesse's writing. He concludes his essay with the discovery: "Perhaps, as I had thought from time to time, there was after all something like a humorist concealed within me, and in that case I was well provided for. My sense of humor was merely not yet fully developed; I still had not suffered enough."

The novel *The Steppenwolf* is a record of the suffering that leads to a full-blown sense of humor. At the very outset Harry Haller learns from the tract that the solution to his misery is humor. He is a man totally devoid of humor and thus unwilling, or unable, to make any concessions to "reality." This recalcitrance, this insistence upon an unequivocal "either-or," leads in the beginning to his frequent speculations on suicide; his unwillingness to compromise puts him in the position of the ideal poet that Hesse had imagined in *The Nuremberg Journey*. The tract points out, however, that only the strongest natures have the courage for suicide or for an existence in the realm of the pure ideal. For most others there remains "a third realm, an imaginary but sovereign world: humor." Humor is "the escape of conciliation. . . . In its imaginary sphere the confused and manifold ideals of the Steppenwolf can be realized." The tract continues with a paean to humor:

"Only humor, that magnificent invention of those who are hindered in their vocation for the Ultimate, of the *almost* tragic, of the most gifted among unhappy men—only humor (perhaps the most unique and most brilliant achievement of mankind) brings about the impossible. . . . To live in the world as though it were not the world, to eschew it as though it were no eschewal—all these popular and often formulated claims of a sublime wisdom can be realized solely through humor."

It is a long time before Harry Haller is willing to accept this view; the novel deals primarily with his suffering. At the end, when he is punished for his failure to make the proper distinctions between reality and the ideal, Harry's sentence is: to be laughed at by the assembled Immortals. Laughter emerges as the symbol of humor, which represents in turn the theme of the novel.

In his succeeding works, though humor remains a central theme, the symbol reflects a more tempered view. Laughter is the proper symbol for a sense of humor—gallows humor, as Hesse put it in his essay—that has just been newly forged out of despair. As it matures laughter gives way to the milder symbol of the smile: the beatific smile of Leo in *The Journey to the East* and the old music master in *The Glass Bead Game* or the ironic smile of the novelist Hesse, which was noted by Gide and Thomas Mann. At the end of *The Journey to the East* the narrator is rebuked for a transgression similar to that of Harry Haller. On this occasion, characteristically, the sentence is milder, for gallows humor has been distilled into the fine essence of irony: "The follies of your novitiate are annulled when we smile about them." In humor Hesse discovered his way out of the dilemma; laughter and smiles represent adequate and appropriate symbols for this pervasive theme.

Hesse's humor, of course, has many features in common with the Romantic irony of Friedrich Schlegel or humor as defined by Novalis; and it is particularly because of their humor that Hesse responded so warmly to the works of Jean Paul and Wilhelm Raabe. In the introduction to an edition of Jean Paul that Hesse edited in 1921 he maintained that Jean Paul became a humorist as the result of his inability to reconcile in his own life the conflict between

his dreams and the reality about him.[8] And in a reminis-
cence that he recorded of a visit with the aged Raabe,
Hesse states clearly that he was most deeply impressed
by Raabe's "devious humor" and by the great faith and
love of humanity that seemed to lie behind his penchant
for bantering irony.[9] Yet Hesse's own variety of humor
emerged organically, as we have seen, as a solution to
his personal dilemma, and it developed in stages from a
desperate gallows humor, through the rousing laughter
of the Immortals, to the beatific smiling irony of *The
Glass Bead Game*. Humor becomes the perspective from
which Hesse chooses to view reality after the consolations
of the elegy have failed and when it becomes apparent
that the idyll can never be attained in our world.

[8] "Über Jean Paul"; GS, VII, 264.
[9] "Besuch bei einem Dichter"; GD, IV, 643-644.

+((

6

The Crisis of Language

THE SENSE of a discrepancy between everyday "reality" and essential reality and the subsequent attempt to render this higher reality in a literary form produce a dilemma that Hesse shares with many other writers of the twentieth century. It turns out, namely, that language, ravaged and trivialized by thoughtless use and conditioned to describe everyday "reality," no longer suffices to express reality of a higher order. It is like a precision tool whose edges have become dulled; the knife once used by the skilled artisan to carve delicate images has been appropriated by clumsy workers who use it to split wood for kindling. In the preceding chapter we saw how this situation produced, in Rilke and Hesse, the need for comparative forms of adjectives and adverbs that are normally absolute.

This so-called "crisis of language" (*Sprachkrise*), like many of the most interesting phenomena of modern literature, was anticipated in certain respects by German Romanticism.[1] Only in more recent times, however, with a boost by Nietzsche as well as advances in the physical sciences, has it become a central dilemma of overwhelming proportions. If language is not an adequate tool to express

[1] In an essay on "James Joyces Epiphanie und die Überwindung der empirischen Welt in der modernen deutschen Prosa," *Deutsche Vierteljahresschrift*, 35 (1961), 594-616, I have discussed this problem in more detail and listed some of the relevant bibliographical items. Walker Gibson's anthology, *The Limits of Language*, is a useful compilation of sources and references in English.

the distinctions of modern science—the conception, for instance, that light consists at the same time of waves and of particles—then how can it possibly satisfy the requisites of literature, which deals with an even more tenuous stuff than light? It is, of course, by no means a peculiarly German phenomenon. T. S. Eliot was referring to the same dilemma when he wrote, in *Four Quartets*:

> . . . . Words strain,
> Crack and sometimes break, under the burden,
> Under the tension, slip, slide, perish,
> Decay with imprecision, will not stay in place,
> Will not stay still.

And he characterizes poetry as

> . . . . . . a raid on the inarticulate
> With shabby equipment always deteriorating
> In the general mess of imprecision of feeling. . . .

Joyce's Stephen Hero is obsessed with the same problem:

"He read Skeat's *Etymological Dictionary* by the hour, and his mind, which had from the first been only too submissive to the infant sense of wonder, was often hypnotized by the most commonplace conversation. People seemed to him strangely ignorant of the value of the words which they used so glibly."

In his collection of essays (*The Treasure of the Meek*), Maurice Maeterlinck uttered a similar concern:

"When we express something, we degrade it strangely. We believe that we have plunged to the very bottom of the abyss, and when we ascend to the surface, the drop of water that sparkles at the tip of our pale fingers no longer resembles the sea from which it was taken. We believe that we have discovered a grotto of marvelous treasures;

and when we return to the light of day, we have brought
forth nothing but false gems and bits of glass; and yet
the treasure glitters, unchanged, in the shadows."[2]

The centrality of the dilemma is emphasized by the fact
that Robert Musil borrowed this sentence from Maeterlinck as the motto for his first novel, *Young Törless*
(1906), which revolves around the duality of reality and
the impossibility of expressing its higher form. Wherever
we look, we find modern writers fascinated by this paradox. For the writer's medium is language; yet he is com-
pelled to distrust its ability to express what is meaningful to him. The situation is not without analogy to that of
a technologist who cannot trust his slide rule, a painter
who is skeptical of his paints, or a musician who cannot
find the proper notes to render the sounds that he hears in
his head. It is no accident that the century which produced
the crisis of language in literature has also witnessed the
development of electronic music, in art the techniques
of Futurism and Constructivism, and in science the tri-
umphant advent of the IBM machine.

Early in his career Rilke wrote a touching poem to
humble words, "die armen Worte, die im Alltag darben,
die unscheinbaren Worte. . . ." Much of his later poetry
shows how concerned he was to rehabilitate these words
that have been ruined by overuse and subsequent neglect.
He finds his own answer to the language crisis, like Georg
Trakl, Konrad Weiss, and others, in the autotelic metaphor,
whose meaning lies totally within itself: the metaphor
exists, as it were, on a different plane from everyday
reality and its significance is thus not impaired by mis-
conceptions latent in that sphere. Similarly, Stefan George
took recourse to a world of private symbols, which need

---

[2] *Le trésor des humbles* (Paris, 1898), pp. 65-66.

no reference to outside reality for their validity. Rimbaud's poetic excesses, Mallarmé's hermetic cabala of language, as well as Valéry's absolute poetry—all these attempts stem ultimately from the same language skepticism, while the young Joyce found his answer in his own unique and very specifically defined secularization of the epiphany. Jean-Paul Sartre discussed the problem in *What is Literature?* (1945) and supplied an answer of sorts in his fiction. Hofmannsthal's *Letter of Lord Chandos* (1902), which is frequently cited to document the final break of modern German literature from the nineteenth century, is at the same time possibly the most despairing statement of the language crisis; and Hofmannsthal, consistently, found the most radical solution: he gave up lyric poetry, which depends upon words alone for its meaning, and turned instead to drama, where the words, supported and interpreted as they are by gesture, pantomime, emotion or silence of the actor, do not carry the full burden of expression.

Hesse thus shares in a characteristic phenomenon of modern literature when he becomes aware of the crisis of language. In each case, of course, the author's unique problematics brings him into conflict with language; for Hesse it was the awareness of the disparity between so-called "reality" and the eternal reality in which he believed. The problem that faced him: how to express eternal reality in terms ordinarily applied to everyday "reality"? For Hesse the language crisis became acute only after his two realities came into conflict—around the time of *Demian*. We can even date it specifically from an essay entitled "Language" that he wrote in 1917.[3] Language is "a shortcoming and residue that causes the poet more distress than anything else. At times he can actually hate

[3] "Sprache"; GS, VII, 56-62.

it, indict it and curse it—or rather, himself, that he is born to work with this miserable tool." Hesse goes on to voice his envy of the painter and the musician, whose works are intelligible beyond all boundaries of language. He envies the musician especially because his medium is used only for one thing: music. The writer, on the other hand, must use for his purposes the same language in which school is taught and business is carried on, in which telegrams are sent and trials conducted. "If he says 'heart,' meaning the quivering life-element in man, his most intimate capacity and weakness—the word at the same time indicates a muscle. . . . He cannot use a single word that . . . does not simultaneously summon up alien, disturbing, hostile associations." Hence the writer is never able to render more than a fraction of what he intends. Here again he comes into conflict with reality, for just as he struggles to find new modes of expression, so too the bourgeois clings to his simplified paradigmatic language, in which everything has its accepted name. The world of everyday reality resents and resists any attempt on the part of the poet to disturb traditional language.

Hesse returns to this problem constantly. In *The Nuremberg Journey* the language crisis goes hand in hand with the development of humor as an escape hatch from a face-to-face conflict between the two realities. What, Hesse asks himself, can he possibly have to say to his audience? Their realities are totally different and, hence, their communication takes place on two different levels. A further complication is raised by the conflicting urges to be absolutely honest and yet to write "beautifully" in the tradition of the past.

"All the writing of my generation vacillates desperately back and forth between these two demands. For if we are prepared to be honest to the point of self-extermination —where can we find the expressions for it? Our literary language, our school language doesn't supply it. Our handwriting has been formed out of the past. Isolated despairing books like Nietzsche's *Ecce Homo* seem to show us a way, but ultimately they point out even more trenchantly the futility of seeking a way out of our dilemma."

The consequence of these reflections, as Hesse recalled years later, was the realization that his way of life and his way of writing did not correspond to one another:

"For the sake of good writing, I had more or less done violence to most of my experiences and I had either to give up writing or to resolve to be a bad writer instead of a good one. My attempts to do so, from *Demian* to *The Journey to the East*, led me farther and farther away from the good and beautiful traditions of the narrative."[4]

It is essential to remember, of course, that Hesse is not appealing to any absolute standards when he speaks in this connection of "good" and "bad" writing. "Good" actually has a double meaning. In *The Nuremberg Journey* it refers, not without a touch of irony, to traditional narrative forms that were liked and, more important, easily understood by the average reader: uncomplicated traditional narrative style. At the same time—and this is implicit in the second passage—Hesse himself loved in many cases the same writers: the nineteenth-century Swiss novelists Gottfried Keller and Jeremias Gotthelf, for instance, or the less sophisticated Romantic tales. These, along with others, represent the "good" and "beautiful" tradition of writing, and the reason is associated with the conception of two realities. For—at the conscious risk of over-

4 "Unterbrochene Schulstunde"; GD, IV, 868.

generalization—the style of these writers is "good" precisely because they are not aware of—or at least do not wish to exploit—any rift between the real and the ideal. They were writing from a real or assumed perspective of unity and hence the words of everyday life served with perfect adequacy to describe the vision of their fiction. As a result, there is no pronounced stylistic tension between the object of their expression and the medium of expression, between vision and reality.[5]

For Hesse, however, and most other modern writers, the situation has changed. The disparity between reality and the vision has become so glaring that words from one realm cannot possibly express the meaning of the other. Radically stated, it is impossible to express ultimate truth in any form at all, as Hesse wrote to a perceptive critic of *The Journey to the East*: "My book, the confessions of an aging writer, attempts . . . to portray that which cannot be portrayed, to call to mind the ineffable."[6] Yet true poetry and philosophy, he continues, are characterized precisely by this attempt to transcend the limits of the possible. The fact that they are doomed inevitably to failure is the tragedy of poetry and philosophy; but their unceasing attempts constitute their responsibility and their nobility.

The only possible course is to renounce the "good" writing of tradition and turn to "bad" writing, that is, to the uncomfortable, often experimental forms of fiction

[5] The problem is actually far more complex than I have indicated, but for the purposes of generalization my remarks are probably valid enough. For an exhaustive discussion of the shifting relationship between objectivity and subjectivity in prose from Goethe to the end of the 19th century, see Richard Brinkmann's important study: *Wirklichkeit und Illusion* (Tübingen, 1957).

[6] Letter of September, 1932; GS, VII, 524.

that may offend the audience. In this sense, of course, Rilke, Trakl, Eliot, Joyce, and the others are "bad" writers. The crisis of language produced a variety of independent solutions: the illogical comparative form, autotelic metaphor, absolute symbols, Joyce's epiphany. One could easily add other techniques that were conceived or adapted for the same purpose: Proust's association, the montage effect of Dos Passos and Alfred Döblin, Musil's essayism, to mention only a few conspicuous examples.

Two of the less radical techniques employed by Hesse and other writers to transcend the impasse of language are the symbol and the archetypal image, for both arouse associations that extend beyond any meaning attached to the words themselves. Both of these techniques are best considered within the specific context in which they occur, but by way of illustration we might anticipate with two examples. The Glass Bead Game is one of Hesse's most effective symbols. It is not defined closely enough to reduce it to a simple allegory, but is presented in terms so general that the reader can produce his own associations from almost any area of modern intellectual life. It stands *par excellence* for the tendency toward abstraction and synthesis characteristic of the years between the two world wars—in non-objective art, in atonal music, in symbolic logic—and thus represents Hesse's conception of totality through magical thinking. The archetypal image, on the other hand, derives its effect from the relationship it establishes between a character in the present and a mythical figure from the past: it evokes a sense of timelessness. The action in the present is viewed, as it were, as an eternal recurrence of an action in the past. This is what Hesse had in mind when he referred to Demian and Mother Eva as figures "that encompass and signify far more than is accessible to rational consideration; they are magical conjurations."[7]

A vastly more fascinating and far-reaching effect of the language crisis in the novel was its impact on the role of the narrator. Once the writer admits that his standpoint, the point of view of the personal or omniscient narrator, is not by necessity that of his audience, then the omniscient narrator becomes an absurdity in fiction. Throughout most of the nineteenth century authors maintained, or at least pretended to maintain, the fiction of an implicit agreement between author and reader. Theodor Fontane's characters continue to live by standards that they acknowledge as false; and similarly Fontane continues to write as though his narrative view of reality were indisputably identical with that of his late nineteenth-century readers. But the twentieth century has witnessed radical changes in the function of the narrator which parallel developments in the natural and social sciences. The discoveries of Einstein, Planck, and Heisenberg destroyed the illusion of a totally "objective" science by including the observer as a factor in the experiment itself. Recent studies of social thought or history, like H. Stuart Hughes' *Consciousness and Society* or G. P. Gooch's *Historians and History in the Nineteenth Century* have likewise taken the narrator into consideration, conceding that the personal views of the writer inevitably must color or slant his presentation, no matter how objective he may strive to be.

The modern novel has been concerned with precisely the same problem. If the omniscient narrator is an absurdity, then he must be replaced. The two most common replacements have been, on the one hand, the first-person narrator who recounts his own story in a style ranging from

7 GS, VII, 515.

ostensible objectivity to stream-of-consciousness; and, on the other hand, the third-person narrator, whose point of view is explicitly located by the author. Thus Thomas Mann's Felix Krull tells us his own story, which in turn is colored by what we learn of Felix from his own words; while the tragic life of Adrian Leverkühn (in *Doctor Faustus*) is related in ironic counterpoint by the pedantic and rather prosaic Serenus Zeitblom. When the invisible narrator does play a role, as in Joyce's *Ulysses* or in Kafka's novels, then he takes up a position so close to his hero as to be indistinguishable from him.[8]

For Hesse the problematic role of the narrator has profound implications, many of which can be examined only in the context of the novels themselves. In general, however, it can be pointed out that the position of the narrator is determined largely by the central dilemma of dualism. Hesse must try to tell his stories under the assumption that the audience will not be familiar with the higher reality that he is trying to depict. Furthermore, as he has indicated himself, the ideal cannot possibly be expressed in the language of everyday, the language that is the writer's tool. As a result, not once in his novels do we find the Third Kingdom portrayed from an absolute point of view. In *The Journey to the East* and *The Glass Bead Game*, the two novels in which he attempted most systematically to render his vision of the Third Kingdom, we have on the one hand a renegade narrator who has deserted the League and hence no longer sees it perfectly; and on the other hand a scholar of a later generation who assembles from the documents at his disposal the record

---

[8] There is, of course, an elaborate bibliography of writings on this matter. I should like to mention only two basic works: Käthe Friedemann, *Die Rolle des Erzählers in der Epik* (Leipzig, 1910) and Friedrich Beissner, *Der Erzähler Franz Kafka* (Stuttgart, 1952).

of a critical period in the history of the Glass Bead Game. In both cases the narrative standpoint has been selected with the greatest care, for Hesse realizes that any individual actually living on the third level would speak a language utterly incomprehensible to the reader who exists on another level of reality. Even the simplest words would have a different meaning. In a letter of 1943, Hesse wrote explicitly about this problem. "What we experience is not relatable in words," he says, "and the problem lies in the word 'I.' " Most people use the word "I" "as though it were a known, objective quantity, which it simply isn't."[9] Actually, he continues, there are two kinds of "I," and the difficulty is to determine where one begins and the other ends. There is "our subjective, empirical, individual I," which vacillates and is subject to a variety of external influences. Then there is a second "I," an eternal *I* that constitutes our share in the Whole, in the Over-personal. This is obviously the "I" of the third level, which emerges strongly when the individual is reunited with the spiritual community. But its language is unintelligible to the "empirical I" of the second level, which is exposed to all the impulses of despair.

All the other novels exploit various devices of indirectness when the narrative approaches the third level. In *Demian* and *The Steppenwolf* the first-person narrator resorts to symbolism; in *Siddhartha* the third-person narrator, who up to the end has maintained a point of view immediately proximate to that of Siddhartha, focuses on Govinda, who sees the realm of simultaneity reflected in the face of his friend Siddhartha. At no point does Hesse, as narrator, attempt to portray directly the experienced Third Kingdom or magical thinking, for the direct rendition

[9] GS, VII, 635-636.

of totality and simultaneity exceeds the capacity of everyday language.

Another narrative device that Hesse exploits, along with such writers as Gide, Huxley, and Thomas Mann, is the multiplicity of views. If no single view of reality is absolute, then possibly one can approximate an absolute view by presenting the discrepancy of various standpoints: somewhere between them lies the truth. (This is the technique of observation which, in physics, Niels Bohr called the principle of complementarity.) In *The Steppenwolf* the life of Harry Haller is presented not only in his own first-person narrative, but also from two further, radically opposed points of view: that of the Immortals, in the Tract, and that of the completely bourgeois "editor" of Haller's manuscript. In *The Glass Bead Game* Hesse returned to this technique, for in addition to contemporary documents about Joseph Knecht's life we have the reaction to his career by an epigonal scholar as well as the appended autobiographical sketches from Knecht's own hand. It is possible, of course, to misunderstand the novels completely if these factors are not taken into consideration and weighed according to their relative points of view, and probably no two of his books have encountered more misinterpretation than *The Steppenwolf* and *The Glass Bead Game*. Hesse, however, is absolutely consistent to his own experience and to the general crisis of language when he resorts to sophisticated narrative devices in an attempt to render his vision of simultaneity and totality if not objectively, as was the tendency in the nineteenth century, then indirectly through multiple or carefully delineated points of view. His own specifically unique contribution to narrative technique was the counterpoint of double perspective, discussed below in the chapter on *The Steppenwolf*.

A further characteristic of the modern novel that goes hand in hand with the crisis of language is the tendency for these problems to precipitate themselves not only functionally but also thematically in the works themselves. Again and again—in Hesse as well as in Gide, in Aldous Huxley as well as Hermann Broch—the narrator comes back to the difficulty, yes even the impossibility, of expressing his ideas through the medium at his disposal. Language and the problems of narration become a theme in themselves—in Hesse this is particularly conspicuous in *The Steppenwolf*, *The Journey to the East*, and *The Glass Bead Game*. The treatment of abstract topics such as the crisis of language within the framework of the novel is one aspect of the tendency toward essayism in modern fiction. If the author feels at a loss to express simultaneity and totality through the narrative alone, then he includes obtrusive passages of a discursive or expository nature, in which he allows himself to reflect upon the implications, in a broader sense, of the specific story that he is telling, hoping thereby to achieve additional dimensions of reality.

What distinguishes Hesse and his literary contemporaries from the writers who happen, as it were, by an accident of birth to be writing in the twentieth century, is principally the realization that the old forms no longer suffice; in other words, the experience of the breakdown of reality, the consequent crisis of language, and the resulting search for new structures and means of expression. This situation produced a distinct generation of writers: Proust, Gide, Huxley, Joyce, Broch, Mann, Hesse, and several others. They differ by virtue of this awareness from the many who continued to write, happy with the forms of traditional narrative and innocent of any problematics in the act of writing itself. And they can be distinguished from the postwar generation—which in

Germany refers to them with the partly admiring, partly derogatory term "calligraphers" (*Kalligraphen*)—to the extent that art as such constitutes the central concern of their works. The crisis of language forced these artists into a heady infatuation with technical experimentation. The ideal that they attempted to render through these new techniques is an autonomous realm of art—Hesse's chiliastic vision, Thomas Mann's "magic mountain," Proust's kingdom of memory—in which the norms of everyday reality are suspended in favor of timelessness and totality. The conviction that man's salvation from the exigencies of time can be found in an autonomous aesthetic world of the spirit bestows an amazing coherence of theme upon the entire generation. If they differ among themselves— and where can one find greater literary variety than in the generation that embraces Proust and Huxley, Gide and Hesse?—it is not so much in theme as in the structures through which the common theme expresses itself. Our study of Hesse's themes has highlighted the bonds of similarity that link him to his generation. To discover his uniqueness within that generation we must turn to the structure of his novels. For Hesse's reaction to the common crisis of language was not so much an abrupt break with the past, as rather a radical transformation or escalation of traditional forms that had grown problematic.

In 1949 Hesse summarized his literary career: "As a writer, I believe, I have always been a traditionalist. With few exceptions I was always satisfied with the traditional form, a standard pattern, a model. It was never important to me to offer novelty of form, or to be an avant-gardist or pioneer."[10] *The Steppenwolf* is the notable exception to which this statement refers. Otherwise the observation is correct. It is this traditionalism that distinguishes Hesse's

[10] GS, VII, 683.

novels, say, from the works of a contemporary like Hermann Broch, who set about writing *The Sleepwalkers* with the explicit intention of creating what he called "a *novum* in the form of the novel." At the same time, as we shall see, the traditional form supplied only the starting point for Hesse. He rarely took over an older form without shaping it, adapting it, modernizing it in accordance with his awareness of the crisis of language. With the vocabulary of Novalis and the structures of E.T.A. Hoffmann he dealt with the problems of psychoanalysis and existential thought. Within the transformed framework of traditional Romantic genres he created paradigms of the twentieth-century dilemma.

PART II. THE STRUCTURES

Kafka's stories are not treatises on religious, metaphysical or moral problems, but works of literature. . . . Kafka speaks to us neither as a theologian nor as a philosopher, but solely as a poet.

(Hesse, "Kafka Interpretations")

❭❭❭❭❭❭❭❭❭❭❭❭❭❭❭❭❭❭❭❭❭❭❭❭❭❭❭❭❭

7

The Gospel of *Demian*

IT IS A TRUISM of European intellectual history that
World War I represented a violent eruption of social
and spiritual forces that had for some time been seething
beneath the apparently placid veneer of prewar society.
Man's view of reality had undergone deep-lying changes
that made it wholly incompatible with the existing structure of society, and a cataclysm was inevitable. The war
itself, with its new and vast proportions, came as a surprise and shock to many; yet it was not so much the
physical phenomenon of battle that dumbfounded a
startled world, but rather the total transformation of a
traditional civilization that was externally the result but
internally the ultimate cause of the war.

Since 1918 the world has witnessed wars that dwarf,
for sheer efficiency and impersonality of killing, the
slaughter of World War I. Yet as an emotional experience
the war of 1914-1918 seems to have penetrated deeper
into the human heart than subsequent wars. The reason,
possibly, is simply that war has become too efficient and
impersonal. This is the implication of the young German
dramatist Tankred Dorst, who denies that the atomic
bomb is too terrible to be treated dramatically. Certainly,
he writes, it is feared no more than people feared the
Swedes during the Thirty Years' War or than an im-
pressionable reader of popular magazines fears cancer.
"On the contrary: these are concrete terrors that people
can comprehend, that affect them directly—whereas I

honestly know no one who arranges his life as though the bomb were going to fall next week."[1] Whatever the reasons may be, the First World War produced literature of a quality and quantity unmatched since 1945—works in which the authors sought indefatigably to uncover the reasons for the world-shaking event.

In Germany and Austria particularly the analysis of prewar civilization supplied the material for many of the major novels written between 1918 and 1933. Most of them, turning with an almost morbid fascination to the past, sought by analysis to expose the fatal flaws of the irretrievably vanished age, to unmask beneath Prussian austerity or Viennese gaiety the dark powers that unleashed a holocaust of unsuspected proportions upon the world, transforming all society in its course. Robert Musil in *The Man without Qualities* (1930-43) and Joseph Roth in *Radetzky March* (1932) portrayed these somber metamorphoses fermenting beneath the Strauss-waltz illusion of the Austro-Hungarian Empire. Under almost laboratory conditions in *The Magic Mountain* (1924) Thomas Mann hermetically isolated and combined the various societal elements that, in reality, exploded into World War I. In the first two volumes of his massive trilogy *The Sleepwalkers* (1931-32) Hermann Broch described the deterioration of outmoded values in his Prussian Junker Pasenow and the Rhineland proletarian mystic Esch; the final volume, which takes place in 1918, shows finally the triumph of Huguenau, the symbol of the new valueless society of postwar Germany, over the forces of the past. In every case it is society that is on trial. The writers seek mercilessly to lay bare the reasons for the upheaval

---

[1] Tankred Dorst, "Die Bühne ist der absolute Ort," in *Grosse Schmährede an der Stadtmauer*, Collection Theater, Texte 5 (Köln, 1962), p. 116.

in values and society that had been unparalleled since the French Revolution. Such a novel is Hermann Hesse's *Demian: The Story of Emil Sinclair's Youth (1919).*

Demian was written in a few months in 1917 as a direct product of Hesse's psychoanalysis and subsequent reexamination of his beliefs. As a result, we find in the book many examples of the influence of Nietzsche, Jung, Bachofen, and other thinkers who most immediately contributed to Hesse's revaluation of values. The title itself, moreover, reveals a break with earlier works, which had revolved subjectively, as a rule, around individuals or situations implied by the title. *Demian* was originally published with the subtitle: "The Story of a Youth by Emil Sinclair." Two points are of interest here. In the first place, the subtitle is left significantly vague to imply that the "youth" is intended generally and symbolically—not specifically. Secondly, the full title raises the question of the relationship between Demian and Emil Sinclair, a question that becomes even more perplexing as the novel progresses. Is it Demian's youth or Sinclair's that is important? Does Demian really exist, or is he a symbolic representation of Sinclair's *daimon*? In what way is either of them an exemplary figure? The various questions implicit in the title can be answered only by a detailed analysis of the text.

The Organization of the Plot

Seen as genre, the novel falls into the category of the *Bildungsroman* (roughly "novel of education"), which flourished particularly during the age of German Romanticism. Characteristically the *Bildungsroman* traces the development of a youth during his formative years from immaturity and uncertainty of purpose to the total integration of his personality and capabilities—precisely the process that we witness in *Demian*. The emphasis and goal may shift from case to case, but basically the form remains constant: it is neither a novel of manners, nor a novel of tight-knit plot, nor a loosely constructed picaresque story. Instead it typically displays an episodic structure that permits a broad exposure of the hero to contemporary cultural influences while deriving its coherence from a central focus on the inner growth of the youth toward an affirmation of life. A specific characteristic of the Romantic *Bildungsroman* that becomes important in *Demian* is the presence of a spiritual mentor who educates the hero according to the principles of the group that he represents; this group (usually a secret society) stands for an ideal rather than the achieved reality of the period. We find this pattern not only in early novels like Goethe's *Wilhelm Meister's Apprenticeship*, Hölderlin's *Hyperion*, and Jean Paul's *Titan*, but also in a twentieth-century example like Thomas Mann's *The Magic Mountain*, in which Hans Castorp's intellectual guides, Settembrini and Naphta, are emissaries respectively of the Freemasons and the Jesuits.

By using this traditional form Hesse consciously placed himself in a narrative tradition to which he felt attuned. Although the form has inspired non-German novels (Romain Rolland's *Jean Christophe*, Somerset Maugham's *Of Human Bondage*, Thomas Wolfe's massive cycles), the *Bildungsroman* is a typically German genre and constitutes Germany's main contribution to the European novel. So Hesse was employing a familiar, almost a national form. This is interesting in itself because he had made use of this obvious form only once before—in *Peter Camenzind* —and for his other major works he resorted to narrative patterns of a different sort. Further: although *Demian* is instantly identifiable as a *Bildungsroman*, Hesse transformed and expanded the dimensions of the traditional form beyond the limits it had hitherto observed. The main changes we shall note are: internalization of the ideal represented by the group; structuring by the use of prefiguration; broadening of the novel's implications by the use of myth and symbol in a characteristically modern way.

Like most of Hesse's novels *Demian* has a bare minimum of exterior action or "plot." It is ostensibly the first-person narrative of a young man named Emil Sinclair, who relates certain episodes from his life between the ages of ten and twenty. Although no dates are mentioned (as is also the case, incidentally, in *The Magic Mountain*) the period is clearly that from 1904 or 1905 to the spring of 1915. The first episode takes place over a period of a few weeks when Sinclair is ten years old. The only son of a prosperous and devout family, he sometimes plays with boys from the lower classes. One of these, Franz Kromer, manages by playing on the younger boy's naïveté to blackmail him for literally no reason. Sinclair had boasted of stealing some apples; this was not true, but since he is ashamed to admit his lie in front of the other boys, he allows Kromer to blackmail him with the threat of exposure. Under the strain of this constant threat Sinclair's whole personality begins to change; his behavior at home becomes bad, and his boyish innocence turns to suspicion and rebellion. These circumstances come to the attention of Max Demian, a new boy in town who is two years older than Sinclair. By observation and shrewd reasoning he ascertains the root of the trouble and manages to free Sinclair from Kromer's clutches.

For several years Sinclair scarcely notices Demian. Then during a communion class they are brought together again, and Demian stirs Sinclair out of his intellectual lethargy by challenging him to think about the deeper meaning of the Bible stories discussed in class. At this time, while he is about fourteen years old, Sinclair forms a strong attachment to Demian, but this gradually dies out when Sinclair is sent away to boarding school.

For a year his life is empty and uneventful. Then, in the fall of the second year Sinclair begins to associate with a group of young rebels in the school. His drinking and generally impossible behavior reach such proportions that he is put on probation and his father is summoned. All of this makes no impression on Sinclair, who is content to wait out his inevitable expulsion. Then suddenly in the spring he falls in love with a girl—or rather, with the idealized image of a girl—whom he meets in the park. Though he never speaks to her, he christens her Beatrice in his heart and worships her secretly. Immediately his behavior changes; his grades rise; he takes up painting in an attempt to capture on paper the image of his beloved. In the process of painting, however, his attachment to the real girl vanishes, and Sinclair finds himself painting pictures of an ideal figure that strangely resembles his friend Demian.

At this point he begins to recall details of his friendship with Demian and remembers one specific incident: Demian's interest in the carved figure of a bird in the keystone above the entrance to the Sinclair home. He decides to paint, from memory, a picture of that bird, which he mails to Demian. Demian's answer reaches Sinclair in a strange way. It is a cryptic note that he finds tucked into his book after a recess in school one day. (Although Hesse, typically, leaves this point quite vague, it is implied that the note was put there by the practice teacher, Dr. Follen, who has just come from the university and probably knew Demian there.) Demian's note links the painting of the bird with the name of a Gnostic deity, Abraxas, which becomes in Sinclair's mind the name of his ideal figure.

At this point Sinclair has reached a certain level of intellectual maturity and independence. The next influence in his life is the renegade theologian Pistorius, whose organ playing attracts Sinclair into the church where Pistorius practices. During this last winter of school when Sinclair is eighteen years old, he is introduced by Pistorius to a wide variety of antiquarian beliefs and myths that stir his imagination greatly. Pistorius, whom we can call an amateur psychoanalyst, helps Sinclair to interpret his frequent dreams, whereby Sinclair realizes that the problems that occupy his mind are actually manifestations of universal problems and myths. During this same period he meets another student, Knauer, who is very much interested in spiritism and whom Sinclair, through an act of almost extra-sensory perception, is able to save from suicide. Ultimately, however, he learns all that he can from Pistorius and the two part when Sinclair leaves school to go to the university.

In the fall of the following year (1913) Sinclair meets Demian in the university town, is introduced for the first time to Demian's mother, Frau Eva, and is accepted into the circle of their intimate friends: a group of widely variegated persons, all of whom share a central interest in the religious rebirth of the individual. Sinclair is immediately drawn to Frau Eva, for she seems to be the personification of the ideal figure that he had sought vainly to capture in all his paintings; this relationship assumes erotic proportions that are almost incestuous since the mother-motif is not the least ingredient of his highly ambivalent feelings toward her.

This idyll lasts through the winter and into the summer

of 1914; it is the fulfillment of Sinclair's dreams. Then the war breaks out. Demian, who is a reserve officer in the cavalry, goes off to the front, and Sinclair soon follows. In the spring of 1915 Sinclair is seriously wounded by a mortar shell. In the hospital where he is taken for treatment he awakens to find Demian on the next bed. Demian, dying, gives Sinclair a farewell embrace, and the two friends are separated forever. Sinclair's memories of his youth and friendship with Demian are written down only after Demian's death.

This brief outline of the rather sketchy plot reveals only a casual relevance to the origins of the war. These matters become clear only in the symbols of the book, which will be discussed separately. We can anticipate, however, by stating that Sinclair explicitly regards his story as characteristic and typological for his entire generation. This is mentioned in the introduction: "Every man's story is important, eternal, divine; and every man, as long as he lives and fulfills the will of nature, is marvelous and deserving of all attention. In each of us the spirit has become incarnate, in each the creatural suffers, in each a Saviour is crucified."[2]

It is obvious from the outline that the plot is not a smoothly flowing, continuous narrative, but rather an episodic focusing on certain incidents. "I shall speak, while I am still lingering over my childhood, only of the new things that came to me, only of those things that drove me forward, tore me loose."[3] Passages like this make it clear that we are dealing not with the evenly paced development of the traditional *Bildungsroman* (such as Stifter's *Indian Summer* or Novalis' *Heinrich von Ofterdingen*), but rather with a frenetic, spasmodic growth. This is indicated in the motto (a passage taken from the text itself) and expressed

[2] GD, III, 102.   [3] GD, III, 143.

repeatedly in the course of the novel: "I wanted only to live the life that clamored within me. Why was that so very difficult?" Nothing is more difficult for the individual than to find the way to himself, to live his own true life according to his inner principles. The natural tendency is for the individual to fall back into the accustomed routine and to accept the standards of his group. Sinclair's early life turns out to be a series of alternating progressions and regressions reflected in the episodes of the plot.

The eight chapters of the novel can be organized loosely into three groups that correspond to Sinclair's age and the place of action. Chapters 1-3 take place in his home town; the first two form a tight unit revolving around the Kromer episode and lasting a few weeks during Sinclair's tenth year, while the third deals with the communion class several years later. The next group of three chapters takes place in the town of St., where Sinclair lives in a boarding house while attending the gymnasium. Chapter 4 describes his initial degradation and the subsequent purification through Beatrice, while Chapters 5 and 6 are again grouped around the central figure of Pistorius and Sinclair's preoccupation with the ideal of Abraxas. The last two chapters, finally, deal with Sinclair's year at the university, his reunion with Demian and Frau Eva, and the war.

These groupings are rather arbitrary, reflecting only superficial plot and rough chronology. The real development of Sinclair as a character takes place on an entirely different level and corresponds only casually to the disposition of chapters. The central theme of this development is the discovery of his true nature: "The true calling for every person is only one thing: to come to himself."[4] But as Sinclair soon realizes, nothing is more difficult than to be oneself; it is a road that means loneliness, alienation,

[4] GD, III, 220-221.

and separation from the community. If the theme of the novel is Sinclair's search for himself with its stages of progressive alienation, then the inner structure of the first part of the book is the rhythm that obtains between his movement away from the community and tradition and his constant relapses into the consolations of solidarity.

Pendulation and Alienation

These considerations bring us to the central problem of the book. The title of the first chapter, "Two Worlds," presents Sinclair's dilemma. As a child he conceives of the world as being divided rather schematically into two halves, one "light" and one "dark." Sinclair gives a number of examples to illustrate this polarity, but it can be reduced roughly to something approximating the traditional Christian dichotomy of good and evil. At the beginning of the novel Sinclair feels himself by training and tradition attuned wholly to the "light" world represented by his parents, his sisters, by law and order, and by solid middle-class society. Since Kromer is an emissary of the other world, Sinclair's involvement with him represents a betrayal of the "good" world: "All the terrors of chaos threatened me, all the forces of ugliness and danger were drawn up against me";[5] "My sin was not specifically this or that; it was my sin that I had given the devil my hand."[6] When Sinclair arrives at home after the fateful meeting with Kromer, his father scolds him for having wet shoes. The thought that he was being reproached like a child at the very moment when Kromer (as he believed) might be reporting him to the police, gives Sinclair a strangely ambivalent feeling of childish security and superiority to his father. This moment, he says, was the most crucial point of that whole episode. "It was the first rent in the

[5] GD, III, 110.   [6] GD, III, 114.

holiness of my father, it was the first blow against the pillars upon which my childhood had rested and which every man, before he can become his true self, must have destroyed. These experiences, which nobody sees, constitute the inner, essential line of our destiny."[7] It is this inner line of his destiny that Sinclair traces in the remainder of the story, and it is characterized by the pendulation that actually determines the order of the episodes.

After this initial rebellion against his father, Sinclair reverts to childishness in a desperate attempt to ignore his plight. "A strange compulsion impelled me to take up again the child's games of my past; I was playing, as it were, the role of a boy who was younger than I, who was still good and free, innocent and secure."[8] This is the beginning of his alienation, for despite his frantic attempts to recapture the innocence of childhood he remained "shy and anguished like a spectre in the ordered peace of our house."[9]

It is Demian who frees Sinclair from his persecutor, but in doing so he deepens the rent already torn in the fabric of the younger boy's innocence. For Demian, by questioning the absolute validity of traditional authority, fortifies Sinclair's inchoate conviction that all is not right in a world in which a child can so easily become guilty. The pendulum swings further. "A strange spirit had come over me. I no longer fitted into our community, which had been so close and for which a raging longing—as for a lost paradise—often overcame me."[10] However, Sinclair is still not strong enough, at the age of ten, to live by these new-found ideas. When Demian frees him from Kromer, thus removing his enforced contact with the other world, he quickly reverts to his former state. "I made

[7] GD, III, 115.　　　[8] GD, III, 120.
[9] GD, III, 122.　　　[10] GD, III, 130.

myself younger, more dependent, more childlike than I was."[11] Ironically, this reversal necessitates a complete break with Demian, who is after all also an outsider by his own acknowledgment. At the end of Chapter 2, then, after his first contact with the "other" world, and a series of violent tremors of vacillation between its dark attraction and the childlike security of his own "light" world, Sinclair is ostensibly back where he started. But the seed has been sown. The "inner, essential line" of his destiny has been deflected from its former course; only on the superficial level is he still an innocent child of ten.

The second blow against the pillars of his childhood comes with the awakening of sexual instincts at the time of puberty, for these overpowering forces cannot be reconciled with the teachings of the traditional society to which Sinclair had forced himself to conform. Again it is Demian who, coming into Sinclair's focus in the communion class, supplies an answer to his gropings by questioning the validity not of the sexual instincts but of the society that condemns them. He proposes to Sinclair the need for a deity who embraces both poles of his experience: the light and the dark, the "good" as well as the "evil." Soon after this the boys part when Sinclair goes off to boarding school. But the transformation has been wrought; he has swung away toward the opposite pole. For the only important memories that he attaches to his communion (a "good" rite) are these conversations with Demian, verging on the "dark" world. "Everything was now changed. My childhood collapsed in ruins about me."[12] At the beginning of the following chapter ("Beatrice") Sinclair reports that "the remarkable emptiness and loneliness" that he perceived for the first time in the vacation after his communion did not pass quickly. His childhood

11 GD, III, 141.   12 GD, III, 162.

has been destroyed, but since there is no adequate replacement for the vacuum it left, he plunges into the opposite extreme. "In this rather unsavory way I was destined to become lonely and to erect between myself and my childhood a closed Gate of Eden with mercilessly glittering watchmen. It was a beginning, an awakening of the longing for my true self."[13] It is still not the right course; this plunge into the abyss of the "dark" world is in its way just as constricting and false as his previous sojourn at the opposite pole of the "light" world. After a year and a hàlf of this alienation and abject debauchery Sinclair has again reached a pivotal nadir. The pendulum swings back. He meets Beatrice.

Chapters 1 and 2 together represent, after a few initial tremors, a full swing of the pendulum from "light" to "dark" and back again. The second full swing, however, lasts from the beginning of Chapter 3 to the middle of Chapter 4. At this point Sinclair's inner development no longer corresponds to the arbitrary form of the external chapter disposition. After the encounter with the girl in the park, who embodies the ideal of his lost innocence, he strives again to recapture that forgotten past. "Again I sought with the most ardent effort to build myself a 'light world' from the rubble of a shattered period of my life; again I lived wholly in the sole desire to do away with the dark and evil within me and to dwell fully in the light, on my knees before gods."[14]

From this point on, Sinclair's story is no longer a pendulation between extremes, but an intensification of his search for himself with the concomitant alienation that this involves. He seeks guides, leaders, ideals, only to outstrip and reject them. In the first part of the book he has learned that a commitment to either pole of his

[13] GD, III, 171.   [14] GD, III, 174.

nature exclusively is a false road. Now he must learn, by the progressive acceptance and rejection of ideals, that the true ideal for his life lies not in exterior reality, but rather within himself. This accounts for the characteristic phenomenon of the novel (and of almost all of Hesse's subsequent writing) that we shall call internalization.

The ideal of Beatrice, which—as Sinclair soon realizes—is more of a synthesis of the two poles than a symbol of the "light" world as he had initially assumed, carries him along for a certain time. "The figure of Beatrice, with which I was so intensively and so fervently occupied for a time, now gradually receded, or rather: she slowly stepped away from me, approached the horizon ever more and became more shadowy, more remote, paler. She no longer satisfied the needs of my soul."[15] Beatrice is gradually replaced, in the course of Chapter 5, by the figure of Abraxas and his exegete, Pistorius, who "taught me to maintain my courage and self-respect."[16] But Pistorius-Abraxas, like every stage, must be transcended, for Sinclair is not seeking an established doctrine to which he can cling, but rather self-knowledge. "Everyone must at some time take the step that separates him from his father, from his teachers; everyone must feel something of the severity of loneliness, even though most men can bear only a little of it and soon creep back to the fold again."[17] Sinclair has freed himself from his family and his childhood. But it is more bitter, he discovers, to liberate oneself from a leader whom one has approached voluntarily out of love and veneration. The parting from Pistorius is the most bitter wrench that Sinclair has as yet had to suffer. "I had already tasted much loneliness. Now I suspected that there was a still deeper loneliness and that it was inescapa-

[15] GD, III, 187.   [16] GD, III, 202.
[17] GD, III, 216.

ble."[18] The decision to leave Pistorius coincides with the end of the second group of three chapters, harmonizing the hitherto contrapuntal rhythm between inner and external form.

The last two chapters represent the final stage of Sinclair's road. He has reached the ultimate point of alienation and is thus fit to appreciate for a short idyllic time the association with others who have suffered the same loneliness in the search for self. "I, who for so long had been alone, learned to know the community of spirit that is possible among men who have tasted total loneliness."[19] This is the period of Sinclair's reunion with Demian in the university town and of his love for Frau Eva. There is no longer the relationship of older boy to younger: they approach each other as equals since Sinclair has developed to a level of independence and self-knowledge that parallels Demian's. But even this ultimate community of spirit is not destined to last; man in search of himself is fated to be alone. And so Demian dies in the war, leaving Sinclair behind—once again in total isolation and alienation, but now strong enough to live out his own life. It should be stressed in this connection that the war, therefore—at least from the point of view of Sinclair's development—is a result rather than the cause of his alienation. Men are destined to be alone; all solidarity is tentative and illusory; war—or its equivalent—thus must come in order to dissolve the bonds, to cast the individual back upon himself.

We have purposely considered the abstract pattern of Sinclair's pendulation and increasing alienation with little reference to the actual substance of the novel in order to allow the basic structure of tension, counterpoint, and intensification to emerge. For it is within the framework of this inner structure—not the superficial disposition of chap-

[18] GD, III, 221.   [19] GD, III, 236.

ters—that the meaning of the book must be examined. To recapitulate: the book now organizes itself roughly into two parts. The first, ending with the nadir of Sinclair's debauchery at school, consists of a series of increasingly wide pendulum swings between the "light" and the "dark" world. Kromer, Demian's influence, and the first year at school represent the negative pole of the swing. The second part consists again of three basic impulses, but here it is no longer a movement of pendulation, but rather an intensification in degree of alienation, represented respectively by the ideals of Beatrice, Pistorius-Abraxas, and Demian, which in turn are progressively superseded. Early in the book parallels between the inner development and external chapter disposition are refracted into a contrapuntal tension between inner and external form; this counterpoint, characteristically, is resolved again in Chapters 7 and 8, in which Sinclair's life, for a short period, is harmonious and no longer in conflict with the world.

The Nietzschean Goal

Even a cursory reading of *Demian* reveals that the content of the structure we have outlined is essentially Nietzschean. The question of Hesse's relationship to Nietzsche is too complex to be discussed exhaustively in the present connection, but a few general remarks are necessary before we can proceed to a further examination of the structure and composition of the novel. Hesse's enthusiasm for Nietzsche dates back at least to his days in Basel (1899-1903), which he called "above all the city of Nietzsche, Jacob Burckhardt and Böcklin."[20] At that time, he says in the same essay, he was "too deeply enchanted by

[20] "Ein paar Basler Erinnerungen" (1951); quoted in *Hermann Hesse. Eine Chronik in Bildern*, ed. Bernard Zeller (Suhrkamp Verlag, 1960), p. 34.

Nietzsche" to be susceptible to Burckhardt. And only two years after the writing of *Demian* Hesse took up Nietzsche's pen to write "Zarathustra's Return" (1919). Nietzsche is also mentioned explicitly several times in the text of *Demian*. At one point Sinclair describes the deep impression that the writings of Novalis made upon him. "Even later I rarely experienced books so profoundly—perhaps only Nietzsche."[21] During his period of profound loneliness after the rupture with Pistorius, the works of Nietzsche provide a source of consolation. "I lived with him, felt the loneliness of his soul, sensed the destiny that drove him irrepressibly on, suffered with him and was overjoyed that there had been a man who went his own way so inexorably."[22]

Apart from explicit references there are also passages in the text that ring unmistakably with the sound of Nietzsche's prose. A conspicuous example is the use of the word "herd" to designate the unthinking masses of humanity. "Everywhere there was this togetherness, everywhere this sitting-around-together, everywhere this disregard of destiny and flight into the warmth of the herd."[23] Another passage recalls the tones of Zarathustra. Pistorius tells Sinclair of the perils of his goal: "It is damnably dangerous! For that reason most people are glad to give up flight and prefer to walk on the sidewalks to the tune of law and order."[24] The icy atmosphere of Zarathustra's mountains is present in other words with which Pistorius exhorts Sinclair: "A person who really desires nothing but his own destiny has no compatriots; he stands quite alone with only the cold cosmos surrounding him."[25]

All of this is part of the grand system outlined in the novel. Man, as Sinclair comes to realize, is not a complete

[21] GD, III, 178. [22] GD, III, 225. [23] GD, III, 225.
[24] GD, III, 201. [25] GD, III, 222.

and perfect being as he comes into the world, but only a trajectory of nature in the direction of the perfect man ("ein Wurf der Natur nach dem Menschen hin"). This is clearly Hesse's way of describing Nietzsche's *Übermensch*. Most people never become true men, but remain on a low level of development—Nietzsche's *Herdenmensch*. True development toward the ideal is possible only after one has transcended the arbitrary limitations established by tradition and society. There are no absolute standards valid for everyone, Demian announces in anticipation of *In Sight of Chaos*. Each man must discover his own inner values. "But you have not yet reached that point at which one perceives what 'allowed' and 'forbidden' actually mean. You have felt only a part of the truth."[26] The realm for which Sinclair is striving is a realm "beyond good and evil" in which it will be possible for him to affirm all of life, and not only that narrow slice of life that is officially approved by representatives of the "light" world.

These passages are unmistakably reminiscent of Nietzsche. At the beginning of *Thus Spake Zarathustra* we read, for instance: "Man is a rope tied between animal and overman—a rope above an abyss.

"A perilous crossing, a perilous on-the-way, a perilous backglance, a perilous tremor and stopping.

"What is great about man is, that he is a bridge and not a goal: what can be loved about man is the fact that he is a transition and a decline."[27]

For Nietzsche men are "arrows of longing toward the other shore,"[28] an image similar to Hesse's "trajectory of nature in the direction of man." And Nietzsche realizes that this road of individuation and development is a lonely

[26] GD, III, 158.
[27] Friedrich Nietzsche, *Werke*, ed. Karl Schlechta (München, 1955), vol. II, p. 281.
[28] *Ibid.*, p. 282.

one. "Do you wish, my brother, to go into loneliness? Do you wish to find the way to yourself? Wait a moment and hear me.

"He who seeks gets lost easily. 'All loneliness is guilt,' says the voice of the herd. And you belonged to the herd for a long time.

"The voice of the herd will still resound within you. And if you say: 'I no longer share your conscience,' then it will be a lament and agony."[29]

Sinclair's pendulation in the first half of the novel has the purpose of exposing him to the full gamut of good and evil, making him aware that both poles actually constitute part of his nature. The intensification of alienation in the second part is the natural course by which he gradually penetrates ever more deeply into his own nature, fulfilling his own personal destiny and leaving behind those goals and teachers whose values he has exhausted. The process involves a "transvaluation of all values" in Nietzsche's sense of the word, and this transvaluation gives us a clue to another structural technique of the novel.

Irony of Style and the Religious Impulse

We have seen that the novel is a network of tensions through which Sinclair advances toward the Nietzschean goal of a life beyond good and evil. The tension of the book, however, is heightened piquantly, though perhaps imperceptibly at first, by Hesse's practice of serving up this Nietzschean doctrine in language lavishly spiced with Christian and Biblical overtones. "It was my sin that I had given the devil my hand." "The grace of God was with all of them, but no longer with me."[30] A longing for the lost innocence of his childhood overwhelms Sinclair "like a raging longing for a lost paradise." After telling Demian

---

[29] *Ibid.*, p. 325.   [30] GD, III, 116.

the secret about Kromer, Sinclair feels: "Now I had almost confessed . . . and a premonition of salvation drifted toward me like a strong fragrance."[31] "From the vale of tears of my damnation" Sinclair rushes back "into the lost paradise that opened again to me."[32] At the nadir of his depravity Sinclair feels: "If henchmen had now come and bound me and led me to the gallows as an abomination and iconoclast (*Tempelschänder*), I would have concurred."[33] With his increasing alienation he realizes that he has created a "closed Gate of Eden" between himself and his childhood, and at the beginning of the Beatrice episode he resolves "to become a temple servant, with the goal of becoming a saint."[34] In his greatest loneliness he feels himself akin to Jesus in the garden of Gethsemane. And scattered through the book are occasional free quotations from the Bible: Europe "had won the whole world, but lost its soul thereby."[35]

Examples of this sort, which could easily be multiplied, prove one thing: even on the level of diction Hesse creates a conscious stylistic tension by pitting Christian phraseology against Nietzschean thought, whereby the tone of the book becomes decidedly religious.

This is no illusion or stylistic trick. In 1930 Hesse wrote: "I myself consider the religious impulse as the decisive characteristic of my life and my work. The realization that the individual, whether faced with the World War or with a flower garden, experiences the external world as a manifestation of the One, the Divine, and fits himself into it, seems to me to be the primary and predominant characteristic of my nature."[36] An attitude of this sort

[31] GD, iii, 137.   [32] GD, iii, 140.   [33] GD, iii, 168.
[34] GD, iii, 175.   [35] GD, iii, 238.
[36] GS, vii, 497. In this connection see especially Maurice Colleville, "Le problème religieux dans la vie et dans l'oeuvre de Hermann Hesse," *Etudes Germaniques*, 7 (1952), 123-148; and

is not at all surprising in the son and grandson of a well-known missionary family.[37] Hesse grew up surrounded by the symbols not only of Christianity, but of oriental religions from the areas where his grandfather had spent the major part of his life. Hesse himself was destined to become a theologian, a future that he escaped by running away from the seminary at Maulbronn where he had been enrolled by his hopeful parents. Dissatisfied though he was with any narrow orthodox Christianity, Hesse spoke not from ignorance, but from a deep knowledge of Christianity and its implications, a piercing examination of its doctrines and symbols. In all his works, as we shall see, the primary impulse is indeed religious in this broad sense of the word. But only in *Demian* does this impulse actually shape the structure of the book. We have already mentioned the texture of the language and its ironic implications. Let us now examine some broader features.

Demian is in one sense a dictionary of religious lore. In the course of his search Sinclair is exposed, at least briefly, to almost every conceivable variety of religious experience. Beginning as an orthodox Christian he proceeds, on the one hand, to an almost saintly asceticism in the Beatrice period and, on the other hand, to the depths of heretical cultism in the adoration of his painted images.

Joseph Mileck, *Hermann Hesse and His Critics*, pp. 173-178. Colleville writes (p. 141): "On pourrait sommairement . . . qualifier d'abord Hesse d'âme religieuse: il y a en effet chez lui, que nous avons déjà appelé un 'Gottsucher', un besoin religieux profond, un instinct religieux incoercible, mais qui . . . ne saurait s'accommoder et se contenter des formes traditionelles et élémentaires de la religion."

[37] Hesse's maternal grandfather, Hermann Gundert (1814-1893), was a noted missionary and scholar of Indic languages; his father, Johannes Hesse (1847-1916), began as a missionary, but was forced for reasons of health to return to Europe, where he directed a religious publishing house.

Through Pistorius his experience is broadened. "Every religion is beautiful," says the renegade theologian. "Religion is soul, regardless of whether one is taking Christian communion or making a pilgrimage to Mecca."[38] Pistorius is a religious epicure who has celebrated cults, as he boasts, for which he could be imprisoned for years; he knows the Gnostics and Zoroaster; he reads to Sinclair from the Vedas and teaches him to utter the sacred Om. With his highly relativistic perspective he is in a position to interpret Christianity as a myth rather than as revealed doctrine. For him "Christ is not a person, but a *heros*, a myth, an immense silhouette in which humanity has painted itself on the wall of eternity."[39] This relativism, of course, makes him unfit for any such position as minister of a Christian church.

Among his acquaintances at boarding school Sinclair enjoys the reputation of being a Spiritist or "at least" a Theosophist. One boy, Knauer, introduces him to the rituals of White Magic. The group of seekers around Demian, finally, is like a gallery of religious types: there are astrologers and cabalists, also an adherent of Count Tolstoy, devotees of new sects, practitioners of Indian exercises, vegetarians and others. "We journeyed through the marvelous, thousand-headed gnarl of gods from the ancient world down to the dawning of the Christian conversion."[40]

Religion not only determines the diction of the language to a great extent; it also constitutes the substance of the book. This is not to say that the novel is extensively informative with regard to these diverse matters. But religion definitely establishes the tone and atmosphere, emphasizing the fact that Sinclair's search is basically a religious one. It is thus fitting that the two main symbols of the novel

[38] GD, III, 204.   [39] GD, III, 204.   [40] GD, III, 237.

should be borrowed from religious sources: Gnosticism and pagan Roman cultism.

The Symbols

Early in the novel, while Sinclair is obsessed with his awakening sexual urges and distressed that this perfectly normal physical phenomenon is denied any place in the traditional "light" world of his family, Demian startles the younger boy by telling him that the Christian God is simply not adequate for our times. As the divine manifestation of all that is good, noble, beautiful and lofty, He is fine. "But the world consists of other qualities. And all that is simply ascribed to the devil. This whole part of the world, this entire half, is denied and buried in silence." Demian, however, feels that all of creation should be affirmed and worshipped.

"I believe that we should venerate and sanctify everything, the whole world, not merely this artificially separated, official half. So in addition to the service of the Lord we also need a service of the Devil. That would suit me just fine. Or, one should create a god who also encompasses within himself the devil, and before whom one wouldn't need to close one's eyes in shame when the most natural things in the world transpire."[41]

This idea completely absorbs Sinclair's attention during the next years, but it is only in his last year at boarding school that he learns the name of such a deity. In connection with a passage in Herodotus, Dr. Follen mentions the god Abraxas, "a deity who had the symbolic function of combining the Godly and the Satanic."[42] It is this new conception that gradually displaces in Sinclair's mind the ideal of Beatrice, who now disappears from his center

[41] GD, III, 156-57.   [42] GD, III, 186.

of interest. The symbolic god who dominates the next section of the book is Abraxas.

An elaborate study could be written on Hesse's interest in Gnosticism and on the historical significance of Abraxas, of which Hesse was aware.[43] In this respect Hesse shared in the general reawakening of interest in Gnosticism and other religious cults that flared up in Europe around the turn of the century as still another manifestation of opposition to the materialistic positivism of the nineteenth century. (Goethe, in his *West-Eastern Divan*, also refers twice to the god Abraxas; the deity already had, so to speak, a firm place in Germany's cultural tradition long before Hesse.) But such an inquiry would exceed the limits of this study and would, moreover, be quite irrelevant. Though Sinclair tells us that together with Pistorius he read a Greek text dealing with Abraxas, it is not the historical deity of numerological significance that is of importance here. Abraxas is for Sinclair nothing more than the symbolic representation of the realm "beyond good and evil" to which he aspires, and as such he defines it repeatedly in the course of his story. "Bliss and horror, man and woman intermingled, the most sacred and the most hideous interwoven, deep guilt trembling through tenderest innocence—this was my beloved's dream image, and this was also Abraxas."[44]

[43] In his essays and letters Hesse refers with some frequency to Gnosticism, and among the writers whose works concerned him —Bachofen, Jung, and Bernoulli, for instance—there is much discussion of Gnostic lore. Abraxas (or Abrasax) was the name given to the supreme demiurgè in certain Gnostic cults. According to the Greek numerological system the letters of his name yield the total of 365, a sum of great magico-mystical importance. See A. Dietrich, *Abraxas: Studien zur Religionsgeschichte des späteren Altertums* (Leipzig, 1891), or Hans Leisegang, *Die Gnosis* (4th ed. Stuttgart, 1955). Hesse, however, ignores this whole aspect; he is interested in the deity only as the being that reigns supreme over the Gnostic dichotomous world of light and dark. Everything else is irrelevant. The name itself does not occur in Herodotus.

[44] GD, III, 188-89.

But Abraxas is only a symbol for Sinclair's goal—not the goal itself. As his insight grows deeper, he transcends this particular manifestation of his ideal. It is fitting that a symbol derived from Gnostic cults should predominate here, for Pistorius, Sinclair's leader at this time, is essentially a religious historian, looking to the past rather than to the future. When Sinclair realizes that he has outstripped Pistorius, he leaves him behind—as well as the god Abraxas, whose place is taken by a new symbol in the last two chapters. Abraxas, like Beatrice, represents a stage that must be left behind, for Sinclair is seeking his own personal god—not a symbol borrowed from an ancient cult.

If Abraxas is the symbol of Sinclair's goal, the symbol of his own development is likewise borrowed from ancient cult usage: the bird breaking its way out of the egg. When Sinclair receives Demian's cryptic message after sending him the painting, it reads: "The bird is breaking its way out of the egg. The egg is the world. He who wishes to be born must destroy a world. The bird flies to god. The god is Abraxas." The association of Abraxas with the myth of the bird and egg is actually Hesse's own free syncretic blending. This myth belongs properly to Roman antiquity—not to Gnostic cultism—and Hesse undoubtedly has his information from J. J. Bachofen, either directly from his writings or indirectly through the psychology of Carl Gustav Jung.

Although Hesse defines the symbol sufficiently for his own purposes within the framework of the novel, it is of interest to note its source in Bachofen since only this connection demonstrates what concerns us here: the religious nature of the symbol. Bachofen (1815-1887) is one of the three Swiss thinkers of the nineteenth century who had a decisive influence on Hesse's thought. We have already mentioned Nietzsche (who was Swiss, of course, by choice and not by birth); Jacob Burckhardt becomes important specifically with regard to *The Glass Bead Game*. Although the influence of Bachofen is not so thoroughly documented as the other cases, the evidence is sufficient. In a selection from his diary for 1920, Hesse writes that he had "spent much time contemplating the ancient matriarchal society by way of Bachofen"[45]—a clear reference to Bachofen's epoch-making study of *Matriarchy* (*Das Mutterrecht*; 1861). Three years later he reviewed in *Vivos Voco* a new edition of the study of *Oknos the Ropemaker* from Bachofen's *Essay on the Grave Symbolism of the Ancients* (*Versuch über die Gräbersymbolik der Alten*; 1859). Both of these references postdate the composition of *Demian*, but they indicate an interest in Bachofen, and the former points specifically to the work that is conspicuous in the novel. (*Oknos the Ropemaker* plays a role, as we shall see, in *The Journey to the East*.)

Hesse's knowledge of the great Swiss religious anthropologist unquestionably goes back a number of years. Most probably Hesse became familiar with his ideas—if not directly with his works—during his years in Basel from 1899 to 1903. At this time Bachofen had just been "discovered" by German intellectuals—this is evident, for instance, in the "Cosmic Circle" (Ludwig Klages, Alfred Schuler, Karl Wolfskehl) with whom Stefan George was associated for a time. Moreover, Bachofen had lived and worked in Basel, contributing extensively to the intellectual life of the city. Hesse was later acquainted with Carl Albrecht Bernoulli (1868-1937), a novelist and professor of the History of Religion who edited Bachofen's works and wrote two studies of his thought.[46] (In one of these studies Bernoulli even mentioned *Demian* specifically as

[45] "Aus einem Tagebuch des Jahres 1920," *Corona*, 3 (1932-33), p. 204.
[46] J. J. *Bachofen und das Natursymbol* (Basel, 1924) and J. J. *Bachofen als Religionsforscher* (Leipzig, 1924).

evidence for Bachofen's thesis that all culture arises from the mother cult.) Finally, Jung himself was deeply indebted to Bachofen's research into ancient cult symbols and the matriarchal state.[47] It is inconceivable that much of this would not have reached Hesse, at least indirectly through Dr. Lang while Hesse was undergoing psychoanalysis. In other words, I believe that we are completely safe in assuming, in the face of overwhelming textual evidence in the novel itself, that Hesse was directly indebted to Bachofen's works.

Just as Sinclair had been prepared for Abraxas by Demian's disquisitions on the need for a new god, so too the symbol of the bird and the egg is carefully anticipated in the course of the novel. At their first meeting early in Chapter 2, Demian calls Sinclair's attention to the remarkable relief sculpture in the keystone above Sinclair's doorway. Sinclair has never observed it closely and knows only that it is "a bird or something like that."[48] Some time later—during the period when Sinclair does not associate with Demian and before the communion class—Sinclair happens to see him one day, standing in front of the house and sketching the figure of the bird. After the Beatrice episode, when Sinclair again feels a need for Demian, he recalls this incident and decides to paint his own picture of the bird. "I no longer knew clearly how it looked, and part of it, as I knew, was no longer readily discernible since it was old and had often been repainted. The bird stood or sat on something, perhaps on a flower or on a basket or nest, or on the top of a tree."[49] In any case, Sinclair begins to paint, and the finished picture turns out to be "a bird of prey, with a sharp, bold hawk-

[47] Ira Progoff, *Jung's Psychology and its Social Meaning* (New York, 1953), esp. pp. 28-35.

[48] GD, III, 124.   [49] GD, III, 183.

face. It was halfway situated in a dark world-orb, from which it was working its way as though from a huge egg, against a blue background of sky.''[50] Shortly thereafter Demian's message arrives, communicating the name of Abraxas for the first time and relating it to the bird and the egg.

Hesse has chosen and employed this symbol with such virtuosity that we might well pause to consider it in more detail. As we have seen, the use of the bird as a symbol is anticipated casually, but effectively several times before it emerges in full force. The symbol, as it is stated in the novel, is quite appropriate, for just as Sinclair must destroy the world of his childhood and traditional society in order to reach his goal, so too must the bird smash the egg in order to be born. But the significance is even deeper. According to Bachofen's chapter on "The Egg as a Nature Symbol" the egg symbolizes the two poles of the world— the "light" and the "dark"—in Roman antiquity.

"There can be no doubt as to their meaning. The alternation of the light and the dark color expresses the transformation from darkness to light, from death to life. It shows us the tellurian creation as the result of eternal becoming and of eternal perishing, as a never-ending movement between two opposite poles.''[51]

"It embraces all parts of the material world: heaven and earth, light and darkness, the male and female powers of nature, the stream of becoming and perishing, the embryo of all tellurian organisms and of the higher and lower creation, as well as the whole world of deities which— being of material origin like all tellurian life—shares with

[50] GD, III, 183.
[51] *Versuch über die Gräbersymbolik der Alten*, in: J. J. Bachofen, *Mutterrecht und Urreligion. Eine Auswahl*, ed. Rudolf Marx (Stuttgart, 1954), p. 25.

men, beasts and plants one and the same mother: the dark egg."[52]

The parallel is quite detailed. It is not simply the "world" that Sinclair smashes, but specifically the world of false polarities. (In this connection it is not entirely out of place to recall that Julius Langbehn, the author of *Rembrandt as Teacher* and prophet of a mystical re-union of fragmentized reality, had himself portrayed with a symbolic egg in his hand—"Der Philosoph mit dem Ei.")

We have spoken of the progressive stages of Sinclair's alienation, each breaking another tie with the past. Actually the image of the bird ridding itself of its shell is a much closer analogy and one that Hesse, again, has introduced subtly at earlier stages. In the introduction to the story Sinclair wrote: "No man has ever been completely and totally himself, but everyone strives to become himself. . . . Each one bears with himself remnants of his birth, the slime and *egg-shells* [italics mine] of a primeval world, to the very end." Already here we have an anticipation of the central symbol, and this particular motif recurs several times in the course of the novel. Recapitulating his friend-ship with Pistorius, for instance, Sinclair claims that these conversations rarely brought him anything wholly new.

"But all of them, even the most banal, pounded with gentle and steady hammer-blows at the same point within me; all helped to form my nature; all helped to peel off the skins, to crack the egg shells; and after each of these talks I raised my head a bit higher, a bit more freely, until my yellow bird stuck his lovely predatory head out of the shattered world-shell."[53]

Thus the bird and the egg—originally a Roman cult

[52] *Ibid.*, p. 29.   [53] GD, III, 200.

symbol for the spiritual rebirth of the individual—is used appropriately here as a symbol for Sinclair's religious search and growth. There is a further implicit dimension: namely, the Jungian collective unconscious. Sinclair has forgotten—he stresses this point—what the bird was resting upon in the keystone. And so his painting of the egg is free creation and not reproduction from memory. Yet the very fact that he then actually paints the bird breaking its way out of an egg, thus linking his painting with the ancient cult symbol, is a practical illustration of the workings of the collective unconscious in Jung's sense of the phrase. It is relevant to our purposes to note how Jung's thought is applied in the novel as a *technical* device for the development of the theme, for a similar case will be discussed below in connection with Frau Eva.

However—and here we must anticipate—Hesse does not employ the bird and the egg as a mere personal symbol for Sinclair. From the very beginning Sinclair makes it clear that he regards his own story as typological: it parallels and reflects the development of his whole generation. In one of his early talks with Demian it comes as a consolation to Sinclair to learn that his struggles are not unique. "The realization that my problem was a problem of all men, a problem of all life and thought, came upon me suddenly like a sacred shadow when I saw and suddenly felt how deeply my own most personal life and thinking were involved in the eternal stream of great ideas."[54]

It comes as no surprise, then, when Sinclair's most private symbol is projected, at the end of the book, onto a universal screen as a harbinger of war. During the last summer (1914) Sinclair experiences a vision in the midst of a storm:

[54] GD, III, 157.

"A loose yellow cloud came drifting across the sky; it piled up against the grey mountain wall, and in a matter of seconds the wind formed from the yellow and blue an image: a gigantic bird that tore itself loose from the blue mass and disappeared into the sky with great wings flapping."[55]

When Sinclair tells Demian of this vision it becomes clear that the bird now symbolizes humanity striving to break out of the bonds of tradition. That this impulse results in war is made obvious a few pages from the end, when Sinclair, on duty in Flanders, again uses the image to explain that the war is merely the superficial manifestation of great changes being wrought in the depths of humanity. Something was being developed, he felt, in the midst of the chaos of war.

"Something like a new humanity. . . . The objects as well as the goals [of the war] were quite incidental. The basic feelings, even the wildest ones, were not directed against the enemy. Their bloody deeds were only a radiation from within, of a soul split within itself, which wanted to rage and kill, destroy and die, in order that it might be born anew. A great bird was fighting its way out of the egg, and the egg was the world, and the world had to be destroyed."[56]

The symbol of the bird and the egg, with all of its associations from Jung and Bachofen, is thus the central symbol of the novel. Introduced almost on the first page, it is maintained to the very end. But whereas in the first half of the book it is a personal symbol, it assumes universal proportions in the second part, a shift that corresponds to the change from a more Freudian psychology

---

[55] GD, iii, 245.   [56] GD, iii, 254.

in the opening chapters to the Jungian revelations of Pistorius, and to the gradual transformation of religion into myth. Yet as a symbol the image remains absolutely consistent. Whether the bird represents Sinclair or all of humanity venting its frustrations in the horrors of war, the shattered egg is the world divided into the traditional dichotomy of "good" and "evil," "light" and "dark"; and the goal toward which the bird soars represents a new level of humanity that stands "beyond good and evil"—in other words, a moral and religious goal. Once again, then, we find confirmation of the essentially religious nature of *Demian*, and the efficacy of this most pervasive symbol is intensified by the fact that it belongs, originally, to the religious sphere.

The Technique of Prefiguration

Literature has developed various techniques for expanding the implications of its substance by reference to larger frameworks. One of the most common of these is the retelling of classical or medieval myths from a contemporary point of view, as Thomas Mann did in his *Joseph* tetralogy. The other face of the same coin, of course, is the modern story that is cast into the mold of traditional myths, as in Joyce's *Ulysses*. A less obvious technique is the use of universal archetypal patterns, which differ from the first type inasmuch as they are not necessarily associated with a specific name or figure or concatenation of events. In her study of *Archetypal Patterns in Poetry* (Oxford University Press, 1934) Maud Bodkin analyzed types such as the archetypes of rebirth, of Paradise-Hades, images of the hero or of woman. Finally there are writers like Franz Kafka, who find in the storehouse of tradition no image that fulfills their needs and who manage to create new myths that are adequate as an expression of their societies.

In addition to all these, which are the more conspicuous techniques of modern literature, there is still another time-honored associative device—one, however, that by definition is so restricted that it cannot often be applied. I speak of the device of figural interpretation, which was perhaps the leading literary technique in Christian literature from Tertullian to Dante and which remained active in Europe to the eighteenth century. According to Erich Auerbach, its aim was "to show that the persons and events of the Old Testament were prefigurations of the New Testament and its history of salvation."[57] It arose to satisfy "the mixture of spirituality and sense of reality" characteristic of the Middle Ages, and it did so by insisting, on the one hand, that the prefiguring event as well as the event prefigured were absolutely real in essence and detail; that, on the other hand, the first event receives its spiritual fulfillment only in the second. The medieval scholiasts combed the Old Testament for deeds, words, and symbols —such as the sacrifice of Isaac—that seemed to anticipate a similar deed, word, or symbol in the life of Jesus. This technique differs from allegory and symbol because both elements of the equation are real. It differs from the archetypal patterns because the relationship is always a specific one. And it differs from traditional myth because it involves not one representative figure, but a medley of associations from the past brought to focus on a single figure in the present.

Later we shall see why Hesse felt justified in using such

[57] Erich Auerbach, "Figura," *Scenes from the Drama of European Literature.* Meridian Books (New York, 1959), p. 30; second quotation, p. 61.

an esoteric technique in *Demian*. For the present, let us merely establish the fact that he does so. The basic structural element of the novel, namely, turns out to be the Biblical *figura*, a series of which is adduced by Hesse to give form to his various episodes. Two points should be stressed. First, Hesse draws his *figurae* not only from the Old Testament, but also from the Gospels—contrary to medieval practice. Second, he makes a pronounced use of the modern author's prerogative to invest the traditional myth, archetype, or *figura* with a new meaning. But as a structural technique his usage reveals a striking similarity to medieval figural interpretation. At the very beginning of their acquaintance, when Demian is giving Sinclair his unique exegesis of the story of Cain, the older boy states:

"You can also interpret this story of Cain differently. Most of the things that they teach us are certainly quite true and right, but you can also look at all of them in a different way than the teachers do, and generally they then make much better sense."[58]

This Nietzschean relativism introduces a principle of method that is much akin to essayism as defined in Musil's *Man without Qualities* or to Hermann Broch's conception of the "Disintegration of Values." It is precisely this "different way of seeing" that distinguishes Demian and his circle from the rest of humanity, that makes them dangerous and feared, just as Prince Myshkin—in Hesse's essay on *The Idiot*—is feared because of his magical thinking. For under their eyes the old established traditions are no longer sacred, but are exposed to transvaluation and reinterpretation—a procedure that is tantamount to an upheaval of existing society. It is quite appropriate in a work such as *Demian*, which is concerned so cen-

[58] GD, III, 125.

trally with questions of a religious nature, that the matters exposed to this reflective consideration should be first and foremost the legends of the Bible. By way of contrast, it is interesting to note that the symbols just discussed, heretical and pagan in nature, are retained roughly in their original significance. Only the Christian *figurae* are subjected to this Nietzschean transvaluation!

In a letter of 1930, Hesse wrote, in connection with the interpretation of Cain advanced in *Demian*: "The myths of the Bible, like all myths of mankind, are worthless for us as long as we do not dare to interpret them personally, for ourselves and our times. But then they can become very important to us."[59] In his important essay on *The Brothers Karamazov* (1919) Hesse advanced the same thought, couched this time in Nietzschean terms that point clearly to the source of Hesse's ideas: "It is possible that the whole 'decline of Europe' will take place 'only' internally, only in the souls of a generation, only in the reinterpretation of worn-out symbols, in the revaluation of spiritual values."[60] Sinclair's "revaluation of spiritual values" is manifestly intended to apply to his whole generation as the inner reason for the outbreak of the war, as we have seen in the case of the bird and the egg.

In the novel *Demian* there are several explicit cases of this "reinterpretation of worn-out symbols." The first of these is Demian's bold analysis of the story of Cain, with which he startles Sinclair in their first conversation. According to Demian it is unrealistic to believe that a man who has committed a heinous crime should be singled out and, in effect, protected by God through a special mark. Rather, he suggests, there was something about this man from the very beginning that set him apart from

[59] GS, VII, 488.   [60] GS, VII, 175.

the others and disturbed them: the radiance of intellectual power or, say, of moral courage. At any rate, he was feared by his fellows for this quality, which distinguished him like a mark. But instead of admitting that they feared him for his accomplishments and powers, people invented an elaborate fiction to explain that this individual—Cain in this case—was being punished by God for some terrible transgression. Unlike the symbols of Abraxas and the Bird and Egg, this new Cain is Hesse's own invention for the text of his fiction. "I know of no literary sources for what I wrote about Cain in *Demian*," he stated to a reader in 1930, "yet I could well imagine that something similar might be found in the Gnostics. What in those days was called theology is more like psychology for men of today, but the basic truths are the same."[61] Hesse is, of course, not the only writer to use the sign of Cain as a distinguishing characteristic of "awakened" man. In *Tonio Kröger* Thomas Mann is also obviously referring to Cain, though he neither mentions the name nor develops the symbol so consistently as Hesse, when Tonio says of artists in general: "Their self-awareness is enflamed because they alone among thousands feel the sign on their forehead and realize that it escapes no one's attention."

What distinguishes Hesse's novel from the merely encyclopedic novel is the fact that this reinterpretation, having been introduced, is not then dropped, but assumes a symbolic function in the texture of the work. The Mark of Cain, from this moment on, recurs like a leitmotiv, identifying those whom destiny has set apart as leaders in the spiritual revaluation that is impending. This first occurs to Sinclair as he recalls the decisive moment when he felt superior to his father for failing to perceive his plunge into sin:

[61] GS, VII, 487-88.

". . . there for a moment it was suddenly as if I had seen through and despised him and his whole light world and wisdom! Yes, at that moment I myself, who was Cain and bore the mark, had imagined that this sign was no stigma, that it was rather a distinction, and that I, as a result of my badness and misfortune, stood higher than my father, higher than the good and the pious."[62]

When Demian and Sinclair meet at the university for the first time in several years, Demian has no trouble recognizing his old friend. "You've changed, but you still have the mark. . . . We used to call it the Mark of Cain, if you remember. It is our sign. You have always had it, and that's why I became your friend."[63] The word *Zeichen* ("sign" or "mark"), which is used so frequently throughout the novel, always has this specific meaning, whether it is written in the full form (*Kainszeichen*) or not. Though it is used at first to designate only Sinclair and Demian, Sinclair gradually realizes, as he perceives that his own problems are actually universal in nature, that there are others about him—notably the group of religious seekers surrounding Demian at the end—who are similarly set apart from the world. Like the bird and the egg, the personal symbol becomes increasingly universal. "We, the ones with the mark, might rightly be considered strange, or even crazy and dangerous in the eyes of the world."[64] In *The Steppenwolf*, ten years later, Hesse calls these people "the ones with an extra dimension"; but it remains, as here, a quality that distinguishes the elect from the masses. "That is why we are marked—just as Cain was marked in order to arouse fear and hatred and to drive the men of his time out of their narrow idyll into dangerous expanses."[65]

[62] GD, III, 127-28.   [63] GD, III, 226.
[64] GD, III, 236.   [65] GD, III, 239.

The second story that Demian reinterprets, the story of the unrepentant thief, has a totally different structural function. Rather than becoming primarily a pervasive leitmotiv, it serves as a typological precedent that fortifies Sinclair's resolves at a time when he needs it most. It will be recalled that Sinclair, after being freed from Kromer's psychological blackmail, swung back to the security of his earlier life within the family in a desperate attempt to shake off the influence of the "dark" world that he had discovered within himself. Not until the communion class, some three or four years later, does he begin the second long pendulum swing, whose momentum carries him into the excesses of debauchery at school. Again, as Sinclair states: "These impulses always came from the 'other world' "[66]—first Kromer, now Demian. For Demian urges him one day to reexamine the lesson that had just been taught: the story of Golgotha. Demian objects to the penitent thief: "First he was a criminal and committed God-only-knows-what sort of heinous deeds. And now he melts away and celebrates lugubrious festivals of betterment and remorse!"[67] What meaning does such repentance have, two steps from the grave? Demian vastly prefers the other thief, who is obviously the only one that a man could trust and in whom one could have any confidence, for he has remained true to his convictions to the bitter end. But, as Demian concludes cynically, men of real character always are the losers in the Bible.

These words reaffirm Sinclair's faith in himself and in the "dark" world that he now knows. He realizes that it was cowardly of him to recant, to deny the "dark" world, and to return to his father's world in the hope of finding happiness. For true happiness and security lie only in fidelity to one's own inner principles—as in the case of

[66] GD, III, 143.   [67] GD, III, 155.

the unrepentant thief. And under the aegis of this unorthodox *figura* Sinclair resumes his search. Soon thereafter he leaves home and parts from Demian, but this new
understanding of the thief who was unwilling to deny the
devil, gives him the strength to carry on his own search for
a deity that embraces both God and the devil.

In the letter quoted above Hesse denied knowledge of
any source for his reinterpretation of the story of Cain.
There is likewise no documentary evidence pointing to a
source for his ideas concerning the unrepentant thief. Yet
interestingly, there are clear hints that this is one of the
matters that came up for discussion during the sessions
with Dr. Lang. In his notebook under the date 28 October
1917, the doctor made the following entry:

"I am the justice of the thief on the left, the one who
takes his sins upon himself. The one who once taught
you to pray: Do not spare me, poor sinner that I am. I
am hammering in your shaft. Someday you will understand
and read the runes that I have beaten out in the stone of
your heart, the primeval writing of mankind that you must
teach them, the Table of Laws of that which is to come."[68]

The second half of this passage is reproduced to give
an example of the tone, so similar to that of *Demian*, in
which this rather remarkable psychoanalyst seems to have
addressed his patients. But the first sentences, with the
reference to the unrepentant thief, demonstrate clearly
that Lang shares Hesse's reinterpretation of the story.
Whether Lang got it from Hesse or vice versa is a moot
point. What does matter is the clear suggestion that this
interpretation is apparently not one invented merely for
the fiction of the book, but rather one that has meaning

[68] Quoted by Hugo Ball, *Hermann Hesse: Sein Leben und sein
Werk* (Suhrkamp Verlag, 1947), p. 158.

for Hesse personally, as do almost all of the "revaluations" that he undertakes. It is quite possible—even probable, as Hesse's friend and first biographer maintains[69]—that Hesse contributed even more to the interviews than he received. Yet the importance of Dr. Lang as a catalytic agent in Hesse's writing cannot be overestimated. Much of the material in *Demian* seems to have its origin either directly or indirectly from the year that Hesse spent in close contact with the psychoanalyst. This supposition is borne out by Jung himself, who wrote about Lang: "He was a very curious, though extremely learned man, who had studied Oriental languages (Hebrew, Arabic, and Syrian) and was particularly interested in gnostic speculation. He got from me a considerable amount of knowledge concerning gnosticism which he also transmitted to Hesse."[70]

The prefigurative episode of the unrepentant thief, which is made explicit by Demian's own exegesis of the Biblical text, runs quite counter to the typological *figura* that has governed Sinclair's pendulation up to this point: the legend of the Prodigal Son. Unlike Cain and the unrepentant thief, the following *figurae*, though clearly intended as such by Hesse, are not introduced so elaborately. Before considering the Prodigal Son, we might review the beginning of the novel from our newly acquired point of view. It is quite apparent, in view of the religious nature of the book, that Sinclair's "Two Worlds" (the title of Chapter 1) represent the traditional Christian dichotomy of good and evil, which Sinclair strives in the course of his development to transcend. He begins in the good, "light" world. From indications in the language that have been

[69] *Ibid.*, p. 155.
[70] Quoted by Benjamin Nelson, "Hesse and Jung. Two Newly Recovered Letters," *The Psychoanalytic Review*, 50 (1963), 15.

quoted above ("Gates of Eden," "lost Paradise," et cetera)
it is apparent that this state of childhood innocence is
equated with the Garden of Eden in Paradise. If we now
ask ourselves what specific incident caused Sinclair's fall
from grace and his expulsion from Paradise, we realize
that it was the theft of apples. As a matter of fact, Sinclair
did not steal the apples, but only boasted of having done
so. Yet it is this ostensible theft that involved him so unfortunately with Kromer, who in other passages is called
"the devil" and "the tormentor." Only in retrospect does
it become clear to the reader how charged with religious
symbolism the texture of the language is, even when
Hesse is recounting the most commonplace incident. As
we have seen, Sinclair regards himself as a typological
figure—both fulfilling established prefigurations and symbolizing his own generation of mankind. When he is led by
a tempter to claim that he has stolen apples, he thus symbolizes the fall from grace of all humanity. In this connection, however, two points must be stressed which bring
out the "revaluation" of myth as Hesse employs it. In
the first place, Sinclair's sin is the *imagined* theft of
apples; that is, a psychological illustration of Hesse's
claim that the spiritual rebirth of Europe will take place
"only" inwardly; for the stolen apples are only in his mind.
Secondly, the fall from grace is regarded, in the light of
the novel, as a good thing; Paradise is a prison, the gates
of Eden lock one *in*; and the most vicious of all dreams is
the dream of a lost paradise in the past, in childhood, for
it distracts us from our true course, which lies ahead and
points into the future.

After Sinclair's fall from grace, it is the Prodigal Son
who prefigures his actions in the next episode. This *figura*
is not made explicit through a chapter heading, but it
emerges clearly from the text itself. The theme is stated in

the opening pages of the novel, even before Sinclair has explored the "dark" world in more than his imagination:

"There were stories of Prodigal Sons to whom this had happened; I had read them with passionate interest. In those tales the return to the Father and to Good was so liberating and splendid that I felt: this alone was proper, good and desirable; and yet the part of the story that took place among the evil and forlorn was far more enticing. And if one could have said so and admitted the fact: it was sometimes actually too bad that the Prodigal Son repented and was found again."[71]

When Sinclair comes home after his first involvement with Kromer, he welcomes the sights and smells of the paternal rooms "like the Prodigal Son."[72] And, after Demian has succeeded in freeing him from Kromer, "I celebrated with lofty feelings the feast of my re-acceptance, the return of the Prodigal Son."[73] What we have seen so far, then, is Sinclair's fall from grace; his first pendulation toward the "dark" world and back under the sign of the Prodigal Son; and the second plunge into the abyss foreshadowed by the unrepentant thief.

The Internalization of Reality

The second major stage of Sinclair's development is heralded, as we have seen, by the internalization of his ideal. During the Beatrice episode and his exploration of the cult of Abraxas with Pistorius, Sinclair was desperately searching to find his ideal in the outside world: in a person, in an established though forgotten cult, in a tailor-made god. But his more mature stage—the realization that his ideal lies only within himself, necessitating the break with Pistorius—takes place in a chapter typo-

[71] GD, III, 105.   [72] GD, III, 113.   [73] GD, III, 140.

logically entitled "Jacob's Struggle with the Angel" (Chapter 6). As a matter of fact, the prefiguration here is merely stated and not nearly so elaborately developed as the other cases we have discussed. After Knauer berates Sinclair for having failed him, Sinclair realizes that his own development is not yet complete. He paints the picture of his last externalized deity—a hermaphroditic being resembling both himself and Demian—and then, as he prepares to worship it, he recalls the words of Jacob: I will not let thee go, except thou bless me (Genesis 32:26).

"The painted face in the lamplight changed at every invocation. It became bright and luminous, black and gloomy, closed pale lids over dead eyes, opened them again and emitted glowing glances; it was woman, man, girl, a small child, an animal, dissolved to a spot, became large and clear again. Finally, following a strong inner call, I closed my eyes and now saw the image within me, stronger and mightier. I wanted to kneel down before it, but it was so very much within me that I could no longer distinguish it from myself, as though it had become pure I."[74]

This is the process that we have called internalization, and it represents Sinclair's symbolic battle with his own angel for its blessing. (His feeling of rapture that succeeds this battle is a passage that in substance, vocabulary, and style strongly recalls the third of Novalis's famous *Hymns to Night*, a work that impressed Hesse deeply.)

Hesse seems to have felt, however, as the reader may well do, that the preceding scene is lacking in vitality or in force of depiction. There the process of internalization is totally cerebral. Only this feeling of insufficiency can account for the duplication that takes place in the succeed-

[74] GD, III, 211-12.

ing passage, which, for our purposes, is far more interesting. In order to make the internalization come to life,
namely, Hesse resorts once more to a prefigurative pattern that renders the process far more vividly. After his
spiritual exertions Sinclair falls into a deep sleep. He wakes
up in the middle of the night and discovers that his painted
image is missing: it is neither on the wall nor on the
table. "Then I thought that I vaguely recollected having
burned it up. Or had it been a dream that I had burned it
in my hands and eaten the ashes?"[75] The scene immediately
changes, and we are left with this tantalizing, disturbing
uncertainty that is surely calculated to lend to the constantly increasing effacement of distinctions between internal
life and external reality in the novel. What seems clear,
however, is the source of this strange vision, a passage
from Revelations 10: 9-11:

"And I went unto the angel, and said unto him, Give
me the little book. And he said unto me, Take it, and
eat it up; and it shall make thy belly bitter, but it shall be
in thy mouth sweet as honey.

"And I took the little book out of the angel's hand, and
ate it up. . . ."

Like John, Sinclair has figuratively wrested his picture
from his angel; this vision, it will be recalled, follows the
struggle with the angel. And it is this new strength that
first confirms his faith in his own messianic mission. The
scene is doubly striking because it is anticipated some
pages earlier when Sinclair dreams that Demian has forced
him to eat the heraldic emblem of the bird above the
entrance to his house.

The Book of Revelations is the obvious source for
religious prefigurations of this visionary quality, and not

[75] GD, III, 212.

unexpectedly the same source is drawn upon again for the most impressive vision of the entire novel, which occurs close to the end of the book. To say that Hesse consciously (I feel sure) employed these suggestive prefigurative devices is by no means to belittle his artistic inventiveness. To operate within frameworks of this sort and to fit them organically into the total structure of the novel demands a degree of craftsmanship and artistic integration that at least equals, if not exceeds, that of free composition. Yet by doing so the writer achieves a depth and sense of timelessness and mystery that would have been otherwise impossible. From the outset Sinclair has stressed his conviction that his life is bound up with other lives, that his existence is typological. The use of prefiguration in the novel itself makes that conviction more than a mere claim or figure of speech; it represents an actual rendering of his typological function. This is certainly the case with the apocalyptic vision at the end.

On the level of realistic action or plot Sinclair is wounded on the Flanders battlefield by a shell burst. On the visionary level, however, he experiences the explosion as a great revelation. Indeed, it is the visionary experience that is first described; only afterwards do we realize that the flashing lights of the vision are in reality the bursts of the mortar shell that wounds Sinclair. Whereas in the first part of the novel external reality was portrayed and then analyzed in terms of its symbolic significance, here at the end inner reality takes precedence over external reality. First the vision is related, and only from the internal visionary experience can we derive the external reality. It is an example of absolute internalization of events.

"In the clouds a great city was visible; millions of people

streamed forth and spread themselves in swarms across vast expanses. Into their midst stepped the figure of a mighty deity, with glittering stars in her hair, large as a mountain, with the features of Frau Eva. The streams of people disappeared within her, as though into a gigantic cave, and were gone. The goddess crouched on the ground; the mark on her forehead shimmered brightly. A dream seemed to have her in its power; she closed her eyes, and her great face was contorted in agony. Suddenly she uttered a penetrating cry, and from her forehead sprang forth stars, many thousands of glittering stars that arched in splendid bows and spheres across the black sky.

"One of the stars roared directly toward me with a bright clanging, seemingly searching for me."[76]

If we compare this passage with John's vision in Revelations 12: 1-2, the analogy is unmistakable:

"And there appeared a great wonder in heaven; a woman clothed with the sun, and the moon under her feet, and upon her head a crown of twelve stars:

"And she being with child cried, travailing in birth, and pained to be delivered."

In both cases we have the symbolic birth of a new humanity from the figure of a Magna Mater. In Revelations it is the Daughter of Zion (cf. Micha 4: 10) who bears the Saviour from the twelve tribes (the twelve stars) of Israel; in *Demian* it is Frau Eva through whom, from the teeming multitudes of the world, a new mankind is born.

The Archetype of Frau Eva

Demian's mother can be fitted into a prefigurational pattern less easily than any other figure or incident in

[76] GD, III, 255.

the book. Her name, to be sure, summons up intentional associations with Eve, the mother of mankind; and this association is heightened by the Cain motif, which is used to designate her son Demian as well as her spiritual children such as Sinclair. In this case, however, Hesse is thinking less of any specific *figura* than merely of the universal archetype of the Magna Mater in Jung's sense. It is this association that accounts for the strong incest motif that figures so prominently in the passages dealing with Frau Eva.

When Sinclair first meets her, toward the end of the book, he realizes that she represents the fulfillment of all the images and ideals he had conceived for himself and then rejected: Beatrice, Abraxas, Demian. Twice he says: "Her look was fulfillment."[77] His relationship to her remains quite ambivalent: "Let her become my mother, my lover, my goddess—if only she is there! If only my road may remain close to hers!"[78] Yet it is quite clear from all of Sinclair's utterances that she represents in his eyes, apart from her fictional reality, a personification of Soul.

The definition of terms such as "soul," "nature," and "spirit" has occasioned much controversy among Hesse scholars, and the problem is complicated by the fact that his own allegiance shifts, in the course of the years, from one pole to the other. In *Demian*, however, as in other writings from this period, Hesse makes it sufficiently clear that his interests at this time are focused exclusively on a rebirth of what he calls Soul, and Frau Eva is the personification of the rebirth.

As we shall see again in the case of Demian, although Sinclair ascribes external reality to Frau Eva, he gradually comes to feel that she is really more a reflection of his own inner being. (This follows from the progressively

[77] GD, III, 232 and 233.   [78] GD, III, 233.

intensified internalization in the novel.) "Sometimes I had the distinct feeling that it was not her person toward which my whole being was attracted and striving, but that she was only a symbol of my inner self and wanted to lead me deeper into myself."[79] (This is, by the way, a psychic transfer that we shall encounter later in the relationship of Harry Haller to Hermine in *The Steppenwolf*.) In the essay "Language" (1917), specifying the notion of an "abyss in one's own inner being" (*Abgrund in seinem eigenen Inneren*), Hesse wrote: "We may call this abyss soul or the unconscious or whatever we like; from it emerges every vital stirring of our life."[80] And in *Demian* the basic quality of Frau Eva is "the atmosphere of maturity and soul that surrounded her."[81] It should be clear by now that Hesse is not anxious to pin this concept down to any specific association with "spirit" or "nature," and that any such attempt must lead away from the central problem. Hesse is interested, in *Demian*, in the essential quality of mankind, the primordial spark of life, which he chooses to call *Seele*. If it has any connection with the polar antithesis *Geist*, which becomes important in his subsequent work, it is the function that Thomas Mann once ascribed to soul: "a mediating and reconciling element between mind and natural drive."[82] More relevant to our considerations, however, is the identification with Jung's *anima*. Here some of the associations are especially revealing inasmuch as they account for the peculiar hermaphroditic quality of Sinclair's ideal.

"*Anima* can be found historically above all in the divine syzygies, the male-female god-couples. These syzygies extend on the one hand back into the darkness of primitive

[79] GD, III, 242.   [80] "Sprache"; GS, VII, 62.   [81] GD, III, 240.
[82] *Die Entstehung des Doktor Faustus* (Berman-Fischer Verlag, 1949), p. 81.

mythology and, on the other hand, into the philosophical speculations of Gnosticism and the classical Chinese philosophy. . . ."[83]

It seems unquestionable that, like so much else in this novel, the hermaphroditic quality of Sinclair's dream-visions and of Frau Eva, all of whom stand for Soul, is influenced by this conception of Jung. This will be borne out below by further parallels with Jung's system.

Now the concept *Seele*, like almost every other important element in *Demian*, has strong Biblical overtones, despite the unorthodox definition it receives. This is strikingly obvious in Sinclair's indictment of the civilization of his age, which is, of course, a reference to the famous passage from Christ's Sermon on the Mount: "It [Europe] has won the whole world, only to lose its soul in so doing."[84] In an essay written in the same year (1917) and entitled "On the Soul,"[85] we read: ". . . it is man's special role and task in life to represent soul." "Man appears to us as that part of the world, as the special province, whose duty it is to develop soul." He goes on to define Soul as "form and potentiality of expression in life . . . a final goal."

Sinclair's ideal, then, as personified by Frau Eva is Soul, and in the final episode he advances rapidly on the way toward the realization of that ideal. At the university he meets Demian, who invites him to see his mother. Arriving at the house beside the river, Sinclair waits in the hall. Framed above the door he notices his painting of the hawk, which he had sent to Demian some months earlier. As his gaze drops, he becomes aware of Frau Eva

[83] *Zentralblatt für Psychotherapie*, 1936, p. 264.

[84] GD, III, 238.

[85] "Von der Seele"; GS, VII, 68-78. The essay ends with the same Biblical quotation.

standing in the doorway. In the course of their conversation she tells him that everyone must find his own dream,
but that no dream is permanent, thus stating the principle
of progressive alienation that we have already observed:
". . . each one is displaced by a new one, and we must
not desire to hold fast to any one dream."[86] Sinclair, who
has fallen in love at first sight with Frau Eva, replies
that he does not know how long his dream will last: "I
wish that it could be eternal. Under the image of the bird
my destiny has received me—like a mother and like a
lover."[87]

This remark is typical of the ambiguity of many utterances in Hesse's fiction, which stems from multidimen-
sional possibilities of reading. It refers both to the present
situation—Frau Eva is, after all, standing beneath the
framed picture of the hawk—and to his first dream, in
which the dream-figure met him in his parental home after
he passed beneath the portal stone with the relief figure.
It is thus exceedingly difficult to pin down the relationships as the story becomes more and more internalized.
The contours seem to shift and melt away as we read, and
every word can be interpreted on various levels. Thus
it can never be ascertained to what extent Frau Eva actually intends the erotic-incestuous implications that Sinclair
ascribes to her remarks; they are all couched in that remarkable language of double-entendre. Regardless of Frau
Eva's character and role on the level of everyday reality
(which is progressively internalized, becoming more and
more vague), Sinclair's own feeling toward her is quite
clear. He regards her as the personification of Soul and as
a mother-image. The latter, to return to Jung, is quite

[86] GD, iii, 234. This is, by the way, an anticipation of the poem
"Stufen" ("Steps"), written years later for inclusion in *The Glass
Bead Game*.
[87] GD, iii, 234.

significant, for the rebirth of the individual as well as of humanity as a whole is to be brought about through the Magna Mater. "It should be stressed," Jung writes,

"that particularly the sun-myth shows us to what extent the basis of 'incestuous' desire is to be found not in co-habitation, but in the unique wish to become a child again, to return to the protection of one's parents, to get back into the mother so as to be born by her once again. On the way to this goal, however, stands incest; that is, the necessity of entering the mother's body once more. One of the simplest ways would be to impregnate the mother and, identical with oneself, to produce oneself again. Here the incest prohibition interferes, and hence the sun myth or rebirth myths invent all conceivable analogies for the mother in order to permit the libido to overflow into new forms and thus to prevent it effectively from descending to more or less actual incest."[88]

I believe that this passage is self-explanatory. If we are to believe the fiction of the book, Sinclair never engages in this semi-incestuous relationship with Frau Eva on the realistic level. But what is the great vision at the end, with which we began this discussion, other than his Jungian "analogy," his attempt by visionary paths to reenter the mother in order to be born again? And projected onto the universal screen, this vision, of course, implies the birth of a whole new humanity from the body of the Magna Mater. Although Jung specifically states that the incest motif is common to many mythical systems, especially the sun-myth, it is characteristic that Hesse should choose an archetypal pattern that fits into the general structure of the novel: namely, a religious one. It is perfectly obvious that Frau Eva does not fit patly into any simple *figura*

[88] *Symbole der Wandlung* (Zürich, 1952), pp. 378-79.

like the other examples we have considered; she is a mixture of the Daughter of Zion, Magna Mater, and the Jungian *anima*, and the elements of these various systems are intermixed in her character. Yet as a structural component in the novel, she fulfills her function just as adequately as the other figures. The sense of mystery that she arouses is actually the result of the planned haziness surrounding her figure.

The Figure of Demian

Up to this point we have mentioned Demian only as the *advocatus diaboli* who appears always at the proper moment to give Sinclair just the little shove that he needs on his inward way, his search for himself. Now, however, we can examine his symbolic function in the novel, for the groundwork has been laid. We have seen that almost every episode and every other major figure in the novel has a typological or archetypal counterpart. It would be unreasonable not to anticipate that Demian, after whom the story of Sinclair's youth is named, should not be similarly prefigured. According to the pattern we have seen, furthermore, we tend obviously to seek this prefiguration in the realm of the religious.

In the course of the book we actually learn surprisingly much about Demian as a plot figure—more than we learn about anyone else in the entire novel. He moves to town when Sinclair is about ten years old and Demian himself two years older. Since he wears a mourning band we assume that his father is recently deceased. In any event, his mother is a widow, and the two of them lead such a secluded life that—as is perfectly natural in the small towns that Hesse knows so well—all sorts of gossip inevitably surrounds them. They are said to be rich, and they do not attend church regularly although Demian subsequently does take communion instruction. Rumor has it that they are Jews or even Mohammedans, but that is, of course, merely a reaction to their alien nature. Some even go so far as to suggest that there is an incestuous relationship between mother and son. Demian is respected, even feared, for his physical strength and self-control, and Sinclair's friends whisper among themselves that he "knows all about girls." We have already seen that he is a questioner and a doubter, and Sinclair regards him as the "representative or harbinger"[89] of his ideal. He is, so to speak, the mouthpiece of the Nietzschean goal toward which Sinclair is striving, and that is his most significant contextual function in the novel.

These external facts help us but little in our identification of Demian's typological function. We must consider instead another group of characteristics that are not explicitly emphasized, but emerge in the course of the narrative. Demian's most salient physical characteristic is the "brightness" (*Helligkeit*) that illumines his forehead; this fact is mentioned repeatedly by Sinclair. Although Sinclair regards some of Demian's deeds as miracles, it is apparent that the feats are accomplished by extreme self-control and an uncanny skill in the psychological assessment of others. By the sheer force of his personality he heals Sinclair after the Kromer affair, and it is the thought of Demian that supports Sinclair later when the two friends are separated. Likewise, all of his major teachings are delivered in the form of parables—taken from the Bible! He talks of Cain, of the unrepentant thief, and of God. The central doctrine of this teaching is the coming of a new religious kingdom for which men must prepare themselves. We are told of disputations in which young Demian surprises his teachers with his questions and

[89] GD, III, 160.

answers. And toward the end of the book Demian has assembled around his person a circle of admirers, all of whom, like him, are striving for the kingdom that he foretells.

It seems clear, in view of these characteristics and the general religious tone of the book, that we are dealing with a Christ-figure. Demian has what amounts to a halo and performs what are commonly regarded as miracles. He is a "healer" by the sheer force of his personality (particularly his impressive eyes are mentioned). He disputes with his teachers, preaches a coming kingdom, and instructs his band of disciples through parables. If this identification can be accepted, it is possible to clarify a few further points that otherwise remain problematic. In the first place, Sinclair writes a plea to Demian, which he recites ritually: "A leader has left me. I am standing completely in the dark. I cannot take a step alone. Help me!"[90] After experiencing the consolation of this plea, Sinclair repeats it constantly: "I now knew the little prayer by heart and often said it to myself. It accompanied me at every hour. I began to understand what prayer is." Secondly, in the last sentence of the book, the personal pronoun referring to Demian is suddenly and inexplicably capitalized—not just once, but twice for emphasis. When he peers deep into his soul, Sinclair writes, he can see his own image, "which now completely resembles Him, Him, my Friend and my Leader."[91] The prayer and the capitalization seem to indicate the deification of Demian, his installation as a Christ-figure in the structure of the book. Going one step further: a book about a Christ written by a disciple is called a gospel. If the novel is indeed a gospel in form, then the tone of the entire work, with its visionary and

[90] GD, III, 223.   [91] GD, III, 257.

messianic zeal as well as its structure of prefiguration, are perfectly in keeping with the Biblical tradition.

This constitutes at the same time, of course, an intensification of the inherent irony of the book. An essentially Nietzschean doctrine is promulgated in a novel whose structure, language, images, and impulses are basically religious; and the central mouthpiece of these doctrines is a figure whose characteristics are based typologically upon those of Christ. Now this identification of Nietzsche and Christ is not far-fetched, at least in Hesse's mind, for the note is sounded within the novel itself. When Demian reminds Sinclair, toward the end, that they must remain true to themselves, he says: "What nature has in mind for mankind is written in the individual, in you and in me. It was in Jesus, it was in Nietzsche."[92] Any mention of Jesus in this way, needless to say, presupposes a secularization of his character. But this, too, has already been anticipated, for Pistorius, as will be recalled, once remarked to Sinclair that he regarded Christ not as a deity but as a myth, a *heros*, as an image that mankind has painted on the walls of eternity.[93] (Pistorius reveals himself by these remarks as an heir of the theological tradition of Strauss, Renan, and Feuerbach.)

If Demian is indeed a Christ-figure, that fact helps not only to account for certain elements of his character but also to explain the central riddle of the entire book: Does Demian actually exist, or is he, as has been suggested, Sinclair's *daimon*? There are several reasons for assuming the latter. Quite early in their acquaintance, when Demian seems almost to be reading Sinclair's mind, the theme is stated: "Wasn't a voice speaking that could only be coming from within me? That knew everything? That knew everything better and more clearly than I myself?"[94] Later, when Sinclair has finished his painting of Demian with its characteristic halo, he reflects: "Gradually the feeling arose within me that it was not Beatrice and not Demian, but—I myself. The picture did not resemble me—it wasn't supposed to, I felt—but it was an essential part of my life, it was my inner being, my destiny or my *daimon*."[95]

Yet all of this speculation leads us nowhere, for Demian has incontestably a formal existence as a character in the fiction. He is too much involved in the plot and with other people to be merely a figment of Sinclair's imagination.[96] If we pursue the gospel analogy to its logical conclusion, however, the whole matter resolves itself. We observed earlier that the tendency of the novel in general is toward gradual internalization of the outer world. This was quite clear in the case of the symbol of Abraxas. Moreover, it is one of Sinclair's (and Hesse's) central beliefs that the boundaries between internal and external reality are merely illusory. "For some time I had been living in such an unreal world with my paintings and my thoughts of Demian that I lost [Beatrice] completely from my sight and mind."[97] Here inner reality is stronger than external "reality." A short time later this impression is repeated: "Conceptions, images or wishes, rose within me and drew me away from the outside world, so that I had a more real and lively contact with these images within,

[94] GD, III, 135.   [95] GD, III, 178.
[96] Here I disagree with Malte Dahrendorf, "Hermann Hesses *Demian* und C. G. Jung," *Germanisch-Romanische Monatsschrift*, 39 (=Neue Folge 8, 1958), 81-97, and Suzanne Debruge, "L'Oeuvre de Hermann Hesse et la psychanalyse," *Etudes Germaniques*, 7 (1952), 252-261. Both interpret Demian purely as a Jungian symbol and as nothing more than an image of Sinclair's conscience, although Mme Debruge concedes (p. 255) that "Demian (daimon) est à la fois figure réelle et symbole."
[97] GD, III, 184.

with these dreams and shadows, than with my real surroundings."[98] Pistorius tells Sinclair that "there is no reality apart from that which we have within us."[99] And when Demian dies, he whispers a similar thought to Sinclair, saying that he will no longer be able to appear in crude physical form to help Sinclair if the need should arise: "You must listen within yourself; then you will see that I am within you."[100] But what we have called internalization on the psychological level, can be translated, in religious terms, as transubstantiation. When Sinclair, in the concluding sentence, states that he can look within himself and find "Him, my Friend and Leader," then he means this in the sense of the authors of the gospels, who have related the life of a living man whom they have known personally, but who is now "within" them. Viewed in this light, it seems unquestionable that Sinclair lives on after the writing of the book.[101] Otherwise Demian's death would be meaningless, both in the sense of the gospel and in the context of the Nietzschean doctrine. Sinclair now possesses the inner strength to continue his lonely way, no longer needing the support from outside. It is now his turn to become the missionary of the new gospel.

On the spiritual level Demian-Christ is certainly a projection of Sinclair's own thoughts: he belongs to the sequence of transcended external ideals like Beatrice and Abraxas. Yet at the same time he has an undeniable fictive existence as a real character who lives and dies.

There remains the question of Sinclair's own name. It is commonly held that Hesse intended this name as a tribute to Hölderlin's friend Isaak von Sinclair, and Hesse has certainly used onomastic devices no less esoteric in his

[98] GD, III, 188.   [99] GD, III, 206.   [100] GD, III, 256.
[101] Richard B. Matzig, *Hermann Hesse in Montagnola* (Basel, 1947), p. 28, believes, for instance, that Sinclair dies at the end.

other works. However, this interpretation adds nothing to our reading of the novel, for whatever Demian may be— he is not a Hölderlin-figure! J. C. Middleton has suggested a far more imaginative solution,[102] which is not only consistent with Hesse's name-giving in general, but which is especially appropriate in view of the theme of the novel: Sinclair is an Anglo-French compound of "sin" and "clair"—the two worlds of the novel, the "dark" and the "light," the two polar aspects of Sinclair's personality that he seeks to reconcile. As such, it is an appropriately symbolic name for a novel like *Demian*, which lives from suggestive symbolic references.

If we now consider the novel as a whole, we see that Sinclair's development falls into three parts. When we meet him he is still living in a state of childish innocence. But he rapidly is plunged into a world of doubt and torment, swinging between the two poles of light and dark until at the very end of the book, through magical thinking, he finds the ultimate synthesis of these conflicting worlds within himself. In the Christian terminology these stages would be the original state of Paradise, the fall, and redemption through Christ. Although by far the greatest part of the book is devoted to the more interesting middle stage, it is clear that all three stages are represented in the novel.

This structure has emerged from an analysis of the text itself, but it corresponds point for point to the triadic rhythm of humanization that Hesse subsequently outlined in "A Bit of Theology" (1932). Sinclair's pendulation is the vain striving of the individual to escape the demands of knowledge by flight back to the world of childish innocence, to the world of the herd-people of whom Demian and

[102] In his unpublished dissertation "Hermann Hesse as Humanist" (Oxford, 1954).

Pistorius speak. His progressive stages of alienation represent the realization that the true goal, a mature and higher
redemption, lies ahead of him on the third level of awareness and not behind in childhood. In the final vision, when
he realizes that the ideal, the justification of his life, lies
within him and not in the external world, he has reached
the chiliastic realm: the "new kind of innocence," the
higher "irresponsibility" of which Hesse speaks in the
essay. This triadic rhythm, as we have seen, underlies all
of Hesse's novels. His mastery reveals itself in the adorn-
ment of the structure, and he repeats himself rarely in
subject or style. The Christian symbolism that pervades
Demian gives way in the following novel to Buddhistic
images. The triadic rhythm of humanization merely supplies what Alfred Döblin has called the "network of tensions" that is established before the author begins to write.
Hesse's ability reveals itself in the body that he constructs
around the skeletal framework. In *Demian* we found the
body of Christ and his disciple; in *Siddhartha* it is the
body of the Buddha.

❖❖❖❖❖❖❖❖❖❖❖❖❖❖❖❖❖❖❖❖❖❖❖❖❖❖❖❖❖❖❖❖❖❖❖❖❖

8

Siddhartha: The Landscape of the Soul

ONE of the most salient characteristics of the reaction against the nineteenth century was a reawakening of interest in the Orient. The East, with its aura of mystery, has been a symbol of revolt against rationalism in Germany at least since the twelfth century, when the authors of medieval romances such as *König Rother* and *Herzog Ernst* sent their heroes off to Constantinople and beyond in search of adventure and magical knowledge that were no longer in evidence in Europe. Not until Herder, however, was a mythical image of India created that inspired, on the one hand, the scholarly investigations of Friedrich Schlegel, Friedrich Majer, and Josef von Hammer-Purgstall, and, on the other hand, the poetic vision that permeates the writings of Novalis, the older Goethe, and Schopenhauer— to mention but a few characteristic examples.[1]

With the reaction against positivism and the advent of modern mysticism that is so conspicuous in the works of Maeterlinck, Yeats, Hofmannsthal, and others, the mystical image of the Orient received a new impulse. Alfred Döblin, with his *The Three Leaps of Wang-lun* (*Die drei Sprünge des Wang-lun*; 1913), was one in a line of expressionists that included poets such as Else Lasker-Schüler and Franz Werfel, who exploited Oriental materials in their effort to find a correlative substance for their new conceptions. This interest was disseminated in popularized

[1] See, in this connection, A. Leslie Willson, *A Mythical Image: The Ideal of India in German Romanticism* (Durham, N.C., 1964).

form to thousands of readers in many languages by Hermann Count Keyserling, whose *Travel Diary of a Philosopher* (1919) gave an account of his trip around the world in 1911 and 1912 as well as an introduction to the mystical thought of the East. The Orient became a popular province for all those—writers, theosophers, and readers alike—who sought a philosophy of unity and totality to offset the fragmentation of existence produced by the scientific and technological progress of the West, whose decline Spengler was gloomily prognosticating.

Hesse and the East

While Keyserling was making his subsequently publicized tour of India, he might have encountered Hermann Hesse, who, with the painter Hans Sturzenegger, was taking a quiet trip through the East in the same year (1911). In his *Picture Book* (*Bilderbuch*; 1926) and in the journal *Out of India* (*Aus Indien*; 1913) Hesse published his own far less spectacular account of his impressions. India was a goal for Hesse, toward which he had long been striving, and at the same time a disappointment. In many of his stories and essays he has told of his childhood, surrounded by the objects that his grandfather Gundert had brought back from thirty years of missionary work in India. India, it can safely be maintained, was one of the most influential conditioning factors in Hesse's childhood. "From the time I was a child I breathed in and absorbed the spiritual side of India just as deeply as Christianity."[2] As a boy he had before him the constant stimulus of that same grandfather, who continued in Germany his scholarly enterprises on Indic languages; and his father also published works dealing with his years

[2] GS, vii, 371.

in the Orient.[3] "For over half of my life I was concerned with Indic and Chinese studies," Hesse wrote in *Picture Book*, "—or, so as not to get the reputation of scholarly authority, I was accustomed to breathe the air of Indian and Chinese poetry and piety."[4] Anyone who takes the trouble to glance at essays like *A Library of World Literature* (*Eine Bibliothek der Weltliteratur*; 1929) can easily obtain a quick synopsis of Hesse's impressive range of reading in Oriental literatures and philosophy.[5] It was only natural that he should desire to see with his own eyes the lands that had so long filled his imagination. And, indeed, he found there the India of which he had dreamed; his disappointment lay in the realization that he himself, as an Occidental, was unable to partake of this Oriental paradise.

"We come to the South and East full of longing, driven by a dark and grateful premonition of home, and we find here a paradise, the abundance and rich voluptuousness of all natural gifts. We find the pure, simple, childlike people of paradise. But we ourselves are different; we are alien here and without any rights of citizenship; we lost our paradise long ago, and the new one that we wish to build is not to be found along the equator and on the warm seas of the East. It lies within us and in our own northern future."[6]

What he brought back from his trip was "a deep rever-

[3] For an account of these matters see Joseph Mileck, *Hermann Hesse and His Critics* (Chapel Hill, North Carolina, 1958), pp. 3-4, and E. A. F. Lützkendorf, *Hermann Hesse als religiöser Mensch in seinen Beziehungen zur Romantik und zum Osten* (Burgdorf, 1932).

[4] "Besuch aus Indien"; GD, III, 856.

[5] "Eine Bibliothek der Weltliteratur"; GS, VII, 307-343.

[6] *Aus Indien*; reprinted extensively in *Bilderbuch* (GD, III, 786-862); here p. 845.

ence for the spirit of the East,"[7] whether in its Indian or Chinese form. But Western Man can never hope to return to that state of primitive innocence; rather, he must seek his own paradise in the future. Not cyclical, but progressive regeneration is his destiny, and that fact separates him irrevocably from the primeval Golden Age of which he dreams.

Hesse's attitude toward the East is at this time not one of enthusiastic affirmation, but rather of critical assessment. The magic of the East, which he clearly regards as an image of a lost and irrecoverable paradise, exerts an ineluctable attraction upon his mind and imagination, and he returns to it again and again. Yet he pores over the lore and wisdom of the East with a skeptical eye, striving to single out those elements that are relevant to his own problems and, in turn, testing and sharpening his own thoughts on the systems that he discovers there. This is particularly evident in his journals from the year 1920, precisely during the composition of *Siddhartha*.

"My preoccupation with India, which has been going on for almost twenty years and has passed through many stages, now seems to me to have reached a new point of development. Previously my reading, searching and sympathies were restricted exclusively to the philosophical aspect of India—the purely intellectual, Vedantic and Buddhistic aspect. The Upanishads, the sayings of Buddha, and the Bhagavad Gita were the focal point of this world. Only recently have I been approaching the actual religious India of the gods, of Vishnu and Indra, Brahma and Krishna. And now Buddhism appears to me more and more as a kind of very pure, highly bred reformation—a purification and spiritualization that has no flaw but its great

[7] GD, III, 851.

zealousness, with which it destroys image-worlds for which it can offer no replacement."[8]

This evaluation is perfectly consistent with Hesse's thoughts as we know them already; it is the reproach that Sinclair, the poet, made to Pistorius, the analyst. A purely abstract vision of the world is insufficient for men who require substance and life. This brings us directly to the story of Siddhartha, the Brahman's son who rebels against the strictures of his caste and predestined office in life.

After all that has been said it is no surprise that Hesse undertook to write a novel about India; by the same token, it would be naïve to read the book as an embodiment or exegesis of Indian philosophy. Hesse found this book difficult to compose because he was engaged in coming to terms with India as he wrote. *Demian* was poured forth within the period of a few months in 1917; *Siddhartha: An Indic Poem* required almost four years of effort although it is shorter than *Demian* by one quarter. Hesse began the book in 1919 and quickly wrote the first four chapters, which were published separately in the *Neue Rundschau* (1920). Then there came a break during which he wrote the expressionistically flavored story "Klingsor's Last Summer"; later in the winter of 1919-1920 he went on to compose the next group of four chapters (the Kamala episode).[9] Then he suddenly found himself unable to go on.

"My Indic poem got along splendidly as long as I was writing what I had experienced: the feelings of Siddhartha, the young Brahman, who seeks the truth, who scourges and torments himself, who has learned reverence, and must

---

[8] "Aus einem Tagebuch des Jahres 1920," *Corona*, 3 (1932), 201-02.

[9] Hugo Ball, *Hermann Hesse* . . . , p. 162.

now acknowledge this as an impediment to the Highest Goal. When I had finished with Siddhartha the Sufferer and Ascetic, with the struggling and suffering Siddhartha, and now wished to portray Siddhartha the victor, the affirmer, the subjugator—I couldn't go on."[10]

It was not until 1922, after a complete revision of his views of India, that Hesse was finally able to finish the last third of his novel and publish it in full.

The Elements of the Plot

Siddhartha, feeling that the teachings of Brahmanism do not lead to salvation, decides to try other paths. He leaves home with his friend Govinda (chapter 1) to join the ascetic Samanas, with whom he spends three years. But gradually realizing that asceticism and yoga are only leading him further away from himself, he goes with Govinda to hear the teachings of Gautama the Buddha (chapter 2). Govinda remains with the great teacher, but Siddhartha perceives that everyone must seek out his own path (chapter 3). Departing from Buddha, Govinda, and a life of the spirit alone, Siddhartha determines to expose himself to the world of the senses and experience (chapter 4).

Crossing a river on a ferry, he reaches a large city where he quickly meets and desires the love of Kamala, a famous courtesan (chapter 5). Aided by Kamala, who has taken an interest in the poor stranger, Siddhartha soon becomes wealthy and is able to afford all the pleasures of life that he desires—including Kamala herself (chapter 6). After many years, however, he realizes that this path was just as foolish as that of asceticism; that his luxurious life has

[10] "Aus einem Tagebuch des Jahres 1920," p. 193. A similar explanation can be found in Hesse's correspondence with Romain Rolland, to whom the first part was dedicated.

lulled his true self to sleep just as perniciously as the exercises of yoga had done before. He decides to break his way out of the world of Sansara and illusion (chapter 7). Unaware that Kamala is now pregnant with his child, Siddhartha steals secretly away from the city and returns to the river where, at the height of his despair, he almost commits suicide. But as he sinks toward the water, he suddenly feels a stirring of his old self and realizes that escape by suicide is impossible (chapter 8).

He decides to stay by the river and to try to learn to understand himself again: he regards his years as ascetic and then as profligate as two necessary evils that cancel each other out, leaving him once again in his original state of innocence—with the added dimension of knowledge of good and evil. Living with the wise ferryman Vasudeva, Siddhartha learns many secrets from the river: primarily that there is no time and that all being is a unity (the awareness of simultaneity and totality!) (chapter 9), but before this knowledge can be of real significance, it must be conditioned by love. After twelve years have passed, Kamala comes to the river with her son in search of Buddha. She dies from a snake bite, and Siddhartha begins to care for the boy. He loves his son desperately, but the spoiled young city boy yearns only to get away from the two senile old boatmen and to return to life in the city. Eventually he succeeds in escaping, and Siddhartha experiences for the first time the pangs of love and, then, pure unselfish devotion (chapter 10). When he has reached this stage, Vasudeva dies, for Siddhartha can now take over the tradition and his knowledge (chapter 11). Govinda passes by one day and, in a mystic revelation, realizes that Siddhartha in his own way, like Buddha, has achieved absolute peace and harmony (chapter 12).

It is immediately apparent that, though the scene has

changed, many elements of the plot are similar to those of *Demian*. Like Demian (and later Sinclair) Siddhartha is characterized by an almost physical illumination that is a reflection of his inner control and mental powers. Here, too, we have a dichotomy between the world of the spirit and that of the senses. Accordingly, Siddhartha passes through the stages of saint and profligate, like Sinclair, on his road to fulfillment. His development also involves the seeking out and consequent transcending of a series of teachers. Vasudeva's death, with the symbolic embrace, has the same significance of mystical transference as the death of Demian. And, finally, Siddhartha's development follows the triadic rhythm that we have already noted as characteristic of Hesse's novels, indeed his whole conception of human growth. Here, to be sure, the initial stage of childlike innocence is not portrayed, for Siddhartha, when we meet him, already has the seeds of knowledge and doubt in his heart. Yet that stage is clearly implied, for instance, in Siddhartha's words after his awakening on the bank of the river: "Now I stand again beneath the sun as I once stood as a small child: nothing is mine. I have no powers, no accomplishments, I have learned nothing."[11] And the harmony that he attains at the end of the book is, of course, the third stage of higher innocence.

Apart from those familiar to us from *Demian*, there are other elements of the plot that are clearly discernible: namely, elements borrowed from the life (or legend) of Gautama Buddha.[12] Siddhartha, in the first place, has the same name as the Buddha, who in addition to the proper name Gautama also bore the epithet Siddhartha

---

[11] GD, III, 688.

[12] I refer especially to the biographical evidence for the life of Buddha in Maurice Percheron, *Buddha in Selbstzeugnissen und Bilddokumenten*, trans. Joachim Rassat (Rowohlt-Monographien, 1958), pp. 17-33.

("the one who has reached the goal"). Both are supposed to have been first among their fellows, as children, in all competition. Buddha left his wife and newly born son to become an ascetic; Siddhartha leaves his beloved Kamala and their still unborn son for the same purpose. Both spent time among the ascetics, learning the practice of yoga. Buddha spent six years meditating on the bank of a river; Siddhartha's last years are spent at the river, where his final revelations come to him. Buddha's revelations came to him under the Bo-tree, while Siddhartha makes his most important decision while sitting under a mango tree. During his three vigils under the Bo-tree Buddha experienced in a vision all of his previous existences, the condition of the present world, and a revelation of the relationship of all things to one another; this is precisely the essence of Siddhartha's final vision in the novel: a view of the world as simultaneity and totality.

These parallels do not mean that Hesse is writing a life of Buddha or using Buddha as a typological prefiguration. On the contrary, any attempt to analyze the novel according to Buddha's life or his teaching about the Four Truths and the Eight-fold Noble Path does violence to the natural structure of the book.[13] The book includes, cer-

[13] Here my interpretation differs from that of Leroy R. Shaw, "Time and the Structure of Hermann Hesse's *Siddhartha,*" *Symposium,* 11 (Fall 1957), 204-224. Shaw regards the novel as an expression of the Four Noble Truths (chapters 1-4) and the Eightfold Path (chapters 5-12) of Buddha. I believe that this view is structurally fallacious for the following reasons. In Buddhism the Eightfold Path is the way to the perception of the Four Noble Truths, which represent fulfillment. If Siddhartha achieves the Truths in the first part of the novel, then it is contextually pointless and structurally inconsistent for the novel to continue. But more important: the whole novel is Hesse's attempt, as we shall see, to reject the Buddhist way. If that is so, then it would be illogical for Siddhartha to follow the Eightfold Path in his own development. Finally, Shaw's interpretation is predicated upon an acceptance of the superficial disposition of the

tainly, an implicit critical exegesis of Buddhism,[14] but Hesse's entire view of life and development is explicitly opposed to that of Gautama. In his diary of 1920 he states categorically that he opposes Buddha's conscious attempt to postulate an established pattern of development, maintaining instead (just as Siddhartha does) that he hopes "to fulfill the will of God precisely by letting myself drift (in one of my stories I called it 'letting oneself fall') . . ."[15] As a matter of fact, recent studies indicate that the *thought* of *Siddhartha* has more in common with Chinese than with Indian philosophical and religious systems.[16] However, questions of this nature are out of place here since, as in *Demian*, Hesse defines his symbols adequately within the framework of his fiction.

The parallels to Buddha's life are, rather, contributing factors to the *legendary* quality of the novel, for the legend is the genre that Hesse seems consciously to be imitating here. The legend, as one can easily verify by a cursory comparison of selections from the *Acta Sanctorum*, consists substantially of an ideal life whose episodes are filled by traditional "motifs" or, in the terminology of André Jolles,[17] by "linguistic gestures." These incidents

---

material: namely, two parts of, respectively, four and eight chapters. I believe, as the following analysis will show, that this approach ignores the essential triadic structure of the novel.

[14] Particularly informative on this point is the dissertation by Johanna Maria Louisa Kunze. *Lebensgestaltung und Weltanschauung in Hermann Hesses Siddhartha* ('s-Hertogenbosch, 1946). Miss Kunze, however, seems, like Shaw, to be unaware of the very important journal of 1920 from which I quote.

[15] "Aus einem Tagebuch des Jahres 1920," p. 206. (The story to which Hesse refers is *Klein and Wagner*.)

[16] See esp. Edmund Gnefkow, *Hermann Hesse: Biographie 1952* (Freiburg in Breisgau, 1952).

[17] *Einfache Formen* (2nd ed. Darmstadt, 1958), esp. pp. 23-61: "Legende." Cf. also the article "Legende" by Hellmut Rosenfeld in *Reallexikon der deutschen Literaturgeschichte*, II (2nd ed. Berlin, 1959).

or motifs are, as a rule, traditional and transferable; precisely in this way Hesse has transplanted various motifs from the life of Buddha to the life of Siddhartha—not as typological prefiguration, but in order to sustain the legendary quality of the narrative. Hesse, of course, is not attempting to write a model legend; he exploits the possibilities of the genre only insofar as he can do so without obstructing the development of the novel. Yet there are certain other features of the legend *per se* that appear as elements in his novel and contribute to its structure. In the first place, Siddhartha is clearly regarded as a "saintly" figure—he is, in Jolles' words again, an *imitabile*—not in the sense that his road can be emulated, but rather his goal of absolute peace. Then, his reunification with the All at the end of the book corresponds to the miraculous union with God in Christian legends. As in Christian canonization trials, his saintliness must be attested by witnesses: namely, Vasudeva, Kamala, and Govinda, all of whom recognize in his face the aspect of godliness and repose. These elements of the plot unquestionably heighten the legendary atmosphere of the story.

The quality is maintained above all, however, in the language. The style here is just as highly consistent with the theme as in *Demian* and hence, properly, is unique and different from the style of the earlier novel. As a matter of fact, in the latter part of the novel one can find passages in which Hesse did not quite succeed in sustaining the pure simplicity of the earlier pages. This is accounted for by the fact that the first part of the book, as we have seen, was written in a mood of reflection whereas the second part was a voyage of discovery for Hesse himself. Thus in the beginning the style is more controlled. It is characterized essentially by extreme parataxis of syntax (which corresponds to the parataxis of structure, as we shall see), consciously archaic phraseology, epic repetition and epic cataloguing of detail (joined by many passages of iterative-durative action to denote the passing of time), Homeric simile, and, in general, by a highly stylized presentation. This is the basic tone of the entire book although in the excitement of the second part Hesse occasionally lapses into discongruous passages of extended hypotaxis and less leisurely presentation.

The River as Symbol

The central symbol around which the plot and substance of the novel are organized is the river. Unlike those in *Demian*, this symbol is not complicated or complemented by other symbols or motifs; it alone bears the full burden of communication. The river, as so often in literature from Heraclitus to Thomas Wolfe, is a symbol for timelessness, and with this symbol Hesse aligns himself with many other modern authors who are obsessed with the problem of the tyranny of time: Proust, T. S. Eliot, Hermann Broch, Thomas Mann, and Faulkner, to mention only a few.[18] In Hesse's case this symbol of simultaneity is expanded to include the realm, already anticipated in *Demian*, in which all polarity ceases: totality. It is a realm of pure existence in which all things coexist in harmony. Fluidity is a corollary of what, in *Demian*, we called magical thinking, or what Siddhartha expresses thus: ". . . of every truth it can be said that the opposite is just as true!"[19] For in any system that regards all polar extremes as invalid, as interchangeable, traditional values are indeed in a state of flux. Hence we find in *Siddhartha*

[18] For a stimulating and informative discussion of this topic, with explicit reference to the river as a symbol, see Hans Meyerhoff, *Time in Literature* (Univ. of California Press, 1955), pp. 14-18.

[19] GD, III, 725.

many symbols of fluidity, and this extends even to the vocabulary, which returns to expressions of fluidity just as consistently as the language of *Demian* to the style of the Bible. Further: another corollary to the principle of magical thinking is metamorphosis. Just as fluidity might be regarded as the mode of totality in space, metamorphosis—in the Indian sense of transmigration of the souls—is its mode in time. Thus the concept of the "cycle of transformations" (*Kreislauf der Verwandlungen*) plays an important role in the argument of the book, for Siddhartha's ultimate goal, as exemplified in the final vision, is to escape the wheel of metempsychosis by realizing that all possible transformations or potentialities of the soul are possible not only consecutively, but simultaneously in the human soul. "In deep meditation there is the possibility of annulling time—to regard everything that has been, that is, and that will be, as simultaneous."[20] Siddhartha explains this idea to Govinda by using the example of a stone: ". . . this stone is stone: it is also animal, it is also God, it is also Buddha. I love and venerate it not because it might someday become this or that—but because it has long been all these things and always will be. . . ."[21] Siddhartha's redemption lies in the fact that he has escaped the circle of metempsychosis: his Nirvana is no more than the recognition that all being exists simultaneously in unity and totality. As Hesse states it in his diary excerpts: "Nirvana, as I understand it, is the liberating step back behind the *principium individuationis*; that is, religiously expressed, the return of the individual soul to the All-soul."[22]

All of this is nothing new: we met it in Demian's magical thinking and in many of Hesse's essayistic utterances.

[20] GD, III, 726.   [21] GD, III, 727.
[22] "Aus einem Tagebuch des Jahres 1920," p. 206.

And in the story "Pictor's Metamorphoses," which was written in the same year (1922), Hesse transports us to a fairy-tale realm where the hero actually does undergo the various transformations that Siddhartha experiences only psychologically. Through the powers of the magic carbuncle Piktor is physically transformed into a tree and other natural objects. But nowhere else has Hesse employed a more appropriate symbol for his ideas than here: for the river is in essence fluidity and simultaneity. This is made clear repeatedly:

"This is what you mean, isn't it: that the river is everywhere at the same time—at its source and at its mouth, at the waterfall, at the ferry, at the rapids, in the sea, in the mountains—everywhere, at the same time—and that for the river there is only the present, without the shadow of a future."[23]

In the river Hesse found the perfect symbol for his views. Demian's Abraxas, Harry Haller's Magic Theater, and the Glass Bead Game itself are all symbols for precisely the same concept; but they are invented or esoteric symbols that have to be explained, whereas the aptness and significance of the river is instantly apparent to the reader. But Hesse did not stop at the symbolic function of the river. He uses it in addition as the central structural element. Substance, symbol, and structure are so closely welded that it is almost impossible to separate these functions, for the meaning is not put into words, as in the other works, but must be derived from the action of the book itself.

It is only on the river, this realm of totality and efface-ment of polarities, that Siddhartha could have experienced

[23] GD, III, 698; for similar passages see pages 699 and 720.

the visionary dream that he has as he departs from Govinda to experience the life of the senses in the city.

"Sad was the appearance of Govinda, sadly he asked: Why did you leave me? Thereupon he embraced Govinda, wrapping his arms about him, and as he drew him to his breast and kissed him, it was no longer Govinda, but a woman, and from the woman's garments there burst a full breast; Siddhartha rested his head upon this breast and drank, sweet and strong tasted the milk of this breast. It tasted of woman and man, of sun and forest, of animal and flower, of every fruit, of every passion. It made him drunk and unconscious."[24]

In this dream, which comes to Siddhartha as he spends the night in the ferryman's hut beside the river, we have a transition from Siddhartha's previous ascetic life, personified by Govinda, to his new life in the arms of Kamala. But here on the river itself the two realms—spirit and senses—are united in the embrace of the strange hermaphroditic figure of his dream (a figure strongly reminiscent of the male-female dream-ideals of Sinclair in *Demian*). This dream plays a key role in the structure of the novel, for it is at once a transition between two parts as well as an anticipation of yet a third part, in which the two worlds will be reconciled in Siddhartha's vision of totality and simultaneity on the river.

The Structural Principle

Superficially the novel is divided into two parts with, respectively, four and eight chapters. Any attempt to analyze the book on this basis, however, is fallacious, for it is quite obvious that the book falls into three natural sections: Siddhartha's life at home, among the Samanas,

[24] GD, III, 652.

and with Buddha (four chapters); his life with Kamala and among the "child people" of the city (four chapters); and his life with Vasudeva on the river (four chapters). We have three parts of roughly equal length, each devoted to a distinct period of Siddhartha's development.

Temporally and spatially the periods are delimited by Siddhartha's initial crossing of the river and by his subsequent return to it.[25] Only with reference to the river is it possible to determine the fact that the three periods are of equal duration. And the river, as the natural symbol of synthesis, is the natural border between the realms of spirit and sense in which Siddhartha attempts to live before he achieves the synthesis upon its very banks. What we have, in other words, is a projection of Siddhartha's inner development into the realm of space: the landscape of the soul.

It can be ascertained that each section encompasses roughly twenty years of Siddhartha's life.[26] There is very

[25] Shaw, p. 212, is mistaken when he writes that "Siddhartha will cross and recross the river many times during his error-laden search. . . ."

[26] See Marianne Wagner, "Zeitmorphologischer Vergleich von Hermann Hesses Demian, Siddharta [sic!], Der Steppenwolf und Narziss und Goldmund zur Aufweisung typischer Gestaltzüge" (Bonn, 1953). In this unpublished dissertation, written under the influence of Günther Müller and his seminar, the author attempts to establish a precise chronology of events by referring to such things as rain seasons and banana crops. She assumes a lapse of one year between parts I and II, states categorically that Siddhartha is 57 years old when Vasudeva dies, and figures Siddhartha's own age at the end as sixty-one. However, the argument is unconvincing despite its subtleties; there is simply not enough evidence for a detailed chronology of this sort. Far more persuasive is the approach of Marianne Overberg in her dissertation for Müller: "Die Bedeutung der Zeit in Hermann Hesses Demian" (Bonn, 1948), for the author assumes that Hesse is interested not in any specific chronological time, but rather in "biological-inner" ("biologisch-innerseelisch") time. Even Miss Overberg is tempted at times to be unnecessarily specific, as when she establishes the first chapter of Demian in the month of September "soon after the apple harvest."

little to go on. When Siddhartha leaves Kamala to go and live by the river he is "only in his forties."[27] Yet when he first meets Kamala he is still a "youth,"[28] and Vasudeva recalls that he had ferried Siddhartha across the river once before: "It must have been more than twenty years ago."[29] Roughly, then, Siddhartha is in his early twenties when he first crosses the river, and approximately twenty years elapse before he returns to it. When Siddhartha sees Kamala again, the son conceived on the night of his departure is eleven years old.[30] After this reference there is no other specific statement: we read only that "long months" passed before the son fled back to the city. And the opening pages of the following chapter are filled with expressions indicating the passage of time. So we should be justified in assuming, for reasons of parallelism if for none other, that at least twenty more years elapse before Siddhartha's final interview with Govinda. Thus, the narrated time in each major section or life-epoch[31] is roughly equivalent.

Within the sections the time scheme is different. It is obvious from the total time structure of the novel that Hesse must operate, in this book more than in any other he has written, with compression of narrated time within the epochs. This is achieved, in the first place, by the frequent occurrence of passages indicating iterative-durative action. A good example is the opening paragraph.

[27] GD, III, 677.   [28] GD, III, 657.
[29] GD, III, 695.   [30] GD, III, 706.
[31] I use here the terms suggested by Eberhard Lämmert in his excellent study, *Bauformen des Erzählens* (Stuttgart, 1955). Lämmert uses the term "epoch" (*Lebensepoche*) to designate the large units of time into which a story naturally falls and the word "phase" (*Lebensphase*) for specific periods of action within the larger epochs. The terms *Zeitraffung* (compression of time by various techniques) as well as iterative-durative compression stem from Günther Müller and are employed by Lämmert and others in a restricted technical sense.

"In the shade of the house, in the sun of the river bank by the boats, in the shade of the Sal forest, in the shade of the fig tree Siddhartha grew up, the handsome son of the Brahman, the young falcon, along with Govinda, his friend, the son of the Brahman. Sun browned his fair shoulders on the river bank, during the bath, during the sacred ablutions, during the holy sacrifices. Shadow flowed into his dark eyes in the mango grove, during the children's games, during the songs of his mother, during the sacred offerings, during the teaching of his father, the scholar, during the conversations of the sages."

Although the novel begins when Siddhartha is about eighteen years old (he spends three years with the Samanas before he crosses the river for the first time), we receive, in passages of this sort, a clear impression of Siddhartha's childhood and an almost tactile sense of time passing.

From this general continuum of time that lasts for some sixty years, certain phases are isolated as characteristic examples for each of the three epochs. In general Hesse is operating here with two-day phases in all three sections, and these phases fall, in general, at the beginning and end of each epoch. The intervening time is filled—never simply omitted or ignored!—with iterative-durative action of the type just mentioned. In the first epoch we find a two-day phase beginning with Siddhartha's decision to leave home and continuing to the next day when he and Govinda join the Samanas. The second phase takes place three years later, when Siddhartha accompanies Govinda to the grove of Jetavana, where they meet Buddha; forty-eight hours after their departure from the Samanas, Siddhartha also takes leave of Buddha and sets out on his new adventure.

The first phase of the second epoch relates the crossing of the river and his first full day in the city. The following twenty years, however, are expressed by time compression:

"Siddhartha thanked him and accepted, and now lived in the merchant's house. Clothes were brought to him, and shoes, and a servant prepared his bath daily. Twice a day a plentiful meal was laid out, but Siddhartha ate only once a day, and neither ate meat nor did he drink wine."[32]

This passage is a particularly good example because it shows a transition from phase style to iterative-durative style. The first sentence is actually the last sentence of the preceding phase and is a specific answer to a specific proposal by Kamaswami. In the next sentence, however, the change takes place. The fact that clothing and shoes were brought to him is still specific, referring to the first day in Kamaswami's house; but the last part of the sentence is already iterative-durative: his bath was prepared not only on this one occasion, but every day for the next few years. From this point on, the epoch is not interrupted by another specific phase until the end of the twenty-year period when Siddhartha, who is now a wealthy merchant with his own house, possessions, servants, suddenly tires of his life and decides to leave it behind in order to start out all over again. This decision is again related in a two-day phase, which begins with Siddhartha's terrifying vision of his degeneracy and lasts until he finds himself on the river bank two days later, after his near-attempt at suicide by drowning, whereupon he decides to remain with Vasudeva, the ferryman.

The last epoch is richer in phases. The first, which takes place when Siddhartha has been with Vasudeva for twelve years, describes Kamala's arrival with her child and her subsequent death. The next phase relates the son's flight, many months later, and Siddhartha's realization

[32] GD, III, 665.

that he cannot keep the boy with him or determine his way in life. The third phase depicts Vasudeva's death some years later; and the final phase is Siddhartha's mystical transfiguration before the eyes of Govinda. Yet between these eight specific phases, which form the slight action of the novel, the sense of time is never suspended, but is kept flowing by a variety of iterative-durative devices that leave us with a full impression of Siddhartha's life over a period of some sixty years.

The flow of time has two important functions in the novel. In the first place, the flow of time in Siddhartha's life must be depicted in order to make the symbol of the river plausible as an analogy for human life; the *tertium comparationis* is flux. In the second place, time is necessary to allow Siddhartha's own development. He must have time to exhaust fully the possibilities of two aspects of life and, in his third epoch, to adjust to the totally new synthesis of which he becomes aware on the banks of the river. In its own way, the novel *Siddhartha* is a *Zeitroman* in Thomas Mann's definition of his *The Magic Mountain* —a novel *about* time.[33] And the time in *Siddhartha* is as carefully structured as that in Mann's novel although the structure is a totally different one.

The temporal structure of the novel, which can be determined only by reference to the river, is paralleled by the spatial structure and what might be called the symbolic geography of the book. We have seen that the river symbolizes the goal of simultaneity and totality that Siddhartha aspires to achieve. Simultaneity and totality, however, imply the resolution of polar opposites. In *Siddhartha* the polar opposites to be reconciled—the spirit and the senses—are restricted geographically to realms divided

[33] Thomas Mann, "Vorwort," *Der Zauberberg* (S. Fischer, 1950), p. xxiii.

by the river. The river by its very nature has part in both realms: it is not an obstacle to be crossed (as in Buddhistic symbolism) but rather constitutes in itself the natural synthesis of extremes. Siddhartha's wanderings in geographical space thus parallel his inner development.

Siddhartha leaves home in the first chapter in search of "Atman, It, the Only One, the All-One,"[34] which he had not discovered in Brahmanism. "And where was Atman to be found, where did It reside, where did Its eternal heart beat, where else but in the own Self, in the innermost being, in the indestructible part that everyone bears within himself?"[35] These are all periphrases for the word "soul" as we have seen it in *Demian* and Hesse's various essays. Accordingly, Siddhartha sets out to find Atman in asceticism and yoga, for he is still persuaded that the answer lies in exercises of the mind and denial of the world of senses. Yet, in the crucial phase at the end of his first epoch he is forced to conclude: "I sought Atman, I sought Brahma, I wished to dismember and unpeel my Self in order to find in its unknown interior the kernel of all shells, Atman, Life, the Divine, the Ultimate. But in doing so I lost myself."[36] As he wanders on he meditates:

"He now had to experience himself. . . . The body was surely not the Self, nor more was the play of the senses; yet thinking was not it either, nor reason, nor acquired wisdom. . . . No, this world of thoughts also was not part of the beyond, and it led to no goal if one killed the random I of the senses in order to fatten the random I of the mind and of erudition. Both of them, thoughts as well as the senses, were nice things. But the ultimate meaning lay hidden behind both of them; it was important to listen to both of them, to play with both, neither to despise nor to

[34] GD, III, 619.   [35] GD, III, 619.   [36] GD, III, 646.

overestimate either—and to perceive in both the secret voices of one's innermost being."[37]

With this perception in mind he crosses the river and proceeds to the city, where he devotes himself to the sense pleasures of the second section. We have here the familiar polarity of spirit and nature, but in *Siddhartha* the two realms are not mingled as was the case in *Demian*, where Sinclair pendulated constantly between the light and dark worlds. Instead, one section (twenty years) is devoted to the cultivation of intellect and another section (twenty more years) to the cultivation of the senses. Geographically, however, these are also different realms, and they are separated by the symbolic river which Siddhartha crosses. Twenty years later, when he returns to the river, he realizes that his life among the "child people" had merely cancelled out his preceding experiences in the realm of spirit and asceticism: "That was why he had had to go into the world, to lose himself in desire and power, in women and money; that is why he had had to become a merchant, a gambler, drunk and avaricious—until the priest and the Samana within him were dead. . . . He had died, and a new Siddhartha had awakened from the sleep."[38] The return to the river is, of course, not accidental; if Hesse had not intended it as a structural element, he would not have described Siddhartha's first crossing and meeting with Vasudeva, which include certain elements anticipatory of the final resolution.

What we have is a geographical parallel to the temporal structure: in the first section Siddhartha spends twenty years in the realm of the spirit on one side of the river; in the second section, twenty more years in the realm of nature and the senses on the other side of the river; and

<hr>

[37] GD, III, 651-52.   [38] GD, III, 692.

the last (twenty) years of his life are spent *on* the river, which represents the synthesis of nature and spirit, the unity, totality, and simultaneity of all being. It is of interest to note that Siddhartha also begins his life on the banks of a river. (In the paragraph quoted above, the river is mentioned several times as an important feature of his childhood.) We have no indication that it is the same river. Yet it is significant that his period of childlike innocence (the first of his three stages) was spent on a river; he leaves the river when the seeds of doubt have sprung in his heart and returns to it only when the poles of spirit and senses have cancelled each other, leaving him again as a child. For although rivers occur elsewhere in the book (there is, of course, a river in Kamala's city), they are mentioned only in passing and play no structural role.

It might be added that the parallelism between the first two epochs extends further to include the characters who play an important role. The significant dream that invades Siddhartha's mind before he first crosses the river calls our attention to the parallel function of Govinda and Kamala:[39] both stand for the essence, or the ideal, of the realm that they respectively represent. Buddha himself, who has achieved fulfillment, does not fit into the realm of the spirit any more than does Vasudeva: both show by anticipation the state upon which Siddhartha will enter when he has advanced far enough. But the Samanas, as representatives of the extremes of asceticism repel Siddhartha just as instinctively as does the village maiden who, at the beginning of his second epoch, invites him to engage in a little amatory sport from the *Kama Sutra*: she is not the essence of sensuality, but its gross extreme.

[39] Kamala's name, like that of Kamaswami, is based on the Sanskrit root *kama*, meaning "love," or Kama, the god of desire.

Through the projection of inner feeling into the realm of geography we have followed Siddhartha's development from the pole of spirit to the pole of nature and back to the synthesis of totality and simultaneity in the symbol of the river. In the final vision of the book Hesse renders Siddhartha's fulfillment visually by reversing the process. For as Govinda looks into Siddhartha's face at the end, what he perceives is no longer the landscape of the soul, but rather: the soul as landscape. Siddhartha has learned the lesson of the river so well that his entire being now reflects the totality and simultaneity that the river symbolizes. As in a painting by Marc Chagall or in Rilke's poem "The Death of the Poet," the landscape is actually reflected in Siddhartha's face. He has reached fulfillment by affirming the totality of the world and by accepting it as part of himself and himself as part of the development of the world.

"He no longer saw his friend Siddhartha's face, he saw instead other faces, many, a long row, a streaming river of faces, hundreds, thousands, all of which came and went, and yet all seemed to be present at the same time, all of them seemed to be changing and renewing themselves constantly, and yet all were Siddhartha. He saw the face of a fish, a carp with its mouth opened wide in infinite pain, a dying fish with breaking eyes—he saw the face of a new born child, red and full of wrinkles, drawn up to cry—he saw the face of a murderer, saw him plunge a knife into the body of a man—he saw, in the same instant, this same criminal kneeling in chains and his head being cut off by an executioner with a blow of the sword—he saw the bodies of men and women naked in the positions and battles of furious love—he saw corpses stretched out, still, cold, empty—he saw heads of animals, of boars,

crocodiles, elephants, bulls, birds—he saw gods, saw
Krishna, saw Agni—he saw all of these forms and faces
in a thousand relationships to one another. . . . and all
these forms and shapes rested, flowed, reproduced, swam
along and streamed one into the other, and over all of them
there was constantly something thin, insubstantial and yet
existing, drawn like a thin glass or piece of ice, like a
transparent skin, a shell or mold or mask of water, and
this mask smiled, and this mask was Siddhartha's smiling
face. . . ."[40]

The Beatific Smile

Siddhartha's smile in the preceding passage is the best
example of the new dimension that we find in this novel.
Here, in brief, we have the same story that we encountered
in *Demian*: a man's search for himself through the stages
of guilt, alienation, despair, to the experience of unity.
The new element here is the insistence upon love as the
synthesizing agent. Hesse regards this element as "natural
growth and development"[41] from his earlier beliefs, and
certainly as no reversal or change of opinion. In the essay
"My Faith" (1931) he admitted "that my *Siddhartha*
puts not cognition, but love in first place: that it disdains
dogma and makes the experience of unity the central point.
. . ."[42] Cognition of unity as in *Demian* is not the ultimate
goal, but rather the loving affirmation of the essential
unity behind the apparent polarity of being. This is the
meaning of Siddhartha's transfiguration at the end of the
book. The passage goes on at length, developing all the
images of horizontal breadth in space and vertical depth
in time that we have indicated. But the whole vision is

[40] GD, III, 731-32.
[41] "Mein Glaube" (1931); GS, VII, 372.
[42] GS, VII, 372.

encompassed and united by "this smile of unity over the streaming shapes, this smile of simultaneity over the thousands of births and deaths."[43]

The beatific smile is the symbol of fulfillment: the visual manifestation of the inner achievement. As a symbol, it too is developed and anticipated before the final scene in which Govinda sees it in Siddhartha's face. It is the outstanding characteristic of the two other figures in the book who have attained peace: Buddha and Vasudeva. When Siddhartha first sees Gautama he notices immediately that his face reveals neither happiness nor sadness, but seems rather "to smile gently inward." Everything about him, "his face and his step, his quietly lowered gaze, his quietly hanging hand, and even every finger on this quiet hand spoke of peace, spoke of perfection."[44] When Siddhartha departs from the Buddha he thinks to himself:

"I have never seen a man gaze and smile, sit and walk like that. . . . truly, I wish that I too might be able to gaze and smile, sit and walk like him. . . . Only a man who has penetrated into his innermost Self gazes and walks in that way. Very well—I too shall seek to penetrate into my innermost Self."[45]

Siddhartha acknowledges in the Buddha a conscious ideal, but it is Buddha's goal and not his path to which the younger man aspires. The symbol of this goal is the beatific smile behind which, almost like the smile of the Cheshire Cat, the individual disappears. The same smile appears again when Vasudeva is portrayed, and we see it grow on Siddhartha's own face.

"And gradually his smile became more and more like that of the ferryman; it became almost as radiant, almost

[43] GD, III, 732.   [44] GD, III, 637.   [45] GD, III, 644.

as illumined with happiness, similarly glowing from a thousand little wrinkles, just as childlike, just as aged. Many travelers, when they saw the two ferrymen, took them to be brothers."[46]

At the moment of Vasudeva's death the unity of this smile is clearly expressed: "His smile shone radiantly as he looked at his friend, and radiantly shone on Siddhartha's face, too, the same smile."[47] The words here are not used in a figurative sense, for it literally is the same smile. The smile is the symbol of inner perfection, but inner perfection for Hesse means the awareness of the unity, totality, and simultaneity of all being. It is thus appropriate that the three men who share this perception should also share the same beatific smile, even though each reached his goal by following a completely different path.

The Epiphany

The beatific smile as the symbol of fulfillment recurs in many of Hesse's novels: we shall find it again in *The Steppenwolf, The Journey to the East,* and *The Glass Bead Game.* But before we leave *Siddhartha* we must discuss one major point: the achievement of Siddhartha's affirmation of existence.

Siddhartha's development to the point of loving affirmation is marked by a technique of modern fiction that James Joyce defined as the epiphany, but which occurs regularly in much prose, German and French as well as English, of the early twentieth century.[48] In the epiphany the protagonist perceives the essence of things that lies hidden behind their empirical reality, and as such the

---

[46] GD, III, 699.   [47] GD, III, 721.

[48] For a full discussion of this term, its use in literature, and relevant bibliography, see my article "James Joyces Epiphanie und die Überwindung der empirischen Welt in der modernen deutschen Prosa," *Deutsche Vierteljahrsschrift,* 35 (1961), 596-616.

epiphany is another symptom of the modern turn away from realism toward a new mysticism. The epiphany reveals the essential integral unity of a given object in a burst of radiance (what Joyce, in the words of Aquinas, calls the *integritas, consonantia,* and *claritas* of the object), and the observer is able to enter into a direct relationship of love with the object thus newly perceived. It is this element of loving perception, missing in the cooler cognition of *Demian,* that we find here in passage after passage. The most striking example occurs in the "awakening" scene of Chapter 4 after Siddhartha has made up his mind not to follow Buddha, but to seek his own way in the world of the senses:

"He looked around as though he were seeing the world for the first time. Lovely was the world, colorful was the world, strange and mysterious was the world! Here was blue, here was yellow, here was green. The sky flowed and the river, the forest towered up and the mountains, everything lovely, everything mysterious, and magical, and in the midst of it all—he, Siddhartha, the Awakening One, on the way to himself. All this, all this yellow and blue, river and forest, entered Siddhartha for the first time through his eyes, was no longer the magic of Mara, no longer the veil of Maja, no longer the senseless and accidental multiplicity of the world of appearances, contemptible for the deep-thinking Brahman who disparages multiplicity and seeks unity. Blue was blue, the river was river, and even if the One and the Divine lay hidden in the blue and river within Siddhartha, it was still simply the manner of the Divine to be yellow here, blue here, sky there, forest there, and Siddhartha here. Sense and Essence were not somewhere behind the things. They were in them—in everything."[49]

[49] GD, III, 647.

The points to be noticed in this and other epiphanies
(including, of course, those written by the young Joyce)
are, first, the impression of radiance aroused by the entire
description, which here is created largely by words such
as "blue," "yellow," and "sky." Then: these are all objects encountered constantly in daily life, but here *perceived* for the first time. And finally: what Siddhartha
realizes is that the meaning of these things is inherent
within them and not some abstract ideal that lies behind
their reality. They are radiant and meaningful as manifestations of the One and the Divine, hence as symbols of
unity and totality.

A further characteristic of the epiphany—one that is
inherent in its very nature but not usually present in the
actual epiphany scene—is the subject's feeling that words,
phrases, and concepts detract from our ultimate perception of the object, that they lie as a veil between the viewer
and true reality. (This is a syndrome that we discussed
earlier as the language crisis.) In *Siddhartha*, as well as
Hesse's works in general, we find this attitude, which provides the background for the experience of the epiphany.
Siddhartha's final interview with Govinda makes it clear
that he has been able to attain his affirmation and union
with the All only because he eschews the easy way of con-
venient words and phrases as explanations of reality.
"Words are not good for the secret meaning. Everything
is always slightly distorted when one utters it in words—
a little falsified, a little silly."[50] He goes on to confide that
he does not make distinctions between thoughts and words.
"To be perfectly frank, I don't have a very high opinion of
thoughts. I like *things* better."[51] And he concludes by
asserting that any ostensible difference between his views
and those of Buddha is only illusory, the product of word-

[50] GD, III, 727.   [51] GD, III, 728. (My italics.)

confusions. In essence, despite all superficial differences, they agree. The final vision, in which Govinda sees totality and simultaneity revealed in his friend's face, is also an epiphany: a direct revelation to Govinda of the essential unity of being that Siddhartha was unable to convey through the medium of words.

It is through epiphanies that Siddhartha breaks out of the rigid schematism of Buddhism and Brahminism (their "highly bred reformation" quality of which Hesse speaks in the diary of 1920) and begins to enter into an immediate contact with the world, though it first leads him to the false extreme of sensualism. Since love is the new dimension of Siddhartha's world, he must, as his final trial, learn to affirm even the rejection of his love by his own son. Only after he has suffered the torment of rejection can he perceive the final truth, which had hitherto been purely intellectual: no two men have the same way to the final goal: not even the father can spare his son the agonies of self-discovery. When Siddhartha accepts this truth, he perceives with visionary clarity that in the realm of simultaneity and totality even he and his own father are one. Just as he had once deserted his father, so had his son left him.

"Siddhartha gazed into the water, and in the flowing water pictures appeared to him: his father appeared, lonely, grieving about his son; he himself appeared, lonely, he too bound by the bonds of longing to his distant son; his son appeared, he too lonely, the boy, storming covetously along the burning course of his young desires; each directed toward his goal, each possessed by his goal, each suffering. . . . The image of the father, his own image, that of the son flowed together; also Kamala's image appeared and merged with the stream, and the image of Govinda, and other images, and flowed one into the other, becoming one with the river. . . ."[52]

Not until he has recognized and then affirmed the loss of his son is Siddhartha ready to enter the state of fulfillment. Only at this point does he affirm with love the insight which had been purely intellectual cognition when he departed from Buddha. For even in the case of his own son he is forced to concede that each man must find his own way in life, that no man's path can be prescribed. Thus the highest lesson of the novel is a direct contradiction of Buddha's theory of the Eightfold Path, to which, as we saw at the beginning of this chapter, Hesse objected in his diary of 1920; it is the whole meaning of the book that Siddhartha can attain Buddha's goal without following his path. If rejection of that doctrine is the essence of the novel, then it is futile to look to Buddhism for clues to the structural organization of the book. Rather, the structural principle is to be found precisely where the meaning of the book lies. Just as Siddhartha learns of the totality and simultaneity of all being—man and nature alike—so too the development of the soul is expressed in geographical terms and, in turn, the landscape is reflected in the human face. The book achieves a unity of style, structure and meaning that Hesse never again attained with such perfection after *Siddhartha*.

It would be futile to deny, on the other hand, that this unity has been achieved at the expense of the narrative realism we customarily expect from fiction. Just as the characters and landscape have been stylized into abstractions by Hesse's poetic vision, likewise the dialogue and action have been reduced—or escalated—to symbolic essentials. As in *Demian* the action is almost wholly inter-

[52] GD, iii, 719.

nalized: the excitement of this externally serene work is entirely within Siddhartha's mind. It is ultimately beside the point to judge this work by the criteria of the traditional realistic novel. Like Hermann Broch, who insisted that his *The Death of Vergil* was a "lyrical work" and that it be read and criticized as such, Hesse had good reasons for calling *Siddhartha* "an Indic poem." In both works there is a stratum of realistic narrative, but each as a whole represents the symbolic projection of an inner vision and not an attempt to capture external reality mimetically. Like his heroes, who vacillate between nature and spirit, Hesse as a narrator feels conflicting impulses toward realism and lyricism. In *Siddhartha* he reached an extreme of symbolic lyricism; his next major work, *The Steppenwolf*, comes closer to realism in its characterization, dialogue, and plot than anything else Hesse has written.

❖❖❖❖❖❖❖❖❖❖❖❖❖❖❖❖❖❖❖❖❖❖❖❖❖❖❖❖❖❖❖❖

9

The Steppenwolf: A Sonata in Prose

TOWARD the beginning of *The Steppenwolf* there is a remarkable passage in which Harry Haller, the author of the first-person narrative, outlines the course of his career. He has often, he begins, experienced periods of extreme despair.

"Once I lost my civic reputation along with my fortune and had to learn to do without the respect of those who had formerly tipped their hats to me. The next time my family life collapsed overnight: my wife, who had become mentally deranged, drove me out of home and happiness. Love and trust were suddenly transformed into hatred and deadly battle. The neighbors looked at me with pity and contempt. At that time my loneliness began. And again—years, hard bitter years later—after I had constructed a new ascetic-spiritual life and ideal in absolute solitude and laborious self-discipline, after I had again attained a certain stillness and loftiness in my life, devoted to abstract exercises of thought and strictly regulated meditation—this form of life, too, fell apart and suddenly lost its noble, sublime meaning."[1]

This passage can be read as a piece of unadulterated autobiography. Hesse is clearly referring to his years of crisis and his struggle, in the period from *Demian* to *Siddhartha*, to construct out of the chaos of those times

---

[1] GD, IV, 253-54.

a new ideal in which he could believe—the ideal that he reached at the end of his Indian novel. As a matter of fact, *The Steppenwolf* is more overtly autobiographical than any of Hesse's other fiction. Almost every detail in the characterization of Harry Haller—from his sciatica and eyeglasses and general physical appearance to his reading habits and political views—is drawn from Hesse's own life and person. As early as 1924 Hesse had begun calling himself "a beast from the steppes"[2] because he felt so alienated from the society into which he had returned from his voluntary exile in the mountains of southern Switzerland. In 1926 he published a group of autobiographical poems in the *Neue Rundschau* under the collective title "The Steppenwolf: A Diary in Verse." (In 1928 the poems were reprinted as part of the volume *Crisis*.) With this word "Steppenwolf," which might best be translated as "lone wolf," Hesse was attempting to delineate his own specific situation: that of a man who felt himself to be so cut off from the world of normal people that he was like a wolf among the lambs of bourgeois society because his very existence threatened their ideals, beliefs, and way of life.

Yet the background and autobiographical details contribute, in the last analysis, only to the texture of the novel. Vastly more significant is the fact that *The Steppenwolf* depicts a general phenomenon of our times: the tragedy of intellect in despair. Harry Haller, the forty-eight-year-old intellectual who can endure life only because he has promised himself the luxury of suicide on his fiftieth birthday, is an extreme case, but his dilemma is typical. How many men, truly devoted to a life of the mind, can honestly say that they have never entertained moments of doubt? How many have not suffered, like Thomas Mann's

[2] In *Kurgast*; GD, IV, 76. See also pages 79 and 108.

Tonio Kröger, from the gnawing awareness that the very qualities they value most highly have cut them off from the world and the pleasures of a less problematic existence? How many have not felt the profound isolation of the intellectual and, at the same time, secretly and frantically asked themselves if the spiritual ideal is really an adequate or even an honest substitute for the life they have forsaken?

Those who have never known these tormenting doubts will find *The Steppenwolf* incomprehensible, or they will see in it, as many readers have, nothing but a eulogy to the pleasures of the flesh. In many of his letters and in his epilogue to the 1941 edition of the novel Hesse lamented the fact that this book has encountered more misunderstanding than any of his other works. There are many, however, who have suffered the same despair—European intellectual history of the twentieth century is a case catalogue—and it is to them that the novel is addressed: to the "madmen" of the dedication, the ones who, in the words of *In Sight of Chaos*, are "mad" because they have learned to affirm the chaos of their nature without questioning the validity of the ideal. On Hesse's second level of individuation men are suspended in a limbo between the world and a higher ideal, still partaking of both realms, but fully at home in neither. The solution to the dilemma for those who, like Harry Haller, are unable to transcend the world completely, is a sense of humor and irony. Hesse's novel recounts the development of Harry Haller from the brink of despair to the heights of humor that make life tolerable.

This intellectual adventure is related in a novel that, as Thomas Mann has pointed out, "does not fall short of

Ulysses and *The Counterfeiters* in experimental daring."[8]
Precisely the form of the work has been subjected to much
criticism despite Hesse's vehement protests that the novel
is the most tightly constructed of his works. It is an almost
universal complaint of authors that their readers, once
they have accommodated themselves to a certain style
or tone, resent the necessity to make adjustments in their
evaluation. It is indeed difficult to think of two works more
different than *Siddhartha* and *The Steppenwolf*. Yet *The
Steppenwolf*, along with *The Glass Bead Game*, is one of
the significant literary documents of the twentieth century,
and in form it is the most elaborate and boldest of Hesse's
works.

First Movement Form

Confusing upon first perusal is the apparent lack of
external organization in *The Steppenwolf*: for instance,
the absence of customary division into parts and chapters.
Instead, we are presented with a running record of a
phantasmagoria of events, interrupted toward the beginning by an apparently incongruous document called "The
Tract of the Steppenwolf" and introduced by the remarks
of a minor figure who appears in the story itself. But if we
look for internal structure, we see that the book falls
naturally into three main sections: the preliminary material, the action, and the so-called "Magic Theater."

The preliminary material, in turn, has three subdivisions: the introduction, the opening passages of Haller's
narrative, and the "Tract." These three subdivisions do
not constitute part of the action or plot of the novel; they
are all introductory in nature. This fact distinguishes them

---

[8] "Hermann Hesse zum siebzigsten Geburtstag," in Thomas
Mann, *Gesammelte Werke* (S. Fischer, 1960), x, 519.

from the second and longest part of the book, which tells
the story and which alone of the three main sections has
a form roughly analogous to the structure of the conventional novel. It relates action covering roughly a month,
and it is essentially a straightforward narrative. The third
section, finally, sets itself apart from the bulk of the novel
by virtue of its fantastic elements: it belongs, properly
speaking, to the action of the novel, for it depicts a situation that takes place in the early hours of the day following the final scene of the plot, and there is no technical
division whatsoever. But the conscious divorce from all
reality separates this section from the more realistic narrative of the middle part.

Beginning with this rough outline, we can proceed to
bring some order into the work. The introduction is
written by a young man who is revealed as a typical bourgeois both by his own words and by the brief mention
that he receives in the book itself. The function of this
introduction is twofold: to explain the circumstances regarding the publication of the book and to portray the
central figure through the eyes of a typical *Bürger*. The
young man is the nephew of the lady from whom a certain
Harry Haller rents an apartment upon his arrival in the
city, which remains nameless but may be thought of as
Zürich. The date of Haller's arrival in the house is given
as several years prior to the writing of the introduction,
and it is stated that Haller lived in the house for nine or
ten months. For the most part the strange tenant lived
quietly in his rooms, surrounded by books, empty wine
bottles, and overflowing ashtrays. However, toward the
end of his stay he underwent a profound change in conduct
and appearance, followed by a period of extreme depression. Shortly thereafter he departed without farewells,
leaving behind nothing but a manuscript which the young

man now chooses to publish as "a document of the times,"[4] for in retrospect he discerns that the affliction which disturbed Haller was symptomatic of the age, and not simply the malady of an individual.

More important than this external information is the view of Haller which we receive through the eyes of a young member of the bourgeoisie before we ever meet him in his own manuscript. The editor, by his own admission, is "a bourgeois, orderly person, accustomed to work and the precise disposition of time":[5] he drinks nothing stronger than mineral water and abhors tobacco; he feels uncomfortable in the presence of illness, whether physical or mental; and he is inclined to be suspicious of anything that does not correspond to the facts of ordinary existence as he knows it. Haller offends all of these sensibilities and many others. He makes it clear that Haller was by no means a man congenial to his own temperament: "I feel myself deeply disturbed and disquieted by him, by the sheer existence of such a being, although I have become quite fond of him."[6]

Despite his bourgeois inhibitions the young man is portrayed as an intelligent and reliable observer. His affection and interest allow him to perceive the conflict that disturbs Haller, and he mentions for the first time in the book the arbitrary dichotomy into Steppenwolf and *Bürger*, by which Haller chooses to designate what he considers the two polar aspects of his personality. The introduction states the two conflicting themes and, without full comprehension of their meaning, portrays Haller in both capacities: as a quiet civil tenant who makes every effort to adapt himself to the orderly routine of the house, and as a tortured outsider who seems unable to take the values of everyday life seriously.

[4] GD, IV, 205.   [5] GD, IV, 196.   [6] GD, IV, 189-90.

The opening pages of the manuscript itself recount one typical evening in the life of the *littérateur* Harry Haller. In atrabilious words he portrays his state of mind, his beliefs and goals, his erratic existence up to the present date. His remarks actually parallel the comments of the introduction, and in many cases the specific events mentioned are identical in both sections. But Haller's remarks are on a different plane: whereas the introduction depicted him externally from the bourgeois standpoint, we now meet him psychologically as he elects to think of himself, and we feel the full effect of his ambivalent attitude toward the bourgeoisie. He acknowledges that he is out of place in normal society, and he leads the life of a lone wolf, always on the fringe of humanity. Yet he is beset by a continual yearning for all that has been left behind:

"I don't know why it is, but I—the homeless Steppenwolf and lonely hater of the petty bourgeois world—I always live in proper middle-class houses. It's an old sentimental weakness of mine. I live neither in palaces nor in proletarian houses, but expressly in these highly decent, highly boring, scrupulously appointed petit-bourgeois nests. . . . Doubtlessly I love this atmosphere from the days of my childhood, and my secret longing for something like a home leads me, hopelessly, constantly, along these stupid old paths."[7]

At the same time—and this produces the tragic dilemma—Haller is not strong enough to live in his total isolation without questioning the value of the ideals to which he has devoted his life.

"Were those things that we called 'Culture,' that we called 'Spirit,' that we called 'Soul' and 'beautiful' and 'sacred'—

[7] GD, IV, 210.

were those things merely a spectre, already long dead
and still considered genuine and alive only by a few fools
like me? Had they perhaps never been genuine and alive?
Had those things with which we fools concerned ourselves
perhaps always been no more than a phantom?"[8]

This dilemma of totally alienated intellect, at home in
neither world yet longing desperately for roots in one or
the other, is elucidated with many pertinent examples as
Haller contemplates his existence and its value in the
course of an evening walk.

These speculations are interrupted by the interpolation
of the "Tract," a document that Haller acquires on this
walk and takes home to read. Since the "Tract" is of
central importance in the novel, it is necessary to recall
briefly how it comes into Haller's hands. Wandering down
a familiar alley that evening, he perceives a doorway in
the wall that he had never noticed before. Above the door
is affixed a placard on which he is able to make out the
fleeting, almost illegible words:

Magic Theater
Admission not for everyone
—not for everyone.

As he steps closer, the evanescent words vanish, but he
glimpses a few letters which seem to dance across the wet
pavement: "For-mad-men-only!" After a time Haller proceeds to his restaurant, still musing over the significance of
the queer letters he had seen or imagined. Out of curiosity,
he passes back through the same alley later in the night
and notes that the door and sign are no longer there.
Suddenly a man emerges from a side street, trudging
wearily and bearing a placard. Haller calls to him and

[8] GD, IV, 221.

asks to be shown the sign. Again he discerns "dancing, reeling letters":

Anarchistic Evening Fun

Magic Theater

Admission not for ev—

But when he greets the bearer and seeks further information, the man mutters indifferently, hands him a small pamphlet, and disappears into a doorway. Upon his return home Haller sees that the pamphlet is entitled "Tract of the Steppenwolf." At this point its text follows in Haller's manuscript.

This "Tract," as Haller reads to his astonishment, offers still a third description of Harry Haller, the Steppenwolf. Whereas the first represented the objective but superficial impressions of a typical *Bürger*, and the second the subjective interpretation of the subject himself, this third depiction is the observation of a higher intelligence which is able to view Haller *sub specie aeternitatis.*

The "Tract," in essence, makes a distinction between three types of beings, differentiated relatively according to their degree of individuation. The cosmology which is developed here can best be visualized by the analogy of a sphere situated on an axis whose poles represent the opposite concepts of nature and spirit. The center of the sphere, as the point farthest removed from all extremes, is the bourgeois ego; the cosmic regions outside the sphere, on the other hand, are inhabited by the "tragic natures" or "Immortals" who have transcended the narrow bourgeois concept of egoism and burst forth into the cosmos by embracing a belief in the fundamental unity of life. They are aware that supreme existence consists in the recognition and acceptance of all aspects of life, and this attitude demands transcendence of the ego in the bourgeois sense. In order to preserve his *Ich*, his ego, the *Bürger* must resist every impulse to lose himself in extremes; he must sway toward neither pole; he wishes to be neither profligate nor saint. In maintaining this position of moderation, the *Bürger* assumes a definite standpoint with regard to the world, relative to which certain of its polar opposites must be condemned as evil.

Thus, for the *Bürger*, whose very way of life requires the utmost order in the world, the opposite extreme of disorder or chaos must be anathema. The Immortals, on the contrary, accept chaos as the natural state of existence, for they inhabit a realm where all polarity has ceased and where every manifestation of life is approved as necessary and good. In their eyes the polarity of nature and spirit does not exist, for their cosmos is expansive enough to encompass all of the apparent polar extremes in the *Bürger*'s limited sphere. (This is, of course, essentially the view developed in *In Sight of Chaos*.)

If the Immortals and the *Bürger* represent the two extremes in Hesse's scale of individuation, the Steppenwolf occupies a tenuous and anomalous perch between them:

"If we examine in this connection the soul of the Steppenwolf, he reveals himself as a person whose high degree of individuation alone marks him as a non-*Bürger*—for all highly developed individuation turns against the Ego and tends towards its destruction."[9]

Not every person of this nature is strong enough to transcend the *principium individuationis* completely: many are destined to remain in the world of the *Bürger* despite their longing for the reaches of the cosmos. If we adapt this fact to the sphere-image, we must place the Steppenwolf in an orbit within the sphere, cruising close to the surface,

[9] GD, IV, 238.

but never penetrating into the cosmos for more than a brief, tantalizing moment. The fact that he belongs to neither realm completely accounts for the Steppenwolf's dissatisfaction with existence and demonstrates why Harry Haller, the case in point, can find no satisfactory solution to his dilemma and often contemplates suicide.

The "Tract" goes on to point out that only humor can make it possible for the Steppenwolf to exist peacefully in a world whose values he despises:

"To live in the world as though it were not the world, to heed the law and yet to stand above it, to possess 'as though one did not possess,' to eschew as though it were no eschewal—all these popular and often formulated claims of a sublime wisdom can be realized solely through humor."[10]

But humor in this sense is possible only if the individual has resolved the conflicts in his own soul, and this resolution can come about only as the result of self-recognition. To this end the "Tract" mentions three possible courses for Haller:

"It's possible that he will one day come to know himself —either by obtaining one of our little mirrors, or by encountering the Immortals, or perhaps by finding in one of our Magic Theaters whatever he needs for the liberation of his ravaged soul."[11]

Thus the "Tract" proposes a reconciliation of the conflicting themes that have been discussed. If Harry Haller can peer deep into the chaos of his own soul by any of the suggested means, then he will be able to live happily in the world or even dare to make "the leap into the cosmos" —that is, to join the Immortals. The final section of the

[10] GD, IV, 240.   [11] GD, IV, 241.

"Tract" explains, however, that this is a more difficult task than Harry had previously imagined, for his personality comprises not merely the two conflicting poles that he had named, but virtually thousands of divergent aspects crying for recognition. It becomes clear that this "Tract" must be understood as the work of the Immortals themselves, for no one else could have this lofty and all-encompassing view of the world. Thus it represents a study of Haller from still a third standpoint.

If we pause now to survey the preliminary material of the novel, a distinct pattern emerges. These three sections (introduction, the opening pages of the manuscript, and the "Tract") present three treatments of the conflicting themes in Haller's soul, as perceived respectively from the three points of view outlined in the theoretical tract: *Bürger*—Steppenwolf—Immortals. The introduction states the two themes; the second section brings the development in which the significance of these themes for Haller's life is interpreted; and the "Tract" recapitulates the themes theoretically and proposes a resolution of the conflict. This scheme, exposition—development—recapitulation, can be found in any book on music under the heading "sonata-form" or "first-movement form," for it is the classical structure for the opening section of the sonata.

The terms "sonata" and "sonata-form" are rather misleading designations in music theory, for the latter does not refer to the form of the former. The sonata is a generic name for any major composition of one to four movements, of which one (usually the first) must be in "sonata-form." If the composition is written for piano, it is a piano sonata; if written for an orchestra, it is called a symphony; and so forth. The term that interests us here, "sonata-form," refers to the structure of the first movement alone. The exposition states two themes with one in the tonic, the other in the dominant; the development follows in which the potentialities of these themes are worked out; and the recapitulation restates the themes as they occurred in the exposition, but this time both are in the tonic, and the conflict has been resolved.

In the novel the difference in keys is approximated by the contrasting attitudes of Harry Haller as Steppenwolf, on the one hand, and as *Bürger*, on the other: the first represents, as it were, the tonic, and the second the dominant. The ABA structure of the sonata, which is achieved through the general repetition of the exposition in the recapitulation, is imitated by Hesse insofar as the exposition and recapitulation are views of Haller from the outside and largely abstract; this lends them an effect of unity. The development differs from these in tone and style since it is written by Haller himself and stresses the practical significance of the two themes for his own life (that is, the development of the themes). The resolution of the tonic and dominant in the recapitulation is an obvious parallel to the proposed reconciliation of Steppenwolf and *Bürger* in Harry Haller's own nature. In view of this rather close correspondence between the musical form and the first part of the novel, it is tempting to suggest that the preliminary material reveals "first-movement form." But is such an analogy justified?

The Musical Analogy

A great deal has been written about Hesse and his attitude toward music, for music is one of the more conspicuous elements in his life and works.[12] There is scarcely a novel whose hero is not in some way musical: *Gertrude*

---

[12] See Joseph Mileck, *Hermann Hesse and His Critics*, pp. 151-157; and Werner Dürr, *Hermann Hesse: Vom Wesen der Musik in der Dichtung* (Stuttgart, 1957).

(1909) is the story of a composer, H. H. in *The Journey to the East* is a violinist, and Joseph Knecht in *The Glass Bead Game* is an accomplished pianist and music theorist. Hesse himself played the violin, his first wife was a gifted pianist, several of his closest friends were prominent professional musicians, and his favorite nephew, Karl Isenberg, aided Hesse in the musical background for *The Glass Bead Game* in much the same way that Theodor Adorno helped Thomas Mann to prepare the material for *Doctor Faustus*. (Both Isenberg and Adorno, by the way, were portrayed by the grateful authors among the characters in the respective novels.)

The course of Hesse's interest in various composers, which began with his early enthusiasm for Chopin, matured to the cult of Mozart in *The Steppenwolf*, and culminated in his eulogy to the supreme art of Bach in *The Glass Bead Game*, is a fascinating theme in itself and one that can be neatly traced in his poems, fiction, letters, and essays. Yet all of these facts, as valuable as they may be for biographical or general cultural reasons, are of little significance here. The central importance of music in *The Steppenwolf*—the jazz of Pablo as well as the sublime harmonies of Mozart—is self-evident. That these two figures and their music correspond to the poles of life and spirit on the thematic level of the book is obvious. Music concerns us here only if we can demonstrate a definite and conscious reflection of the musical theme in the structure of the work, and I believe that it is possible.

Among the many passages in which Hesse remonstrated against the charge of formlessness in his novel, the following is one of the more interesting: "From the standpoint of pure artistry *The Steppenwolf* is at least as good as *Goldmund*; it is constructed around the intermezzo of the Tract as strictly and rigidly as a sonata and develops its theme neatly."[13] In this letter Hesse refers to the sonata metaphorically. In another letter from the same period (but not included among his collected letters) he mentions the same form as a more technical comparison: "*Goldmund* delights people. To be sure, it is in no way better than *The Steppenwolf*, which delineates its theme even more clearly and which is compositionally constructed like a sonata. . . ."[14] Such words must not be taken lightly from a man so well informed about music as Hesse. Generally a pernicious double standard exists, which has often worked to Hesse's discredit. Because Thomas Mann, in his book on the genesis of *Doctor Faustus*, outlined in detail the musical studies that he undertook in order to write his novel, critics have outdone themselves to uncover the musical structure of the work. Since Hesse has made only casual references to the form of his work, most critics have found it simple to dismiss the novel as formless or, at best, to ignore the possibility that the structure, despite its almost incredible technical complexity, is basically very tightly organized.

Hesse, of course, was not a professional musician, yet despite his protests one can see clearly from some of his statements that he was technically competent in the matters that concern us here. "My theoretical interest in music is very limited," he wrote in 1934,

"and it would have little value since I am not a practicing musician. I am interested in counterpoint, the fugue, the change of the harmonic modes; but behind these purely

[13] GS, VII, 495.
[14] Letter of November 4, 1930; published in *Hermann Hesse: Werk und Persönlichkeit* (Stuttgart, 1957), p. 30. This volume, a prospectus of the exhibition in honor of Hesse's eightieth birthday, contains unpublished material from the Hesse Archive of the Schiller-Nationalmuseum in Marbach.

aesthetic questions there are others that also engage me: the actual spirit of true music, its morality."[15]

This was written during the composition of *The Glass Bead Game*, in which Hesse was more directly concerned with music as theme than as technique. Yet the passage is revealing because it demonstrates that Hesse was interested precisely in the technical problems and forms that determine the structure of *The Steppenwolf*: counterpoint, the fugue, and harmonic changes. In view of this acknowledged technical interest and the passages in which Hesse explicitly compares the structure of his novel to that of the sonata, it would seem that our inductive analysis of the introductory material as displaying first-movement form is methodologically acceptable and that it corresponds to a structural pattern present in Hesse's own mind.

In case this assertion seems to force one art-form willfully into the Procrustean bed of another, it might be recalled in passing that first-movement form has been discovered in various literary genres before now. Otto Ludwig, in his essay on "The General Form of Shakespearean Composition"[16] evolves a structural tendency in Shakespeare's plays which he compares to sonata form. Oskar Walzel, ever the advocate of "reciprocal illumination of the arts," suggests that the same application can be made to certain poems.[17] It has been shown that Thomas Mann's *Tonio Kröger* was consciously constructed according to the pattern of sonata form,[18] and Hermann Broch, in his

[15] GS, VII, 570-71.
[16] "Allgemeine Struktur der Shakespearischen Komposition," *Gesammelte Schriften*, ed. Adolf Stern (Leipzig, 1891), V, 89-91.
[17] *Gehalt und Gestalt im Kunstwerk des Dichters* (Berlin, 1923), pp. 351-54.
[18] H. A. Basilius, "Thomas Mann's Use of Musical Structure and Techniques in *Tonio Kröger*," *Germanic Review*, 19 (1944), 284-308.

letters and essays, has explicitly stated that his work *The Death of Vergil* was written as a prose symphony in four movements; the first section, moreover, displays "sonata-form." Calvin S. Brown, finally, devotes an entire chapter of *Music and Literature: A Comparison of the Arts* (Athens, Georgia, 1948) to the analysis of literary works—mainly poems—that employ this structure more or less successfully.

On the other hand, there have been objections to the application of musical form to literary works; one of the most lucid and persuasive of these is advanced by René Wellek and Austin Warren in *Theory of Literature* (New York, 1949). With regard to Romantic notions concerning musical form, the authors contend quite reasonably that "blurred outlines, vagueness of meaning, and illogicality are not, in a literal sense, 'musical' at all." But we have seen that Hesse presents his material clearly, is specific in meaning, and proceeds according to a highly logical system. Wellek and Warren go on to say:

"Literary imitations of musical structures like leitmotiv, the sonata, or symphonic form seem to be more concrete; but it is hard to see why repetitive motifs or a certain contrasting and balancing of moods, though by avowed intention imitative of musical composition, are not essentially the familiar literary devices of recurrence, contrast, and the like which are common to all the arts."

The authors fail to take account of works that go beyond the use of "repetitive motifs or a certain contrasting and balancing of moods." Hesse, in any case, though he makes ample use of the leitmotiv (e.g. the mark of Cain in *Demian*), depends neither upon this nor upon contrast to produce his musical effect; nor is he concerned, except in some of his early poems, with vague synaesthesia. Rather, he has devised a novel that consciously adheres to the rigid structure of sonata-form with an exposition, development, and recapitulation. The other musical devices that he employs are merely embellishments within the general framework.

Double Perception

Before going on to the second part of *The Steppenwolf*, we must pause to consider a matter that contains the key to the entire work: the question of double perception.

In the "Tract" Haller reads: "And all of this is quite familiar to the Steppenwolf, even if he should never get a glimpse of this summary of his inner biography."[19] This seems to suggest a satisfactory solution to the mystery of the "Tract." The device of causing a figure in a novel to read his own biography, written by some unknown hand, is an approved Romantic practice, and Hesse, as we shall see in the epilogue, is in certain respects an heir of Romanticism. Yet it must not be forgotten that up to this point the entire work has taken place on the level of everyday reality. Why should there be this sudden intrusion of the supernatural? Is it not more reasonable to assume that Haller himself reads this strange message into the text of the pamphlet since it is all supposed to be known to him? This is an intriguing speculation, but it requires substantiation.

In his essay "On Reading Books" (1920)[20] Hesse considers three types of readers. The first is the naïve person who accepts the book and its story objectively; the second category comprises those who read with the imagination of a child and comprehend the hundreds of symbolic connotations latent in every word and image.

[19] GD, IV, 241.
[20] "Vom Bücherlesen"; GS, VII, 245.

But the third reader is one who uses the book simply as a *terminus ab quo*: on this level "we no longer read what lies on the paper in front of us, but swim along in the stream of the stimulations and ideas that come to us from what we have read. They can come from the text, they can even arise merely from the shape of the type." For such readers, Hesse adds, an advertisement in a newspaper can become a revelation.

This delightful conceit is not the whim of an instant; it is a recurrent theme in Hesse's works. An example can be found, for instance, as much as ten years later in *Narziss and Goldmund* (1930). After his rude awakening by Narziss, Goldmund lives in a new world of the imagination: "A Latin initial became the fragrant visage of his mother, an extended tone in the Ave became the Gate of Paradise, a Greek letter became a racing horse, a rearing serpent. Quietly it slithered away under the blossoms, and in its place there stood once more the lifeless page of the grammar."[21]

In the light of this idea, why should the action in *The Steppenwolf* not be construed similarly? Let us briefly reconstruct the scene. In a fit of depression Haller goes out for his evening stroll; he is willing to grasp eagerly after any ray of hope that would alleviate his desperate condition. When he notices a smudge or crack in the wall of the alley, set off by the sparkle of the damp plaster, his overwrought mind reads an imaginary message in fleeting letters. In the course of the evening he consumes a considerable portion of wine and finally has a vision of the "golden trace" that comes to him in moments of despair to remind him of the eternal values in which he believes. In this rhapsodic state he meets a weary placard-bearer,

[21] GD, v, 67.

quite by chance, in the same alley, where the mysterious message on the wall, to his disappointment, has vanished. The tired worker, anxious to get rid of the troublesome drunk, brusquely shoves a pamphlet into his hands—*any* pamphlet—which Haller's acrobatic and stimulated mind converts, at home, into the message of the "Tract." For, as the tract states, these are ideas that are already known to Haller: essential thoughts from a remote and more perceptive area of his intelligence—an area usually blocked by the problematics of his dual personality and the exigencies of existence. Here, for an instant, his higher acumen seeps through. It is worth noting, in this connection, that Haller does not include the pamphlet itself in his manuscript, but a *copy* of it—that is, his metaphysical translation of it. No one besides Haller ever sees the original, for it is, as Haller suggests, nothing more than a booklet with a title like "How Can I Become Twenty Years Younger In One Week?" (The fact that Hesse allowed the tract, in some editions of the novel, to be set off by different type and a binding of its own does not disturb this argument. That was no more than a puzzle for the reader, inspired by Dadaism, with which Hesse flirted from time to time.)

This concept of double perception plays an increasingly important role in the novel, for it is necessary throughout the remainder of the book to make a sharp distinction between two levels of reality: the everyday plane of the *Bürger* or the placard-bearer, and the exalted, supernal plane of the Immortals and the magic theater. Haller is an eidetic, an individual capable of producing subjective images that in their vividness rival objective reality. Accordingly, his experiences on the upper level of reality assume fully as much intensity for him as the action on the level of mundane reality. In this novel, in other words, we are dealing with an externalization of Hesse's magical thinking, a concrete rendering in reality of the metaphors of his mind.

Here again we are concerned with a highly musical device corresponding closely to counterpoint, which the *Harvard Dictionary of Music* defines as "the combination into a single musical fabric of lines or parts which have distinctive melodic significance." By means of double perception almost any given action of the book may be interpreted on two distinct levels—a technique that we saw anticipated in many of the ambiguous utterances of Frau Eva in *Demian*. This produces the effect of simultaneity or concomitance of the two planes or melodic lines. This particular device comes much closer to the musical definition of "point counter point" than the technique employed, for instance, by Aldous Huxley in his novel of that title or by André Gide or by many of their imitators. The latter achieve their effect by the sudden juxtaposition of various moods and points of view. Hesse consciously attempts to produce authentic counterpoint by bringing the two lines of action into play at the same time.

It is not idle speculation that Hesse conceived of this technique in terms of musical counterpoint. In a crucial passage at the end of his essay *At the Spa* (1924) Hesse discusses his disappointment in the volume and the frustrations that he had encountered in writing it.

"If I were a musician, I could write a two-voice melody without difficulty: a melody that consists of two lines, two rows of tones and notes that correspond to each other, supplement each other, oppose and determine each other; yet at every instant, at every point in the row they stand in the most intimate, most lively reciprocity and mutual relationship. And anybody who knows how to read music could read my double melody; he would see and hear in every tone constantly the countertone, the brother, the enemy, the antipode. Now it is just this two-voicedness and eternally progressive antithesis, this double-line that I should like to express with my material, with words. . . . I should like to find an expression for the duality, I should like to write chapters and sentences in which melody and countermelody would be constantly and simultaneously visible, in which all variegation is paired with unity, all jest with seriousness. For only therein does life consist for me: in the fluctuation between two poles, in the back and forth between the two pillars of the world."[22]

In his essay Hesse felt that he had failed to express the polarity in an adequate form. Because of the very nature of language it was necessary to express first one idea and then its antithesis; it seemed impossible, through the medium of words, to achieve the simultaneity of musical counterpoint that he desired. I believe that the technique of double perception, exploited so extensively and consistently in the second part of *The Steppenwolf*, represents the fulfillment of that wish.

In his chapter on "Timbre, Harmony, and Counterpoint," Calvin S. Brown denies the possibility of true counterpoint in literature, but he cites the literary pun as the closest approach. The limiting element in the case of the pun is the fact that we have "not two things, but one word with different relationships." On the basis of this parallel, it might be argued that double perception achieves the effect of a sustained pun, and the interplay of the two levels of reality produces a genuine contrapuntal effect. If this is not precisely what is understood by the musical concept of counterpoint, it at least represents an advance beyond any previous literary counterpart.

[22] GD, IV, 113-14.

The Märchen

To insist on a realistic basis for the surrealistic episodes
of the novel in no way constitutes a deprecation of Hesse's
visionary powers. These symbolic projections of Haller's
inner world, the imaginative expression of higher reality,
contain the true meaning of the work, as Hesse argued in
letters to readers who saw in the book no more than a
paean to prostitutes and jazz musicians. All too often,
however, critics have overlooked the realistic basis, thus
ignoring the technique of double perception and missing
precisely the ambiguous quality of "reality" that Hesse
was so intent upon rendering. Only the interaction of the
two levels of reality produces the characteristic tension of
the novel, and the source of Haller's schizophrenic depression becomes understandable only when we see him
enmeshed in the turmoil of everyday reality. For that
reason Hesse comes closer to literary realism in many
passages of this novel than anywhere else in his works.
The emotional release of magical thinking is psychologically plausible only when we are aware of the reality from
which it frees itself. The grandeur of the surreal vision is
lessened in no way if we assume that it is catalyzed by
narcotics or alcohol from the elements of realistic experience.

If there is anything "Romantic" about *The Steppenwolf*,
it is precisely this pronounced juxtaposition of the real
and the imaginary. We have seen—and shall often have
occasion to observe—how Hesse transformed traditional
narrative forms in order to express his own themes: in
Demian the *Bildungsroman* and in *Siddhartha* the legend.
In *The Steppenwolf* the thematic development is that of
the sonata: but the literary form within which this is pos-

sible—if we want to give it a label and put the novel into
the proper tradition—is that of the Romantic *Märchen*.

The *Märchen* (roughly "fairy tale") constitutes, next to
lyric poetry, the most popular genre of German Romanticism; practically every major Romantic writer turned out
at least one anthology-piece. In the *Märchen*, unlike the
drama or most prose fiction, it was possible to represent
symbolically the central theme of Romanticism: the reunification of nature and spirit. When birds and beasts
can communicate with men, when people can be transformed into plants or animals and back again, all boundaries
between these realms are effaced and a total synthesis can
be achieved. Yet these fairy tales differ radically among
themselves, and no single definition embraces them all adequately. The two formal extremes are represented by the
simple folk fairy tales collected by the Grimm brothers
and the highly symbolic *Märchen* of Goethe (in his *Conversations of German Emigrants*) and Novalis (Klingsohr's tale in *Heinrich von Ofterdingen*). Between these
two extremes lie most of the well known *Märchen* of Tieck,
Brentano, Fouqué, and others. Exploiting older sources
for traditional motifs and inspired by the naïve tone of
the folk tales, they created new works in which they sought
—often with conscious allegory or symbolism—to render
the Romantic ideal. (Fouqué, for instance, used the legend
of the marriage of water nymphs and human beings, as
related by Paracelsus, to symbolize the struggle of nature
to acquire a human soul in *Undine*.) Characteristic of all
these tales is the intentional setting of the story in a time
and place remote from the present—the abstract symbolic
realm of Goethe and Novalis, or the vague idealized
Germanic past of the Grimms, Brentano, and Fouqué—
in which the fantastic or "fairy-tale" element does not seem
out of place.

One of the most brilliant *Märchen* authors—the one whom Hesse called "the Romantic narrator of the greatest virtuosity"—fits into none of these categories: E. T. A. Hoffmann. Hoffmann's major *Märchen*—*The Golden Jug*, *Little Zaches*, *Princess Brambilla*, and *Master Flea*—revolve, like the others, around the fundamental Romantic theme of the reunification of nature and spirit in the realm of the fantastic. But unlike earlier *Märchen*, they are all extended narratives set squarely in the present—an undertaking of whose boldness Hoffmann was fully aware. The locales of his tales are, respectively, Dresden, an unnamed German university town, Rome, and Frankfurt; and the time is specifically the beginning of the nineteenth century. In other words, Hoffmann has come a long way from "Once upon a time in a distant land. . . ." His stories typically begin at three o'clock in the afternoon of Ascension Day at the northwest gate of the city of Dresden (*The Golden Jug*). In line with the specification of time and place we also find highly individualized characters. We are not dealing with traditional fairy-tale figures like "a princess," "the lily," "a miller," and so forth—but with well defined people of the everyday world like the student Anselmus and his friends, who are described in often humorous and inevitably realistic detail.

In each of Hoffmann's *Märchen* a myth is fulfilled, in the course of the tale, by the figures of the story. Practically all Romantic fairy tales, of course, have a mythic basis—usually a myth of redemption. But in Novalis, Grimm, or Brentano the myth is identical with the plot of the fairy tale and emerges from it. The characters represent allegorically the elements of the myth, and the myth is not related separately. In Hoffmann the myth is narrated as an interpolated story by one of the figures of the realistic framework. The plot parallels the action outlined in the myth, but the action remains clearly realistic. Thus Anselmus fulfills the myth of Atlantis told by Archivarius Lindhorst, while Giglio Fava and Giacinta (in *Princess Brambilla*) act out the legend of King Ophioch and Queen Liris as narrated by Celionati, and so forth. But the fulfillment is only symbolic! Anselmus experiences the poetic kingdom of Atlantis in his mind, but we are not to imagine that he is physically transported from Dresden to an imaginary realm, any more than Giglio and Giacinta must leave Rome in order to achieve their symbolic reunification.

The fantastic elements of these tales are not relegated to an imaginary realm, but rise immediately out of the everyday life of contemporary bourgeois society. Hoffmann felt so strongly about this that he postulated a principle of narration that he called "in Callot's manner" (after the French satiric artist Jacques Callot): to present "the figures of ordinary life" "in a strange, marvelous dressing." In effect we find scenes that resemble in all external detail the fantastic episodes of the traditional fairy tale, but it is a fantastic interpretation of reality and not a transposition into a fairy-tale realm. This *Märchen*-atmosphere goes back to what Hoffmann, in *Princess Brambilla*, calls the "chronic dualism" of his heroes. For not all the characters of the tales experience reality as fantastic: only the heroes who are blest with a poetic spirit are able to perceive the miraculous in everyday life. Ordinary people consider these heroes demented. And indeed, such an air of ambiguity surrounds these fantastic events that all of them can be justified rationally as visions of the hero inspired by something that he sees in reality. Thus when the Archivarius Lindhorst scurries away in the dusk, it seems to Anselmus as though he were transformed into a great bird; but Hoffmann tells us that at that moment a great vulture flew up into the sky; Anselmus blends the two realistic events to create a fantastic image. At another point Anselmus falls into a faint because a door-knocker seems to have turned into the head of an ugly old peddlar-woman; when he is discovered lying unconscious in the street, the woman of this description is indeed bending over him, trying to offer aid. Anselmus's febrile imagination transforms reality into fantasy at the slightest instigation. The world in which he lives is truly a fairy-tale world of witches, magicians, mysterious transformations, singing serpents, and lovely princesses—but only in his imagination. In reality—and Hoffmann takes great pains to make this clear—everything that Anselmus and the other heroes experience can be explained rationally by psychological means on the basis of contemporary life in nineteenth-century Germany. The miraculous is a capacity for poetic vision in everyday life, and not a realm set apart by itself. This is made clear by the ending of *The Golden Jug*: "In this kingdom that the spirit so often, at least in dreams, reveals to us, gracious reader, try to recognize the familiar figures that wander about you daily—as they say, in ordinary life."

Many contemporary readers misunderstood Hoffmann's intentions and interpreted the visionary projections of his heroes' imagination as an absolute "fairy-tale" kingdom. Hoffmann objected to this and, as a result, wrote progressively more and more realistic fairy tales in an effort to highlight their basis in everyday life. *Princess Brambilla*, as a matter of fact, is not called a *Märchen*, but "A Capriccio." This is purely a matter of nomenclature, for in form it is identical in every respect with the other *Märchen*. Hoffmann expresses the hope, in the fourth chapter, that the reader will not be disturbed by "a thing that calls itself a capriccio, but resembles a

Märchen to a hair, as though it were one itself." Why does he call it a capriccio? So that the reader will not automatically assume, as one might if it were called a *Märchen*, that the fantastic events take place on another level of reality altogether. Instead, Hoffmann writes, "the scene is sometimes transposed into the inner being of the figures who appear." And he states his belief that "the human spirit is the most marvelous *Märchen* that there can be." *Princess Brambilla*—which Baudelaire once called "a catechism of aesthetics" and which the hero of Hesse's early novel *Hermann Lauscher* (1901) treasures most highly of all Romantic prose—is, in other words, just as much a *Märchen* in Hoffmann's sense as the other so-labeled tales. But Hoffmann wanted to make it absolutely clear, by calling it a capriccio, that the fairy-tale elements are not to be dismissed as fantastic, but are to be understood as projections of the characters' own inner visions. This applies to all his *Märchen*. Thus Anselmus is said, at the end of *The Golden Jug*, to be inhabiting a knightly estate in the fairy-tale kingdom of Atlantis. But Hoffmann takes it back again by suggesting: "Is Anselmus's bliss anything more than a life in poetry, in which the divine harmony of all beings reveals itself as the deepest mystery of nature?" Atlantis, in other words, is a frame of mind, an inner vision—not reality in the sense of the traditional fairy tale.

If we recapitulate, we find that the *Märchen*, according to Hoffmann's practice, is no longer a "tale" in the etymological sense, but a long realistic narrative of contemporary life in which a dualistic view of reality is rendered through a contrast between everyday reality and the inner vision of the hero. The fairy-tale atmosphere is created technically by the fact that the inner vision is projected as though it were real in the ordinary sense of the word; the author identifies himself at crucial points with the hero's point of view, describing the world as fantastically as the hero sees it in his vision. The implications of the whole are broadened by reference to an interpolated myth which is fulfilled symbolically by the characters of the realistic framework story. This definition, now, could be a description of Hesse's *The Steppenwolf*. We begin with a dualistic view of reality. The myth of reunification is anticipated in an interpolated document. The setting is contemporary and realistic, but in the course of the story inner vision assumes greater significance for Harry Haller than the external reality that surrounds him; he interacts more naturally with the figures of his imagination than with those of external reality.

To this extent we can regard Hoffmann's unique form of the *Märchen* as the traditional structure within which Hesse is operating—especially since he had already exploited the form in *Hermann Lauscher* (1901), giving explicit credit to Hoffmann. But we must remember that precisely this form of the *Märchen* requires a sound basis in reality, for the entire fairy tale—in Hoffmann and Hesse—is an internal vision that is projected into everyday life. Reality supplies the material from which the vision is constructed in the minds of Anselmus and Haller. Only the contrast between reality and vision makes possible the frustrations of their heroes and the irony in which the authors delight. We can thus conclude, somewhat paradoxically, that to deny the realistic basis of *The Steppenwolf* is to deny Hesse's most conspicuous debt to German Romanticism: his exploitation of Romantic forms and techniques.

The Second Movement: Counterpoint

The second and longest part of *The Steppenwolf* might be called Harry Haller's Apprenticeship.[23] It is interesting to note that the verbs "learn" and "teach" actually occur scores of times in this section of the book. Here Haller learns to accept many facets of life that certain inhibitions of his personality had previously caused him to reject; he discovers to his astonishment that the poles of his being are not so irreconcilable as he had imagined. This phase of Haller's education is rather elementary; it is kept on the level of everyday life in preparation for and in conscious anticipation of the more metaphysical scope of the Magic Theater.

The motif of "chance" and "destiny," as in *Wilhelm Meister's Apprenticeship*, lends an aura of inevitability to the initial events of the denouement, and it is an obvious corollary to the technique of double perception. One day Haller happens to see a man who resembles the placard-bearer of his recent adventure. With a conspiratorial wink Haller asks him if there is no entertainment for that evening: " 'Entertainment,' the man muttered and looked uncomprehendingly into my face. 'Buddy, go to the Schwarzer Adler if you've got problems.' "[24] The repeated use of the word "seemed" in connection with these incidents implies that Haller is not dealing with the same man as before. It is just chance that the stolid citizen happens to respond indignantly to the misunderstood question, advising Haller to go to an obviously

[23] Egon Schwarz, "Zur Erklärung von Hesses *Steppenwolf*," *Monatshefte*, 53 (1961), 191-198, considers especially the parallels between Hesse's novel and Goethe's *Wilhelm Meister's Apprenticeship*.
[24] GD, IV, 260.

notorious brothel if he wishes to satisfy his needs. It is likewise chance (or destiny?) that leads Haller that very evening to this particular night club, where he meets Hermine, who becomes his teacher during this period of apprenticeship.

The entire first day of the action represents an accumulation of impossible situations which bring Haller to the point of suicide. One incident after another convinces him that his life has become intolerable. The conflict of themes introduced in the preliminary material is elevated in the course of this first day to an unbearable pitch. Late in the night Haller weaves wearily from bar to bar, determined to put an end to his miserable existence, yet hesitant to go home and do so. Then he finds himself outside the bar *Zum schwarzen Adler*, and since he recalls the name from that morning, he goes in.

It is made sufficiently clear in the course of the book that Hermine is a high-class prostitute or call girl, and she greets the errant Haller with an intimate, hearty tone that has no deep metaphysical implications whatsoever, but is simply customary in her profession. She immediately perceives that he is weary, dejected, and drunk; like any sensible woman she advises him to sleep it off. Haller, drunk as he is and happy to be able to stave off his suicide as long as possible, is delighted to obey her. He feels that her immediate comprehension of his situation is almost preternatural. Actually, any reader will recognize that most of Hermine's remarks, like the utterances of the Delphic oracle, are open to two interpretations. In this case Hermine's words are precisely what one would expect from a prostitute with long experience in handling drunks and mothering would-be suicides. Only Haller's lonely despondency allows him to ascribe any higher significance to her casual remarks.

Hermine, who becomes genuinely interested in Haller, makes a tremendous impression on the naïve intellectual. In his eyes she stands for a wholly new aspect of life—one that he had previously regarded with distrust. His experiences with her must be viewed continually in double perspective. The whole episode is anticipated in the "Tract," which, as an example of Haller's dual nature and bourgeois inhibitions, cites his attitude toward prostitutes: "Theoretically he did not have the least thing against prostitution, but he would have been incapable of personally taking a whore seriously and really regarding her as one of his kind."[25]

This conflict of theory and reality is precipitated, at this point, in a dream that is at once a technical and thematic *tour de force*. Earlier in the evening, during a visit with some friends, Haller had seen a picture of the older Goethe, executed in a way that infuriated him. The picture, namely, revealed in Haller's eyes none of the demonic, problematic qualities of the poet he loved, but only a typically bourgeois view of a complacent elderly prig. Now, as he slumps against the wall in the bar, he encounters that same Goethe in a dream constructed of complicated literary associations. Somehow, in his dream, he expects to find the lovely Molly, celebrated in the tempestuous life of the pre-Romantic poet Gottfried August Bürger, in Goethe's house. When he sees a scorpion, he instantly assumes that it has some connection with Molly. (This association of sensuality and danger, of course, reflects his fascination with the girl he has just met in reality [Hermine] and his fear of her because of bourgeois prejudices.) When Goethe appears, it is the Goethe of the picture that Haller had seen earlier in the evening: stiff, pretentious, self-satisfied. Haller re-

[25] GD, IV, 235.

proaches him for not being honest, for not corresponding to the image that he, Haller, had formed of Goethe. After teasing Haller a bit, Goethe whispers in his ear that Haller takes him far too seriously. We Immortals, he adds, love jokes, not seriousness. He shows Haller a tiny model of a woman's leg, carved out of ivory, and as Haller eagerly reaches for it, the leg is suddenly transformed into the scorpion, from which he recoils in fright as Goethe laughs at him. Technically the dream is composed of elements of experience already presented in the book: the picture of Goethe and Haller's ambivalent attitude toward Hermine. Structurally and thematically, however, it anticipates and parallels the grand vision of Mozart in which the novel culminates. In both cases Haller encounters Immortals; in both cases he is laughed at for his reluctance to forsake his bourgeois prejudices, for his inability to laugh at appearances and look for a deeper reality beneath the surface of things.

In order to overcome his bourgeois inhibitions he must expand his soul to the point of embracing every aspect of life. Hermine is a test case; on a higher level Haller's acceptance of her and her world—dancing and jazz, the love orgies of Pablo and Maria, narcotics and the elemental pleasures of life—is symbolic for his repudiation of the entire narrow world of the *Bürger* and his new dimensions as an aspirant to the kingdom of the Immortals.

Haller learns much from and through Hermine. She teaches him to enjoy and appreciate many new aspects of life, and her friends, Pablo and Maria, aid her in Haller's education. For Haller she becomes almost a symbol; he calls her "a door . . . through which Life came in to me!"[26] On the brink of a suicide of despair he has found someone who can bring him back to life.

[26] GD, IV, 290.

Hermine realizes why he needs her: "You need me in order to learn how to dance, to laugh, to live."[27] At first she feels that the task is almost insurmountable; for Haller does not understand even the simplest pleasures of life, such as eating. (He had, like Hesse himself, previously been a vegetarian.) It is the art of life in which Hermine is Haller's preceptress:

"It is my responsibility to see to it that you learn a little more about the easy arts and games of life. In this area I am your teacher, and I will be a better teacher for you than your ideal beloved was. You can count on that! . . . How to love ideally and tragically—I'm sure that you know all about that. My respects! You will now learn how to love in a more common and human way."[28]

All that Haller learns from Hermine on this level of mundane reality is symbolic for an entire new world of experience that rushes in upon him: "Just as the gramophone ruined the air of ascetic intellectuality in my study . . . new disrupting things that I had feared penetrated from all sides into my previously so sharply defined and strictly secluded life."[29] At the same time, this new experience brings about a reexamination of his previous beliefs, and many of them, Haller finds, no longer stand up under close scrutiny. He had been an opponent of war, yet he had not been consistent enough in his convictions to face death, but had sought a compromise instead. Likewise he was an enemy of power and exploitation, yet he lived comfortably from the interest that he received from a number of valuable industrial stocks.

"Harry Haller had disguised himself marvelously as an idealist and scorner of the world, as a melancholy hermit

[27] GD, IV, 300.   [28] GD, IV, 318.   [29] GD, IV, 319.

and as a grumbling prophet. But basically he was a bourgeois, he found an existence like Hermine's reprehensible, begrudged the nights that he had wasted in restaurants as well as the dollars that he had handed out. He had an uneasy conscience and longed by no means for liberation and perfection, but wished, on the contrary, to get back to the comfortable days when his intellectual frivolities had given him pleasure and brought him renown."[30]

On the everyday level, Haller's experiences with Hermine constitute the first blows against the illusory and oversimplified existence that Haller had constructed for himself in his flight from the world. Through her he sees that his "ideals" were largely a pose, that he actually lived in a world just as tight as that of the average bourgeois—but lonelier.

On a higher level Hermine and Pablo, the jazz musician to whom she introduces Haller, are equally important: as reflections of his own thoughts. Occasionally these two representatives of the sensual world utter deep and significant statements that ill conform to the realistic picture drawn of them. Hermine, for example, expresses quite lucidly the central tenet of the novel, which Haller is unable to formulate articulately for himself; she confirms his inchoate belief in the eternal spiritual kingdom of the Immortals, telling him what people of their sort, the Steppenwolf-natures, live for: not fame, but eternity—the third kingdom of the spirit according to Hesse's chiliastic vision.

Just as Haller read his own speculations on the Steppenwolf into an indifferent pamphlet, so has he transplanted his own thoughts into the words of a clever

[30] GD, IV, 320-21.

courtesan. This fact is stressed: "All of these, it seemed to me, were perhaps not her own thoughts, but mine, which the clairvoyant girl had read and breathed in and which she was now restoring to me so that they had form and stood before me as though new."[31] Even Hermine understands this, for she reminds Haller why she is important to him; she is a kind of mirror for him because there is some part of her that understands and responds to him.[32]

In the case of Pablo, who is presented consistently as a monosyllabic sensualist, it is even more striking. At the beginning of the magic theater, when Pablo is speaking so astutely on the nature of the personality, Haller muses:

"Was it not perhaps I who made him speak, who spoke from within him? Did not my own soul look out at me from his black eyes . . . just as from Hermine's gray eyes? . . . He, whom I never heard utter a consecutive sentence, who was interested in no dispute and no formulation, to whom I had scarcely attributed the ability to think—he talked now. With his good warm voice he spoke fluently and without a slip."[33]

Hermine, Pablo, Maria, and the entire demimonde of *The Steppenwolf* exist on a realistic plane consistently throughout the book. Only Haller's sense of double perception bestows upon them the added dimension by which they assume symbolic proportions. In the "Tract" he tells himself that he must expand his soul to encompass the world; accident with an element of destiny places him in a posi-

---

[31] GD, IV, 346.
[32] Ralph Freedman, *The Lyrical Novel* (Princeton, 1963), devotes several pages to a detailed analysis of the symbolic function of mirrors in *The Steppenwolf* (pp. 76-94).
[33] GD, IV, 367-68.

tion to carry out this self-admonishment, and he sparks his contact with this other world with reflections that he imputes to the minds of his new acquaintances. This entire sequence of development, on both levels of reality, culminates in the experience of the Magic Theater, which takes place a little less than four weeks after the initial encounter with Hermine.

The occasion that Haller designates as "the Magic Theater" on the upper level of reality is no more than the aftermath of a great ball—according to the season, probably a *Faschingsball*. Haller is prepared for it on both levels; he has learned to dance and to love; by implication he has embraced and affirmed all aspects of life. Symbolic for this acceptance of the cosmos, including its most abysmal depths, is the fact that Haller must descend to a basement bar, called quite pointedly "Hell," in order to meet Hermine. From there they gradually ascend to a small room in the upper stories where Haller later experiences the Magic Theater. This upward progression is interrupted by a symbolic wedding dance which Haller performs with Hermine and which represents the imminent marriage of the two poles of existence in his soul: the intellectual or spiritual with the sensual or natural. In this passage Hermine is no longer "*a* woman"; she is "womankind." "All the women of this feverish night had . . . melted together and become a single one, who blossomed in my arms."[34]

At the same time, there are distinct implications of homosexuality in the relationship—implications that become explicit in the course of the Magic Theater. Since the first night of their acquaintance Hermine's boyish appearance had aroused certain vague memories from

[34] GD, IV, 365.

Haller's youth. Gradually he realizes that she reminds him of his boyhood friend Hermann—a similarity intensified by the very name Hermine—and this resemblance accounts in part for her attraction. On the eve of the ball, finally, Hermine is dressed as a young man, and Haller's exclamation when he catches sight of her is "Hermann!" (It might be mentioned in passing that this relationship is strongly reminiscent of the affair between Hans Castorp and Clawdia Chauchat in Thomas Mann's *The Magic Mountain*. Mme Chauchat interests Hans Castorp because she invokes forgotten memories of his boyhood acquaintance Pribislav Hippe.)

In the course of their symbolic ascent from "Hell" to the Magic Theater, on both planes, Haller loses the last vestiges of his bourgeois notion of individuality. Here the concept of fluidity, so important in other works by Hesse (e.g., *Siddhartha*), is touched upon: "I was no longer myself. My personality had dissolved in the intoxication of the celebration like salt in water."[35] These rites are the final stage in Haller's initiation for the supreme experience. Only now can he agree to Pablo's invitation to the Magic Theater, which involves the stipulation: "Admission only for madmen; you pay with your reason."

The words "only for madmen," which occur like a leitmotiv at several significant points in the book, sum up another major theme of the novel: the concept of magical thinking. These "madmen" are those rare individuals, like Myshkin in Dostoevsky's *The Idiot*, who have perceived the total relativity of good and evil. In the terms of *The Steppenwolf*, they are the inhabitants of this world who have learned to look at life with the eyes of the Immortals. They live for a higher reality where polar opposites have ceased to be reciprocally hostile,

[35] GD, IV, 362.

where every aspect of life is affirmed, where there is no dichotomy between *fas* and *nefas*.

After his symbolic descent into Hell and the wedding dance with his opposite and complement, Hermine, Haller is able to think "magically." He accepts Pablo's invitation, even on the condition that he become "mad." This acceptance concludes Haller's apprenticeship. The second part of the novel has portrayed the full course of his development from a schizophrenic intellectual morosely contemplating suicide because of an imaginary conflict between two poles of his being, to a man with a healthy awareness and appreciation of the world around him. He is now ready to plumb the very depths of the potentialities of his life. The Magic Theater is the vehicle through which he is to be introduced symbolically to the full extent of his personality in all its manifestations, and the consummation of his symbolic marriage to Hermine is to represent the complete welding of all aspects of his nature.

As the second movement of this fictional sonata, then, we find an extended narrative that consciously exploits the technique of double perception—a device, as we have seen, that Hesse explicitly conceived in musical terms as the literary equivalent of counterpoint. In this section the themes of the first movement—Haller's notion of the polarity between Steppenwolf and *Bürger*, as well as the broader view of reality and illusion—are skillfully developed with constant interplay and reciprocity.

The Finale: Theme with Variations

The Magic Theater, like every other incident in the novel, is open to interpretation on two levels. On the realistic plane it is nothing more than an opium fantasy in which Haller indulges after the ball in the company of Pablo and Hermine. From the very beginning of Haller's acquaintance with Pablo it is emphasized that the jazz musician is familiar with all the exotic refinements of narcotics. At their first meeting Pablo offers Haller a powder to improve his spirits, and Hermine informs him that Pablo is an expert in the concoction of various drugs —drugs specifically intended "to produce beautiful dreams." Later Haller admits that he frequently partook of Pablo's narcotic cocktails. On the last evening Pablo again offers Haller one of his stimulants. "Now each of us, leaning back in our chairs, slowly smoked his cigarette, whose smoke was as thick as incense, and drank in slow sips the tartly sweet liquid of marvelously strange and unfamiliar taste. It actually did have an infinitely invigorating and cheering effect, as though one were filled with gas and lost all weight."[36]

Everything Haller is to see in the Magic Theater is a reflection of his own inner life and a product of his eidetic vision under the influence of narcotics. Pablo makes this clear when he tells Haller that he can give him nothing that does not already exist within him. "I help you to make your own world visible, that's all."[37] This scene has been carefully prepared and anticipated by earlier scenes in which Haller's capacity for eidetic vision under stimulation was revealed: the message in fleeting letters on the wall of the alley, the dream of Goethe, and the "Tract" itself.

The "Tract," as we recall, stated that the Immortals are those who have transcended the *principium individuationis*. Pablo now restates this theme, telling Haller that all dreams of overcoming time or of being liberated from reality are actually only the wish to be freed from one's own "so-called" personality. The Magic Theater gives Haller a chance to do precisely this. Peering into Pablo's

[36] GD, IV, 368.   [37] GD, IV, 369.

magic mirror, Haller perceives simultaneously thousands of facets of his personality: he sees himself as a child, a youth, an adult, an old man; as a scholar and buffoon; bald and with long hair. Every potentiality of development and expression is there in the mirrored image. When Haller accepts the fact that all of these Harrys are part of his own personality, he is prepared to enter the Magic Theater and to enjoy the multifarious activities offered there for his amusement.

Physically the theater that he visualizes in his dream is on the order of a penny arcade. There are thousands of booths which he has only to enter in order to undergo a new experience. Hesse mentions fifteen of these sideshows by name, and Haller enters only four of them. But it is obvious that these few sensations are symbolic for the whole world of experience that lies open to him.

Individually each sideshow recapitulates a motif that has been developed in the course of the novel, and each one can be analyzed separately in order to demonstrate how carefully Hesse has constructed his work. Let us examine the first one as a typical example. While Haller is peering into Pablo's magic mirror, two aspects of the personality reflected there leap out of the mirror: one, an elegant young man, embraces Pablo and goes off with him; the other, a charming youth of sixteen or seventeen, dashes down the corridor to a booth marked "All Girls Are Yours!" In the second part of the novel it is indicated that Pablo, apart from his proficiency in heterosexual love, is also homosexually inclined; on two specific occasions he makes overtures to Haller, who rejects them indignantly. Now Haller sees that part of his personality is not only willing but eager to explore this particular side of life. At the same time another part of his nature goes into a booth where (as we learn later when Haller finally comes back to the same booth himself) he experiences the love of every woman he has ever known or even seen and desired during his life. The complete resolution of any polarity in matters of physical love is clearly implied.

The following sideshows pick up various other motifs from the novel: in the second one Haller learns that he, the confirmed pacifist, is able to enjoy war and killing. The motifs of metamorphosis, suicide, the decline of Western civilization, the nature of music, humor, the structure of the personality—all these are mentioned, and each one, whether Haller actually enters the booth or not, conjures up a very concrete image because it represents the culmination of a motif or theme that has been subtly suggested again and again throughout the book. Only one of the shows differs slightly: "The Marvels of Steppenwolf Training" is a surrealistic externalization of the main metaphor of the book in a scene not unlike, say, a play by Kokoschka or Ionesco.

In the final tableau the two levels of reality become so entangled as to be almost inextricable. As the effect of the drug begins to wear off, Harry has his most sublime experience: direct contact with the Immortals in the person of Mozart (like his earlier encounter with Goethe in the dream). But this exposure is too much for his over-taxed nerves; he feels despondent of ever attaining the stature of the Immortals, whom, for an instant, he felt that he had approximated. In this fit of despair he suddenly becomes aware that Pablo and Hermine, far from spending their time in idle dreams, are locked in a passionate embrace on the carpet. On the dream level Haller seems to take a knife and kill Hermine. The actual event probably amounts to no more than an exclamation of jealousy and disgust when he realizes that the woman whom he had elevated to symbolic stature, rather than being the ethereal personification of an ideal, is indeed very much of the flesh. It is, to be sure, a murder on this symbolic level of reality, for in his mind he eradicates the idealized image of Hermine which had obsessed him. As he contemplates her (imagined) corpse, he reflects: "Even before she had become completely mine, I had killed my beloved."[38] Yet not the least indication—it must be stressed—justifies us to assume that a murder has taken place on the realistic level.

The symbolic murder marks the climax of the novel, for the whole structure is calculated to bring Haller to the consummation of his wedding with Hermine, to the total acceptance of all that she represents to him: namely, the opposite of every pole of his personality. He fails because he allows a touch of bourgeois reality to creep into the images of the Magic Theater; he allows pedestrian jealousy to destroy the image of Hermine as the complement of his being. Just as he had recoiled, in his dream about Goethe, from Molly's leg (sensuality) when it revealed itself as a scorpion (danger), in this new vision he destroys Hermine when she shows herself to him in a sensual capacity, rather than as a spiritual ideal.

After the deed Haller slumps back in his chair, and, when Pablo fetches a blanket to cover Hermine from the cool morning air (on the level of ordinary reality), he interprets it to be a cover to conceal the knife wound (on the dream level). When Pablo brings in a radio (first level), Haller thinks that it is Mozart again (second level), and the ensuing conversation is once more on the plane of dream or higher reality. Mozart-Pablo's message is a reiteration of the thought that Haller had once before inferred from Hermine's words. Mozart experiments with the radio and, at length, locates a Munich broadcast,

[38] GD, IV, 406.

where the strains of a Handel concerto are scarcely recognizable through the maddening static of the instrument. When Haller objects to this, Mozart replies: "You are hearing and seeing, my esteemed friend, a splendid image of all life. When you listen to the radio, you hear and see the primordial struggle between Idea and Appearance, between Eternity and Time, between the Divine and the Human."[39]

Haller must learn to perceive the eternal spirit behind the spurious phenomena of external reality; he must learn to take seriously only those things which deserve it: the essence, not the appearance. Mozart goes on to chastise Haller for the murder of the image of Hermine, and it is stressed that the stabbing took place only on the dream level. Before the jury of Immortals he accuses Haller of insulting art by confusing the Magic Theater with so-called reality and "by stabbing an imagined girl with an imagined knife."[40] For this crime against the higher reality of the Immortals Haller is punished by being laughed at, just as Goethe had laughed at him in his earlier dream. The only penalty imposed is that Haller must remain in the world and learn how to laugh at it. "You shall learn to listen to the accursed radio music of life, to venerate the spirit behind it, to laugh at the nonsense in it."[41]

At this point Haller begins to realize that the figure which he had taken for Mozart is actually none other than Pablo, reproaching him for his previous outburst against Hermine. He comprehends that he was too weak to sustain the rarefied stratosphere of the Immortals; he had confused the two levels of reality and had taken seriously the prostitute Hermine of the first level, whereas he should merely have laughed at her. By taking her seriously and allowing himself a tirade against her, he had

[39] GD, IV, 409.   [40] GD, IV, 412.   [41] GD, IV, 413-14.

destroyed the image of Hermine as the symbolic woman, which he had meticulously constructed during his four-week acquaintance with her.

The novel ends on an optimistic note, for Haller now understands his situation and his shortcomings. He knows now that Mozart and Pablo are only two aspects of the same person (just like Narziss and Goldmund in Hesse's next novel): between the two of them they represent a complete union of the poles of spirit and nature, of life and the eternal. Haller's last words, with their tacit understanding and affirmation of this metaphysical union, indicate that he, too, may hope to learn magical thinking and to enter the ranks of the Immortals. He has experienced it briefly, but must transcend himself in order to be able to maintain constantly this new view of life. "Someday I would play the game of figures better. Someday I would learn how to laugh. Pablo was waiting for me. Mozart was waiting for me."

Thus the novel ends. In retrospect the structure of the Magic Theater emerges as a theme with variations. The theme, borrowed from the "Tract," is the notion that Haller's personality comprises a multiplicity of opposite elements. When he views these opposites from the new perspective gained through the magic mirror, from the standpoint of the Immortals, he realizes that they are not mutually exclusive. For the duration of the Magic Theater —until the murder of Hermine's image—he observes life from a point outside the polar sphere of the *Bürger*, and he is able to accept all its aspects. Each booth in the Magic Theater represents a variation on this theme: in each one he sees a specific instance of the opposite tendencies in his nature, and yet he affirms all of them completely.

The *Harvard Dictionary of Music* defines the theme

with variations as "a musical form based upon the principle of presenting a musical idea (theme) in an arbitrary number of modifications (from 4 to 30 or more), each of these being a 'variation.' " It also mentions that the variation is sometimes employed as the form of the finale in the sonata or symphony. Calvin S. Brown suggests that the obvious danger of formal repetition and variation in the literary genres is tedium, and in conventional works of literature that criticism holds true. By making use of a dream sequence Hesse is able to maintain a constant theme while providing in each case a different setting and new details. The setting and details, in turn, are drawn from material carefully anticipated in the preceding parts of the novel. Thus, the finale knits the book into a tightly constructed whole.

The Steppenwolf can be compared to a sonata in three movements. The first movement shows the unmistakable first-movement form, or so-called "sonata-form"; the second movement, though it does not reveal any form typical of the adagio of the sonata, employs the highly musical device of double perception or counterpoint throughout; the third movement, finally, is constructed according to a pattern remarkably similar to a finale in variations. As in the modern symphony, the themes are not limited to one movement alone, but appear in all the parts, thus creating an effect of structural unity in the whole; the second and third movements are based, respectively, upon the first and second points of the "Tract." Although the work abounds in so-called "musical" devices, like leitmotiv and contrast, it does not depend upon such hazy concepts in order to attain its musical effect. Instead, it reveals a structure that corresponds in general to a specific musical form and, in certain places, seems to adhere rigidly to the accepted pattern of musical composition. Since Hesse has clearly and repeatedly stressed the structural tightness of the novel with specific reference to musical forms, it is in keeping with his own intent to regard *The Steppenwolf*, aesthetically his most perfect work, as a sonata in prose.

The Super-novel

In a review of Gide's *The Counterfeiters*, Ernst Robert Curtius[42] developed a distinction between what he called the super-novel (*Uberroman*) and the action-novel (*Aktionsroman*). The action-novel embraces the narrative elements of the work while the super-novel comprises its reflections and theoretical passages. In *The Counterfeiters*, according to Curtius, the action-novel, losing its traditional precedence, takes second place.

"It is no longer there for its own sake but only as a point of reference for the reflection of the super-novel. The interest that this action-novel can still elicit no longer lies in itself, but in the unpredictable development that it attains as the crystallization nucleus of the super-novel."

Reflection has been an important element of the novel, of course, at least since *Tom Jones* and *Tristram Shandy*, although during the nineteenth century it frequently disappeared out of deference to the cult of realism. Not until modern times, however, has the burden of emphasis shifted from the action to the reflection, and it was this shift that Curtius characterized in his review of Gide's novel. Gide is by no means an isolated example. The same relationship of super-novel to action-novel can be ascertained, for instance, in Aldous Huxley's *Point Counter Point* or in Robert Musil's *The Man without Qualities*; and Hermann Broch's *The Sleepwalkers* has been per-

[42] In *Die neue Rundschau*, 37 (1926), 655.

suasively analyzed with specific reference to Curtius' terms.[43]

Postwar American and European literature seems, for the most part, to have turned away from the use of the novel as a vehicle for pure speculation. In the limited historical perspective that we can attain from our standpoint in the 1960's it looks as though the preponderance of the super-novel is a characteristic of the experimental literature of the twenties and thirties, and the most spectacular examples were produced in the period from 1926 (*The Counterfeiters*) to 1932 (*The Sleepwalkers* and *The Man without Qualities*).

Hesse's *The Steppenwolf*, written in the years following 1924 and published in 1927, fits right into this period. It is also of interest to note that a relationship of great personal esteem existed between Hesse and Gide[44] although their first exchange of letters did not take place until 1933. In any case, there is no evidence of literary "influence." Parts of Hesse's novel appeared as early as 1926, and the composition extends well back beyond the publication of Gide's novel. It is another of those cases, so frequent in the arts, of the simultaneous development and emergence of similar new forms as an answer to common needs. In Hesse's novel the "Tract" fulfills the function of a super-novel precisely in the sense defined by Curtius. The problem of Harry Haller is analyzed there in theoretical form and his development—from his initial despair to the ultimate redemption through humor —is anticipated. Structurally, moreover, the "Tract" re-

[43] Karl Robert Mandelkow, *Hermann Brochs Romantrilogie 'Die Schlafwandler'* (Heidelberg, 1962), pp. 49-50.

[44] From 1931 to 1933 Hesse wrote at least six different reviews of various works and editions of Gide. In 1951 on the occasion of Gide's death, he contributed articles to several newspapers and commemorative radio programs.

capitulates all the themes that are developed as counterpoint in the central part of the novel and displayed as
variations in the Magic Theater. *The Steppenwolf*, of
course, does not have the subtle interplay between action
and reflection that is the principle of Gide's novel, whose
narrator is constantly forced by the actions of his characters to revise his own ideas. What matters is the fact
that in all of these novels the action takes place for the
sake of the reflections, and not vice versa. We do not
have, as in the traditional novel, a story which the narrator
seeks to explain, comment, or interpret through his reflective remarks; but rather an author with a theory that
he hopes to illustrate by means of his narrative. The fact
that the "Tract" turns out ultimately to be the product of
Haller's own mind does not affect this interpretation.
Structurally, as we have seen, it represents a sovereign
point of view that is able to regard Haller's life with the
analytical detachment of the super-novel.

When Haller first becomes aware of the thoughts of the
"Tract," he is inclined to reject them in part. He is
rather pleased with what he considers his tragic dilemma—
longing for a bourgeois life that he cannot hope to rejoin
and doubting the ideal that he cannot hope to attain. He
does not realize that his tragedy of intellect is actually a
pose brought about by his own recalcitrance. As soon
as his wall of illusions begins to cave in, as soon as he
realizes that his "convictions" are often no more than
self-deceit, he begins to perceive that the solution proposed by the "Tract" is possible after all. His dichotomy
of Steppenwolf and *Bürger* may be unorthodox, but it is
no less an illusion than the false ideal of European Man
discussed in the essays on Dostoevsky. The "Tract" mentions two basic problems. First Haller must learn to stop
viewing life as a dichotomy and to accept all aspects of

his personality as justifiable and natural. This is the lesson that he learns through Hermine and Pablo's Magic Theater. The second step is to acquire a sense of humor that will permit him to laugh at those aspects of life that tend to obscure the eternal values. The Immortals are always there; if they are invisible, it is our perception that is at fault. Like Goethe in Haller's dream, they enjoy both spiritual and sensual life, both divine poetry and Molly's leg. Like Mozart they can appreciate both classical music and jazz. One must simply be able to distinguish the true values of life even though, like the Handel concerto, they may be distorted by superficial or technological deficiencies. Harry fails to succeed in this second step even though he learns the lesson of the first. The fact that he fails is immaterial, however, because his path is anticipated in the super-novel. Ultimately he will gain the sense of humor, he will be able to distinguish between reality and illusion, he will throw away his razor blade. The real center of the novel is thus the theoretical tract. The action-novel merely introduces the specific examples by showing us Haller's reaction to a certain set of circumstances. It is a concretization of a characteristic group of abstractions from the super-novel.

In his perceptive study of *The Lyrical Novel* (Princeton, 1963) Ralph Freedman analyzes the works of Hesse and Gide according to criteria that go hand in hand with Curtius' observations. In the lyrical novel "the 'I' of the lyric becomes the protagonist, who refashions the world through his perceptions and renders it as a form of the imagination" (p. 271). By this definition, the lyrical "I" would correspond to the "super-novel" as conceived by Curtius, which in turn projects the "action-novel" as a form of the imagination, as an externalization of the inner images of the hero. The technique of double perception permits Haller to "refashion the world through his perceptions." Seen either as the lyrical "I" or as the "super-novel," the tract constitutes the visionary center of *The Steppenwolf*, around which the action revolves. The action itself, however, is related in a severely realistic form in order to maintain the tension between the two realities that underlie Harry Haller's despair. This sort of novel, of course, makes heavy demands upon the reader, who is expected to recreate an ordinary reality from the materials supplied in the visionary scenes.

From this view of fiction, which represents a major step toward the disintegration of traditional narrative forms, it is only a short distance to the dilemma of the narrator in *The Journey to the East*, who doubts the very possibility of communicating with the reader. Hesse recovered from the problematics of the contemporary intellectual with a flight into the medieval world of *Narziss and Goldmund*, a work that in many senses marks a break in his development—almost a retreat before the consequences of his own thought. Only after that interlude will he return to an essentially modern radicalism of form again.

Narziss and Goldmund: A Medieval Allegory

NARZISS AND GOLDMUND (1930) is at once the most popular and, I think, the most imperfect of Hesse's later novels.[1] The reasons for its public success are directly related to its artistic shortcomings—a paradox reflected in the title of the first English translation: *Death and the Lover* (reprinted in 1959 as *Goldmund*). The English title, namely, refers only to Goldmund, the erotic hero who is obsessed by an initial fear of death that develops into a subsequent fascination; the significance of his counterpart, Narziss, is ignored. This implicit interpretation is contrary to Hesse's own conception of the book. In his letters he repeatedly stresses the equal validity of Narziss and all that he represents: "The book and its world become meaningless if one splits it like that: Narziss must be taken just as seriously as Goldmund; he is the counterpole."[2] Yet the protests demonstrate that even German readers who were not influenced by a misleading title persisted in reading the book in the same way as the English translator. It was Hesse's intention

---

[1] Here I disagree with critics such as Joseph Mileck, *Hermann Hesse and His Critics*, p. 10, and Ernst Robert Curtius, "Hermann Hesse," *Kritische Essays zur europäischen Literatur* (Bern, 1950), who explicitly single out this novel as Hesse's best. Though I object to Karlheinz Deschner's unreasonable and bitter attack on Hesse in his polemical *Kitsch, Konvention und Kunst* (München, 1957), it is perhaps not without significance that he chooses *Narziss and Goldmund* as the particular object of his scorn.

[2] Letter of 1934; GS, VII, 584.

to portray, through the dual figures of the German title, the equally balanced poles of nature and spirit, which approach each other and reach a synthesis in the realm of art. This theme, which is clearly developed in the novel, fits organically into the development of Hesse's thought. But as fiction—as plot and structure—the work fails to express the theme adequately. The reader senses a rift between content and form, a rift indicated by the English title, which—by no means unperceptively—regards Goldmund as the single hero and the novel as a picaresque story spiced heavily with erotic escapades and framed by an almost irrelevant monastic setting.

The reasons for this structural flaw are clear, I believe, and we shall go into them in connection with the genesis of the work. Here, however, another matter remains to be clarified. It is essential to point out the differences between the relationship Narziss-Goldmund and the other so frequent pairs in Hesse's fiction. Sinclair and Demian, Harry Haller and Pablo-Mozart, or—as we shall see in *The Journey to the East*—H.H. and Leo are distinguished by their varying degrees of self-fulfillment. There is no difference in quality between these pairs; they have simply reached different levels in the scale of individuation, but they all share in the full range of human potentiality. Sinclair may pendulate between the "light" and "dark" worlds; Siddhartha may cross the river from the sterile land of yoga into the lush valley of Kama Sutra; Harry Haller may vacillate between the sensuous Maria and his library of Novalis and Goethe. But the lures of these different realms are contained within them all. Narziss and Goldmund, by contrast, represent opposite poles of being: Narziss, the priest, is spirit personified, while Goldmund, the renegade monk and artist, belongs part and parcel to the world of nature and the flesh. The function of the protagonist, in other words, is split much as in the novels of the Romantic eccentric Jean Paul, whose *Years of Indiscretion (Flegeljahre)*, with its twin heroes Walt and Vult, Hesse once described as the book in which "Germany's soul expresses itself most strongly and steadfastly."[3] In no other novel except *Siddhartha* has Hesse so rigidly polarized the worlds of nature and spirit, and there, of course, the polarization was spatial and external; the personality of the hero who experienced both areas lent coherence and totality to the novel. Here, however, the reader is forced to make a choice and to identify himself, as it were, with Narziss or Goldmund, for their worlds are so completely different as to be mutually exclusive. The necessity for this choice lies in the highly structured nature of the novel, which is again reminiscent of *Siddhartha*. The protagonists, who are sharply, even paradigmatically characterized, function in totally different areas, to be sure: Narziss in the monastery and Goldmund in the wide world outside. Yet the reader has the uneasy feeling that these figures are drawn more from the mind than from reality. Their types are too pure and their characterization too schematic.

To begin with their names, Narziss is the introspective spirit, devolving "narcissistically" upon itself and content within itself, while the extravert Goldmund ("Golden Mouth," Chrysostomos) is in constant contact with the world about him. Narziss explicitly considers his the realm of the Father, the personification of mind and spirit, while Goldmund spends his life in search of the memory of his mother and, beyond her, of the Primal Mother of mankind. Narziss thinks in conceptual terms, which he articulates in precise words; Goldmund sees visions and images that exist outside of language. He becomes an artist, work-

---

[3] "Über Jean Paul" (1921); GS, VII, 254.

ing in a medium that needs no words, and in his pursuit of nature and love he even develops a feeling of antagonism toward language. Narziss' activity consists largely of making distinctions, of defining differences, categorizing, scholasticizing; whereas Goldmund, in both love and art, seeks to efface all differences in unification and flux.

The heroes themselves are very much aware of their differences, and their constant theorizing about the dichotomy lends an air of didacticism and embarrassed self-conciousness to the dialogue.

" 'Your home is the earth, and ours is the idea. Your danger is to drown in the world of the senses, and ours it is to suffocate in airless space. You are an artist; I am a thinker. You sleep at the mother's breast while I lie awake in the desert. The sun shines for me, for you the moon and the stars. Your dreams are of girls, mine of boys. . . .' "[4]

This often tedious polarization, which is reflected to a great extent in the parataxis of the style and in the vocabulary, extends into the world of the novel. What we actually have, instead of the symbolism that Hesse doubtlessly hoped for, is an allegory, and the abstract conception of the heroes, which is more vivid than their flesh and blood, seems generally to determine their behavior. As a result, the work is a veritable gold mine for scholiasts who are more concerned with Hesse's ideas than with his art. As a novel, however, it suffers from this symbolism flattened into allegory.

The Medieval Background

None of Hesse's novels makes a specific reference to time. Although the sequence of time within the works is

[4] GD, v, 51.

always quite clear, the absence of external dates contributes to the timeless effect that Hesse strives to achieve.
Thus *Demian* ends with the outbreak of a war not otherwise specified, though it clearly refers to World War I;
The Journey to the East begins shortly after that same
"Great War." *Siddhartha* takes place approximately during the lifetime of Buddha, while *The Steppenwolf* plays
in a more contemporary, yet still unspecified age. (We
hear only that Harry Haller, like Hesse himself, was
accused of treason during the war.) It would be false to
make upon *Narziss and Goldmund* the demands for historical realism that we are accustomed to expect of
historical fiction generally. We get a certain atmosphere
of the age, but no more. The time is roughly the age that
Huizinga has called the "waning of the Middle Ages."
One sole reference to the Battle of Pavia calls to mind
(if we consult our history books) the sixteenth century,
but the aura of the novel—the Black Death, the persecu-
tion of the Jews, the social background—is that of the
fourteenth century. It is pointless to try to fix an absolute
date. We are dealing with a period when monasteries are
in full sway, when Catholicism has not yet been split by
Protestantism, when the emergent artisans are consoli-
dating themselves into a new bourgeoisie—in other words,
with the period bounded, to mention two of Hesse's favorite men of the age, by Thomas Aquinas and François
Villon. At the same time, Aquinas and Villon are not
totally inadequate parallels to the spiritual and mundane
protagonists of the novel: Narziss and Goldmund.

The absence of historical requisites is no sign of ignorance on Hesse's part. On the contrary, his familiarity with
the intellectual heritage of the later Middle Ages lends
the work the unmistakable atmosphere of authenticity.[5]

[5] In this connection see the remarks by Curtius in his essay.

Hesse owned and knew the major works of medieval literature, from the great French and German courtly and heroic epics to the troubadours and Minnesinger, from Dante to the Goliards.[6] At the beginning of his career he wrote booklets on Boccaccio and Saint Francis, relying on sources in the original Italian and Latin.[7] Later he translated selections from Caesarius of Heisterbach's delightful *Dialogus miraculorum* for the German audience,[8] edited a selection from the *Gesta Romanorum*,[9] and, in 1919 and 1925, published two short collections of stories *From the Middle Ages*.[10] During the actual writing of *Narziss and Goldmund* he was concerned for months with Sertillanges' study of Thomas Aquinas;[11] how much this preoccupation with Aquinas impressed him is revealed by the statement, several years later, that "scholastic philosophy is perhaps, besides music, the discipline in which Christian Europe achieved the greatest perfection."[12] Of particular interest is the fact that Hesse read and reviewed, in the twenties, Johannes Bühler's important source-work, *Monastic Life in Medieval Germany* as well

---

Curtius, an eminent medievalist, is unquestionably a qualified judge in this matter.

[6] "Eine Bibliothek der Weltliteratur" (1929); GS, VII, esp. pp. 317-319.

[7] In the series *Die Dichtung* (nos. 7 and 13), published by Schuster & Loeffler (Berlin, 1904).

[8] In 1908 Hesse published an essay on Caesarius in his periodical *März*, III, 33-38. In that same year he published several translations from the *Dialogus miraculorum* in the same journal. In 1921 and 1922 several other translations appeared in various journals (including *Die neue Rundschau*).

[9] *Gesta Romanorum. Das älteste Märchen- und Legendenbuch des christlichen Mittelalters*. Nach der Übersetzung von J. G. Th. Graesse ausgewählt. (Leipzig, 1915, 1920, 1924).

[10] *Aus dem Mittelalter*. Bücherei für deutsche Kriegsgefangene, 19. *Geschichten aus dem Mittelalter* (Konstanz, 1925).

[11] Letter of 1928; GS, VII, 483-84.

[12] Letter of October, 1939; GS, VII, 615.

as Max Picard's volume on *Medieval Wood Carvings*.[13]
A perusal of his collected essays or dozens of relevant
book reviews in *März, Vivos Voco*, and the *Neue Rundschau* affords further evidence for the breadth of his
familiarity with the period mentioned. Hesse was as much
at home in the medieval world as many lesser novelists
whose works jangle with the clank of bosses and cuisses.

His choice of the period was not motivated, however,
by a desire to provide an exciting or exotic setting, but
simply by the opportunity offered in the monastic life of
the age for an outward manifestation of spiritual order.
Here, for the first time, he formalized his conception of
the eternal world of the spirit into an order symbolized
by the monastery. In *The Journey to the East* with its
League and in *The Glass Bead Game* with its Utopian
Castalia he continued along the same path. These three
last novels thus form a group in contrast to the earlier
works in which the Third Kingdom was not institutionalized into anything more rigid than the vague community
of spirit in *Demian* or the realm of the Immortals in *The
Steppenwolf*. In *Narziss and Goldmund* the symbol is still
not fully developed. It represents properly only the spirit
and the world of Narziss—the pole from which Goldmund
departs and to which he returns. The monastery is the
focal point of the novel, much like the river in *Siddhartha*,
and Goldmund's immersion in the world of nature varies
in direct proportion to his geographical distance from the
opposite pole. In the two last works, as we shall see, the
conflicting poles are subsumed in the concept of an order
that reigns sovereign above all opposites.

[13] *Klosterleben im deutschen Mittelalter* (Leipzig, 1921), reviewed in *Vivos voco*, 2 (1921/22), 482; *Mittelalterliche Holz-
figuren* (Erlenbach-Zürich, 1920), reviewed in *Vivos voco*, 1
(1919/20), 335.

It was quite natural for Hesse to choose the medieval monastery as his symbol of spirit. We have mentioned his familiarity with the Middle Ages, and it is significant that the novel takes place in a period during which the order of the spirit, though challenged by political forces, was still whole within itself—that is, before the Reformation. But more than this: Hesse was dealing with a physical environment familiar to him since his boyhood. Mariabronn, the monastery of the novel, is based in setting upon Maulbronn, the famous theological seminary in Württemberg, where Hesse spent two years of his youth and from which he, like Goldmund, fled, realizing that it was not his way of life. In the novel *The Prodigy* (*Unterm Rad*, 1906) Hesse had already portrayed the school. That novel, by the way, anticipates the duality of the hero in *Narziss and Goldmund* more than any other work by Hesse: there too Hesse polarized his own personality into the complementary figures of Hans Giebenrath and Hermann Heilner. (Note here the initials H. H. that will recur in Harry Haller and in the narrator of *The Journey to the East*.)

Maulbronn trained boys for further study at Tübingen and for the Protestant clergy, while Mariabronn is wholly Catholic. Even though the religious aspect of the novel—in all but Hesse's restricted sense, according to which all of his novels are documents of his religious development—is minimal, there is a further characteristic reason for this choice of a setting. Hesse deserted the Protestant faith of his family at an early age and subsequently never belonged to any church. But the idea of Catholicism, and particularly its ritual and symbolic aspects, appealed to him immensely. In letters and essays he repeatedly asserted that he would join the Catholic Church if he should ever feel the need for an institutionalized religion. "As a church, as form, as tradition, as a power that both creates and preserves culture, Catholic Christianity is vastly superior to the Protestant type."[14] Hesse is not speaking of the dogma of the Church, but of its aesthetic form, just as his praise of scholasticism implies his admiration for the formal perfection of its thought. His own faith in values that transcend the doctrines of any specific confession precludes his conversion to any church since organized religion is by nature restrictive. Yet among institutionalized religions Roman Catholicism is "the only one that, as such, I can acknowledge and respect."[15] Even this respect for the form of the Church is tempered by Hesse's historism, which realizes that no human institution is eternal. "Despite all my respect, even love for the Roman form of Christianity, I in no way consider this form to be indestructible and eternal."[16] Yet the implications are clear. Among orders existent upon earth, the Catholic Church represents for Hesse the most satisfactory as a form. For purely aesthetic reasons it lent itself to the symbolization that he sought for his own belief in an eternal order. In *Narziss and Goldmund* he borrowed the form and the accoutrements of Catholicism, specifically of Catholic monasticism, just as in *The Journey to the East* he was able to use the external form of secret societies. But in both cases he filled these adapted and modified forms with ideas of a uniquely personal nature.

[14] Letter of October, 1939; GS, VII, 616. Maurice Colleville, "Le problème religieux dans la vie et dans l'oeuvre de Hermann Hesse," *Etudes Germaniques*, 7 (1952), p. 140, actually speaks of Hesse's "tentation" to Catholicism—which is probably a bit strongly stated.

[15] Letter of March 3, 1935; GS, VII, 589.

[16] Letter of November 22, 1934; GS, VII, 580.

The Indomitable Picaro

Narziss and Goldmund begins, roughly speaking, where *Demian* ends. The earlier work culminated in Sinclair's spiritual liberation from his friend, symbolized by Demian's dying kiss. The present novel reaches a similar point in Chapter 4, when Narziss succeeds in convincing his friend that their ways of life are totally different, thus freeing Goldmund for an independent life outside the monastery. At this point Goldmund is eighteen years old, only a year or so younger than Sinclair at the end of his autobiography. The remainder of the novel is devoted to Goldmund's adventures after this first crucial event.

The novel falls into three clearly distinguishable parts comprising, respectively, six, ten, and four chapters. The opening section portrays Goldmund's arrival at Mariabronn and his ostensible desire, for the first three years, to devote himself to a life of the spirit. Narziss soon realizes, however, that this goal is alien to Goldmund's whole personality and that it stems actually from a repression of his love for his mother, for whom his father instilled in him a deep aversion. By Chapter 4 Narziss has succeeded in bringing this psychic distress to the surface of Goldmund's mind, where it initially precipitates a violent shock. Soon afterward Goldmund recovers and realizes that it is his true inner wish to follow the path of his lovely, erotic, forgotten mother. Chapters 5 and 6 depict, first, his inner decision to leave the monastery and to seek his fortunes in the world of the senses and, then, his external leave-taking.

The long middle section, which seems in retrospect to be the true body of the novel merely framed by the beginning and ending in the monastery, relates Goldmund's adventures during the ten years or so that he lives outside the monastery. Most memorable among these are the countless amorous escapades that he encounters from one day to the next; but equally important is his growing interest in art, which finally, after about four years, prompts him to seek out the famous Master Niklaus, from whom he receives instruction in the art of wood-carving, developing his talent to a point beyond that of the master. The two central themes of eros and art are interlaced with other episodes: two killings, the effects of the plague on the populace, and the constant threat of death. It should be mentioned that a very strong seasonal movement carries the narrative along: although Hesse interjects a reference to the passing years here and there, it is especially the succession of snows, blossoms, drought, and falling leaves that makes us aware of the passage of time.

The last four chapters, finally, find the two friends reunited within the walls of the monastery again. Narziss has been able to rescue Goldmund from execution and has now given him a studio in the monastery where he carries out his last works of art. During these three years the two friends engage in various discussions in which it becomes clear to them that their respective positions of nature and spirit are not so far apart as they had both initially assumed. The novel ends when Goldmund dies from the effects of injuries sustained when he attempts, older and weakened as he is, to recapture the spirit and adventure of his youth.

This external organization, which reveals Goldmund's central importance, exposes a structural flaw in the work. Despite Hesse's protests that the world of Narziss is of equal importance, the plot fails to make this clear. The narrative begins when Goldmund arrives at the monastery, and it ends with his death. In between, by far the greater part of the narrative deals with his adventures, whereas Narziss never has the stage for himself. While Goldmund's development is recounted for its own sake, Narziss appears only when he has some bearing upon Goldmund; he himself undergoes no development in the course of the novel, but remains constant from beginning to end. This structure could be justified by saying that the spirit is eternal while life is transitory; that, therefore, it is fitting that Narziss should be present constantly, unchanging, both before and after Goldmund's appearance. Hesse probably had something like that in mind, yet the structural emphasis is out of proportion.

The fact that the novel was originally conceived to revolve around Goldmund helps to explain this asymmetry. In an essay written during the composition of the novel ("An Evening of Work"; 1928)[17] Hesse describes his process of composition. "For me a new work begins to arise at the moment when a figure becomes visible in my mind, which for awhile can become the symbol and bearer of my experience, my thoughts, my problems." This is "the creative moment from which everything is developed," and in the case of the present novel that figure was not Narziss but Goldmund. This comes as no surprise. Some twenty years earlier Hesse had begun a novel on roughly the same subject. *Berthold*, which never got beyond the first three chapters, anticipates significantly many of the narrative elements of *Narziss and Goldmund*.[18] It too begins as a monastic story, and although the time is the seventeenth century, the background is monolithically Catholic (it takes place in Cologne) with only one passing reference to Protestantism (one of the heresies

[17] "Eine Arbeitsnacht"; GS, vii, 302-307.
[18] "Berthold. Ein Romanfragment" (1907-1908); GD, i, 831-883.

that the students take up in the course of their training).
Like Goldmund, Berthold grows up motherless and is
sent by his father into the monastery. They are both
strong, handsome young men, inexperienced in the ways
of the world, but inordinately responsive to sensual love;
for both of them life begins when they are seduced by
older girls. Berthold's closest friend in the school is
Johannes, a professional churchman who has the name
that Narziss adopted after his investiture as a priest; the
most salient physical characteristic of Narziss-Johannes is
a thin ascetic face with dark eyes and long black eyelashes.
It is Johannes, like Narziss, who first awakens Goldmund
to the realization that monastic life is not his true calling,
while he himself is happily reconciled to the life of a
prince of the church. In both novels a major crisis is
precipitated by a girl named Agnes. There are, of course,
certain differences: the early fragment breaks off when
Berthold kills Johannes. Yet the act of killing also belongs
to the character and development of Goldmund. The fragment ends when Berthold flees from Cologne to enter the
Thirty Years' War, just as Goldmund left the monastery
and became involved in the worldly events of his age.

Despite the differences in time and emphasis, the basic
plot elements of the later novel are anticipated in *Berthold*,
and the similarities are far more striking and numerous
than the differences. In the fragment, however, Berthold
was clearly conceived as the sole hero—just as the figure
of Goldmund first took shape in Hesse's mind years later
—while Johannes was merely an important secondary
character. When Hesse began writing *Narziss and Goldmund*, he obviously—consciously or unconsciously—tried
to adapt the original plot and structure to his new
ideas, but the inner changes were so great that they shattered the form of the original conception; vice versa, the

original fragment could not be distended sufficiently to embrace what Hesse now had in mind: namely, the portrayal of two parallel and equally important realms of life. Goldmund, like Berthold, leaves the monastery when he realizes that he is destined for a different life; up to that point the two works are parallel. But in order to ascribe equal validity to the realm of the spirit, Hesse had to resurrect the figure of Johannes, and the resurrection seems quite contrived since it plays no functional role until the very end of the novel when Narziss appears not unlike a *deus ex machina* to rescue Goldmund from execution.

Hesse was attempting, in other words, to adapt an originally picaresque narrative to the exigencies of a double-novel (*Doppelroman*) in the sense of Jean Paul's *Years of Indiscretion*, which he so greatly admired. There, by contrast, Jean Paul keeps his two protagonists, Walt and Vult, constantly in the foreground so that the reader is ever aware of the tensions and resolutions that exist between them. Many modern novels—think of Gide, Huxley, Dos Passos, or Broch—also manage by means of a network of intersecting parallel plots to keep a multiplicity of protagonists in equal prominence. These contrasts, I think, highlight the basic structural deficiency of Hesse's novel. In this case the readers were right. Despite his intentions Hesse did not succeed in rendering convincingly the realms of nature and spirit because the original plot forces the reader to identify with Goldmund. In *The Steppenwolf*, on the other hand, where there is only a single protagonist who experiences all extremes, the reader is at fault if he does not perceive that Mozart and the Immortals are just as important for Harry Haller as jazz and the demimonde of Hermine and Maria. For a variety of reasons *Narziss and Goldmund* represents structurally a break in Hesse's development. Logically it belongs between *Demian* and *Siddhartha*: it begins, as we saw, where *Demian* ended; the rigid dichotomy of the world into nature and spirit corresponds to the view in those works rather than to the more mature conception of chaos and harmony in *The Steppenwolf* and succeeding works. The ideal of Goldmund's primal mother is an extension of Mother Eva in *Demian*. And, finally, it is a young man's book, unlike the last three novels, which treat mature individuals.

After dealing with a middle-aged intellectual such as Haller, Hesse wanted to portray the same situation from another point of view. His inchoate feeling for an order of the spirit impelled him to take up the old plot in his desk drawer with the ready-made symbol of the Church as the pole of spirit. But the figure of Goldmund was too vigorous and the old picaresque plot too intractable to be molded readily into another shape. As a result, the novel remains an imperfect anomaly in Hesse's works; at the same time, because of its structural simplicity, its picaresque nature, and its emphasis on the erotic, it became Hesse's most popular work, far outselling anything else that he published. (Apart from the standard edition, which has reached 222,000 copies, it has been reprinted in eleven different editions.)

The Threat of Death

The central section of the work—the ten chapters devoted to Goldmund alone—are episodic in form and, like the rest of the novel, show a two-chapter rhythm. Few words are needed about the surface action. As Goldmund wanders ever farther from the symbolic pole of the monastery, his encounters with the many women of the novel—Lise, Julie, Lydia, Christine, Lene, Rebekka,

Agnes, and unnamed others—lead him, through love, ever closer to the pole of nature exemplified in his mind by the image of his mother, which gradually is escalated into the symbol of the primal mother of mankind. Equally important, however, is the theme of death, which alone, as its counterpart, puts love into the proper perspective. Life of the spirit inside the monastery has an eternal quality not jeopardized by death. Characteristically, the deaths that occur there are related in gentle tones that contrast sharply with the descriptions of the violent deaths that Goldmund experiences in the world outside. In the world of nature, which does not have the consolation of the eternal, death looms darkly as the frightful and inevitable end of everything. For this reason the narrative stresses the changes of the seasons so strikingly; the heat of the summer and the cold of the winter make Goldmund, the wanderer, bitterly aware of the passing of time, while Narziss, secure in the constant spiritual and physical temperature of the monastery, exists hermetically outside of time, as it were.

Goldmund first becomes aware of the connection between love and death—represented in this first case by pain—when he observes the face of a woman in the agonies of labor. "The expression of great pain in a face was indeed more violent and more disfiguring than the expression of great desire—but basically they were not different."[19] As Goldmund's horizons in the world of experience broaden, as he himself kills, makes love, watches pogroms, observes the death of a woman he loves, and finally is exposed directly to the threat of death himself, he becomes increasingly aware of the inextricable entanglement of life, love, and death in the world of nature.

[19] GD, v, 136.

In Goldmund's imagination the image of his mother becomes the symbol of this blissful and violent life.

"The mother of life could be called love or desire, but one could also call her a grave and decay. The mother was Eve, she was the source of bliss and the source of death; she bore eternally, killed eternally; in her, love and cruelty were one, and her shape became for him an image and sacred symbol, the longer he carried her within himself."[20]

Goldmund hears in his heart "the wild song of death," and this death is ambivalent, for not only does it represent terror and the dreaded end; it is also an enticing love-call. In the course of his journeys, Goldmund realizes ever more clearly that his path must lead inevitably toward death, for he has chosen the way of nature.

Ironically, the way of life brings one in constant contact with death. It is here that love plays such an important role, for as in the novels of Hermann Broch— notably *The Sleepwalkers*—Goldmund seeks to suspend death through love. Late in his life he confides this to Narziss. "Because the world is so full of death and horror, I try again and again to console my heart and to pluck the lovely flowers that exist in the midst of this hell. I find desire, and for an hour I can forget the horror. But that doesn't mean that the horror is any less real."[21] While Narziss' life of the spirit protects him against death, it at the same time cuts him off from the world. Goldmund has thundered through life with heightened sensibilities, but he has become all the more keenly aware of death. This is the dilemma of the novel; neither pure life of the spirit nor a total abandonment to nature represents the proper answer. Goldmund achieves totality, but it is im-

[20] GD, v, 176.   [21] GD, v, 277.

permanent; while Narziss resides in a timeless realm that is limited in its extent.

The Mediation of Art

Art is the medium through which opposites are reconciled and the threat of death annulled, in which totality of life is eternalized and simultaneity of spirit broadened to include nature. Since the powers of love are only a temporary alleviation of the menace, it is necessary for Goldmund to find a means of permanently opposing the annihilation of death. Four years after his departure from Mariabronn he begins to study woodcarving. Art is the logical means of expression for Goldmund since his thinking, in contrast to that of Narziss, is in images rather than words. Early in his journeys Goldmund realizes that words are futile in the world of love. On the night of his departure from the monastery he finds Lise in the dark by screeching like an owl. "He had entered a world where people did not speak, where man and woman enticed each other with owl cries, where words had no meaning."[22] As he wanders further in the world of the senses, it becomes apparent to him how unnecessary words are, in contrast to the monastery, where verbal articulation is everything. "The woman had needed only a single word— to designate the place of the rendezvous. Everything else she had said without words."[23] The obvious medium of expression for man whose ultimate conviction it is that nothing can be said in words is visual art. The paintings and carvings that he executes belong themselves to the palpable world of things that he entered when he forsook the monastic life of the spirit.

But art represents for Goldmund more than merely a mode of expression. As he overcomes the difficulties of

[22] GD, v, 88.   [23] GD, v, 102.

the novice and attains mastery and ease of expression, he realizes that art is the solution to his dilemma between life and death. Contemplating his own mirrored image in a well, it occurs to Goldmund that people are constantly changing—that the water reflected a man totally different from Goldmund of the monastery or Goldmund in the early days of his wanderings. By contrast, the image of man created by an artist remains always the same. "Perhaps that is the root of all art and possibly also of all spirit," he thinks—"fear of death."[24]

Everything in man's experience is a sign of his own transitoriness: the withering of flowers, the falling of leaves, the changing image of his own face. And for this reason, as we saw earlier, the principal unit of time in the novel is the season, that is, the visible unit of time in nature. The blossoming of flowers, the heat of the summer sun, the first snow—these are the temporal incidents that punctuate the rhythm of the book, and each seasonal change makes Goldmund keenly aware of the passing of time and the approach of death. "When, as artists, we create images or, as thinkers, seek laws and formulate thoughts we do so in order to save something from the great Dance of Death, to establish something that has a longer duration than we ourselves."[25]

Toward the end of his life Goldmund explains to Narziss what his art has meant to him. "It was the overcoming of transitoriness. I saw that something remained and outlived the fool's game and death dance of man: the works of art."[26] These, too, of course, ultimately vanish, but they last so much longer than the life of man that they can be legitimately regarded, if only in a relative sense, as an "eternalization of the transitory."

[24] GD, v, 162.   [25] GD, v, 162.   [26] GD, v, 278.

On the one hand, then, art is the medium that suspends the tyranny of time and the threat of death by preserving in lasting images isolated moments of temporal life. On the other hand, art is also the force that mediates between nature and spirit, making possible an ultimate understanding between Narziss and Goldmund, who begin at such different poles. For art is "a unification of the worlds of the Father and of the Mother, of mind and blood; it could begin in the most sensuous experience and lead to the most abstract, or it could have its origin in a pure world of ideas and end in bloodiest flesh."[27] Goldmund's final definition regards art as the realm in which "sensuality can be inspirited,"[28] or, in other words, as the eternalization of totality. Art emerges as the supreme mediator in the novel: the foe of death and the synthesis of the apparently irreconcilable poles of nature and spirit.

In this synthesis, however, art goes one step further: it becomes epistemological, a way of knowing. In the highest forms of art there is expressed the quality of mystery found otherwise only in dreams. Goldmund first becomes aware of this quality when he considers the difference between masterpieces and those works that manifest mere technical perfection. In the former he perceived a mysterious quality absent from the latter. This thought emerges from a late discussion between the two protagonists. Goldmund maintains that the primal conception (*Urbild*) of a great work of art rises not from flesh and blood, but rather from the spirit, as an image in the soul of the artist. The job of the artist is "to render visible in images his inner world."[29] This claim brings us to the final implication of the novel and points the way to Hesse's subsequent works.

[27] GD, v, 176-77.   [28] GD, v, 318.   [29] GD, v, 280.

It is clear, first, that Hesse has given us here a definition of his own art. He is not concerned with rendering reality naturalistically or impressionistically but rather with finding equations and correlatives in the external world, through which to portray his own inner experience.[30] This should not be construed in too narrow a sense: though Hesse had certain ties with expressionism, he is no representative of the movement. Instead he is like Rilke's Malte Laurids Brigge, who sought "vocables for his anguish" in the world of things and of history. Again we find confirmation of the fact that for Hesse inner reality is more meaningful than "so-called everyday reality."

A further point, however, is Hesse's conception of the role of the artist. Already here we find an anticipation of the motto of *The Glass Bead Game*, which states that it is the responsibility of good men to try to bring about what is still a non-existent ideal by treating it as though it were real. In answer to Goldmund's explanation of his view of art, Narziss points out that the conception of primal images is precisely the same as the philosophical "ideas" with which he is accustomed to deal in the realm of the mind.

"You spoke of 'primal images,' of images, that is, that are present nowhere but in the creative mind, but which can be realized and made visible in matter. Long before a figure of art becomes visible and attains reality it is already present as an image in the soul of the artist."[31]

Hesse is describing, within the novel, the process through which his own composition takes place. His works always

---

[30] In this connection it is relevant to recall Ralph Freedman's definition of the lyrical novel, quoted at the end of the preceding chapter.

[31] GD, v, 279.

emerge from an initial compelling image of a central figure—in this case, of Goldmund. Through this conception of the creative spirit both Narziss and Goldmund find their way out of the chaos of the world of experience, for it is the responsibility of the creative mind to treat the ideal spirit as though it were eternally present. Art is thus not merely, negatively, a counterbalance to death. Positively it posits and treats as real the ideal world of the spirit in which all opposites are reconciled.

This theme, in contrast to the plot and characterization, which have close ties with much earlier works, is the element that binds *Narziss and Goldmund* to Hesse's succeeding novels, for the apotheosis of art becomes the central theme in *The Journey to the East* and *The Glass Bead Game*. Here, still in the process of formulation, it represents a forced ending to the novel that was begun under completely different assumptions. The ending itself is unsatisfactory. Goldmund has been led to Narziss' spiritual "ideas": he has made his peace, so to speak, with the world of the spirit, the world of the Father. Narziss, in turn, has seen that Goldmund's life was likewise a justifiable avenue of approaching truth. "Both ways are human ways and insufficient, but art is more innocent."[32] Goldmund is thus able to die in peace, reconciled with both worlds. But his last words to Narziss are like a Parthian shot: he seems unwilling to concede that Narziss, by way of the spirit, might also have made his peace with the world of nature and the Mother. "How will you die, Narziss, if you have no mother? Without a mother one cannot love. Without a mother one cannot die."[33] In these last words the plot seems to do violence to the theme that was developed in the closing pages. From the thematic point of view Narziss has approached the world of nature and art

[32] GD, v, 300.   [33] GD, v, 322.

at least as directly as Goldmund has experienced the world of the mind. Goldmund, after all, came to the spirit through his friendship with Narziss. Why should not the same liberty be extended to Narziss, who experienced the world of nature vicariously through the art of Goldmund? Thematically the book should have ended with a perfect resolution: only the exigencies of structure and plot demanded a different ending. I consider this to be a major structural flaw.

Goldmund's entire life, after his initial psychoanalysis by Narziss, is devoted to the pursuit of his mother's image. Gradually the image, like Sinclair's painting of Beatrice, is transformed and generalized until it assumes aspects of universal validity. At the end of the novel it is no longer Goldmund's own mother, but "the great Eve-Mother" that he seeks—an image that has been enriched by all his experience of love and death, bliss and agony, in the world of nature. It was Goldmund's dream as an artist to create a figure of this Magna Mater, but until the image had coalesced within him, its representation was, of course, impossible. Yet the image is not perfect until Goldmund himself is at the point of death: only the total collapse of his life in the world can bring the image within to perfection. Now he would be able to create her figure, but he lacks the physical strength to do so. "She doesn't want me to make her secret visible."[34] Here we have the final irony in Hesse's aesthetic system. It is the responsibility of the artist, as we saw before, to serve the ideal by treating it as though it existed, by rendering it visible and tangible in art. Yet the ultimate mystery, Hesse implies in the last pages, remains locked in the artist's heart. Goldmund is unable to depict the figure that

[34] GD, v, 321.

he has spent his life pursuing: his mother. The ineffability of the ideal, which emerges in the last pages of *Narziss and Goldmund*, becomes a central theme in the next novel, whose narrator, H. H. finds it impossible to tell the story of his "Journey to the East."

●⟩)●⟩

The Symbolic Autobiography of *The Journey to the East*

IN THE earlier novels Hesse portrayed individuals striving toward a strongly felt but imperfectly achieved ideal; the individual and his striving stood in the foreground while the ideal entered the novel only at intervals by contrived means like the narcotic dreams of *The Steppenwolf*, the epiphany at the end of *Siddhartha*, the visions in *Demian*, or Goldmund's dream of the primal mother. "In most of my works before *The Journey to the East*," Hesse wrote in 1935, "I gave evidence more of my weaknesses and difficulties than of the faith that, despite its weaknesses, made my existence possible and fortified it."[1] In his last two major works, however, the emphasis shifts: the ideal itself moves to the center of the narrative—imperfectly observed, yet still central—while the individual recedes toward the periphery. This shift is reflected in the titles themselves. Whereas the earlier works were named after people, the last two get their titles from things: *The Journey to the East* and *The Glass Bead Game*. (The English translation of *Das Glasperlenspiel* obscures and distorts the original meaning by naming the book after the central figure: *Magister Ludi*.) This tendency reflects a development in Hesse's attitude, for the collective has taken precedence over the individual, a fact emphasized by the thematic stress on the

[1] Letter of November 19, 1935; GS, VII, 595.

ideal of service. The fulfilled individual who has completed the process of individuation need no longer insist vociferously upon his precious personality. Secure in himself, he can devote himself selflessly to the community like Leo in *The Journey to the East* or young Joseph Knecht and the old Music Master in *The Glass Bead Game*. In these two novels we no longer have a hero striving toward a vague ideal, but a central ideal that the narrator tries to define and express.

As we would expect, *The Journey to the East* uses in an almost overwhelming torrent the words and phrases that we adduced in earlier chapters to define Hesse's chiliastic vision and magical thinking. There is mention of a Third Kingdom (*Drittes Reich*—almost the last time that Hesse used that phrase), which exists in the form of a "psychocracy."[2] This kingdom of souls is merely a part of the eternal stream of souls—and by "soul" Hesse means the indestructible spiritual element of mankind as it is manifested in the greatest works of art. He explicitly does not refer to any intangible religious concept. The psychocracy is not only a "unification of all times"[3]—that is, vertical simultaneity in time. It is also horizontal totality in space, embracing all places and all people now living, a state of "magic" that makes possible a "confusion of life and poetry."[4] In this realm there exists "the liberty of experiencing everything imaginable simultaneously, of exchanging inner and outer reality playfully, of shifting time and space like stage sets."[5] It is pointless to repeat the familiar phrases; clearly we are dealing with the first really exemplary rendition of Hesse's ideal, which up to now had been more hinted at than stated or shown.

[2] GD, vi, 10.   [3] GD, vi, 24.   [4] GD, vi, 18.
[5] GD, vi, 24.

The Bundesroman

The Journey to the East is a narrative, not a philosophical tract. Hence the ideal must be rendered in concrete terms and not merely as an abstraction. In fact, since Hesse's ideal is very much an immanent one, existing only to the extent that it manifests itself in the products of the human spirit, it cannot be expressed in purely abstract terms: it cries for substantiation. Confronted with a new narrative situation—an ideal in the foreground rather than a human destiny—and the necessity to render this situation in fictional form, Hesse reached back into tradition again, where he found an old form that could be adapted for his own purposes: the *Bundesroman*, or League Novel. As Marianne Thalmann demonstrated in her definitive study, the Lodge or League Novel is a fictional type with distinctive characteristics.[6] It emerged during the latter half of the eighteenth century at the time when secret orders were at the peak of their influence; most of the important men of the age (Frederick the Great, Goethe, Herder, Pestalozzi, Mozart—in fact, almost everybody but Schiller) belonged to one order or the other. Arising as they did as a reaction against sterile rationalism, these secret societies constitute a rather striking parallel to twentieth-century mysticism in its rebellion against positivism. It was inevitable, in any case, that such a popular movement should be reflected in the literature of the day, and the exotically titled novels like Meyern's *Dya-Na-Sore* and Grosse's *The Genius* rapidly soared to the top of contemporary bestseller lists, like Lewis's *The Monk* in England.

[6] Marianne Thalmann, *Der Trivialroman des 18. Jahrhunderts und der romantische Roman. Ein Beitrag zur Entwicklungsgeschichte der Geheimbundmystik* (Berlin, 1923).

Most of these *Bundesromane* are totally devoid of literary merit, though they are by no means without interest. However, they had such a pronounced form—or formula, in the jargon of present-day popular fiction—that many of their characteristics were absorbed, consciously or unconsciously, by the great writers of the time. Goethe's *Wilhelm Meister's Apprenticeship*, Jean Paul's *Titan,* E. T. A. Hoffmann's *The Devil's Elixirs*—even such ethereal works as Novalis' *Heinrich von Ofterdingen* and Hölderlin's *Hyperion*!—are inconceivable without the influence of the League Novel. (These titles constitute, by the way, a list of Hesse's favorite works from that period.) Central to the *Bundesroman* and adapted in one way or another to the needs of the aforementioned works is the idea of a secret society that somehow guides—or seeks to control—the life of the hero. This produces a constant tension between the central figure and the order, which traditionally represents the ideal to which the hero is being educated. In almost all of these novels the secret society is described according to established patterns that are based, in turn, upon the actual hierarchy of the real orders—most particularly the orders of strict observance such as the Rosicrucians. At the head of the order is a High Tribunal of Elders, whose Superior represents the incarnation of the spiritual principle of the order. The order has its seat in a mysterious building, often a castle, that includes an extensive archive and various secret chambers. Before the novice is accepted, he must submit to an examination and swear an oath of loyalty. He is given a Letter of Apprenticeship and the appropriate insignia, is allowed to participate in the festivals of the Lodge, and must often undertake secret journeys in the service of the order. The journeys, in turn, are often based symbolically upon the legend of Christian Rosenkranz, pater eponymous of the Rosicrucians, who traveled to the Orient and brought back the Arabic and Indic lore that furnishes the basis of the practices of the order. The novice, or hero, is accompanied or guided on his wanderings by a stock figure: the emissary or genius, who represents the human incarnation of the order, in contrast to the Superior who exemplifies its spiritual principle. This emissary is traditionally characterized by various set features, among which the most salient are his omnipotence, his omnipresence, his timeless appearance, his sparkling glance, his foreign origin, and the quality of mutability. These are all the standard paraphernalia of the popular *Bundesroman*, where they occur in unadulterated form. Anyone can see the resemblance, *mutatis mutandis*, to the fictional structure of the contemporary novels of higher literary quality, such as *Wilhelm Meister*, where most of these elements were absorbed without any extensive sublimation. Although the League Novel, and the orders themselves, represented a reaction against pure rationalism and, as such, gloried in mystery and secrecy, the writers of the eighteenth century were not able to be absolutely consistent in their reaction: they almost always supply, just as Goethe did, a rationalistic solution to the various mysteries at the end. This rationalistic solution is another standard characteristic of the typical *Bundesroman*.

The rationalistic basis was abandoned by the Romantic novel, which took over the external forms of the *Bundesroman* but converted them for its own purposes. The order itself is no longer a human organization, but a symbol of some transcendental ideal, as in *Heinrich von Ofterdingen*, while the earthly manifestation of the ideal is usually concentrated into the single figure of the emissary, like Novalis' Klingsohr or the figure of the

Doppelgänger in works by E. T. A. Hoffmann. In line with this internalization or sublimation, the rational exegesis is dropped, and the novel ends in an aura of mystery, as it began. Structurally, however, even the Romantic novel retained many features of the traditional *Bundesroman*, although it transformed them radically for its own needs.

The period we have been discussing—1750 to 1850—is the age in which Hesse, as he has repeatedly stated, feels spiritually most at home. Harry Haller's library consisted principally of complete editions of Goethe, Jean Paul, and Novalis, with further works by Lessing, Jacobi and Lichtenberg—even the six volumes *Sophie's Journey from Memel to Saxony* by Johann Timotheus Hermes. We saw in Chapter 1 that the principal source of Hesse's early melancholy was his conviction that his works, the products of an epigonal generation, could never attain the heights of the great masters of the past. In his delightful and informative essay on *A Library of World Literature* (1929) Hesse again stresses his love for that period. As a child he spent hours in his grandfather's library which included thousands of volumes from the eighteenth century, and here Hesse made his "first valuable discovery in the realm of poetry . . . the German literature of the eighteenth century."[7] It is important for our purposes —not merely because it is impressive—to consider the scope of Hesse's acquaintance with that period. It began with such obvious works as Klopstock's poems, *Werther*, and old almanacs with engravings by Chodowiecki. Hesse went on to read Hamann, Jung-Stilling, Lessing, Weisse, Rabener, Ramler, Gellert, Hermes, contemporary newspapers, as well as Jean Paul, Bodmer, Gessner's idylls, Georg Forster's travels, Matthias Claudius, Hippel, and

[7] GS, VII, 336.

—another *Bundesroman!*—Müller's *Siegwart*. Hesse explicitly states that he also read much of inferior quality, but without any subsequent regrets, for he is aware of the advantages that lie in knowing a certain historical period exhaustively. In his essays and editions of Goethe, Jean Paul, Hölderlin, Novalis, and Brentano; in his letters, his casual utterances, Hesse has indicated again and again how faithfully and lovingly he returned from his far-reaching forays in world literature—the Middle Ages, the classics, the Orient—to the literature that he knew and loved best: the German Romantic period. In any case, there is documentary evidence enough, should internal proof not suffice, that Hesse was well familiar with the culture and technique of the *Bundesroman.*

In *The Journey to the East* he exploited that form as a fictional framework: there are extensive parallels. The reason for this should be obvious: somehow it was necessary to give substance to his ideal, to project it into the realm of reality, to lend a form to his chiliastic vision. The *Bundesroman,* which had fulfilled precisely this function in the eighteenth century and which had served Goethe, Jean Paul, Novalis, Hölderlin, and others admirably, supplied the very equipment that he needed. The organization of the Order from which H. H. deserted and which he now strives to reenter emerges clearly in the course of the story. It has the traditional hierarchy ranging down from the Superior and a High Tribunal to the novices. The four articles of faith are set forth in the Letter of the Order, and are symbolized by the four stones in the ring given to each novice. The novice is admitted to the Order only after he has satisfied the superiors, in an interview, that his intentions are honest; and he must undergo a year of trial after absolving the oath of loyalty. The Order itself is housed in a building that is more Kafkaesque than medieval in its setting, but the effect of mystery is achieved, and a vast archive, almost surrealistically flexible, contains a complete record of the activities of the Order and its members.

As in the Romantic novel, the figures of the Superior (the spiritual incarnation of the order) and the emissary (its physical manifestation) are merged in the person of Leo. Yet Hesse remains close to the older form because Leo has two quite distinct hypostases. As emissary he is the humble servant who obliges everyone, making himself the lowliest of the lowly. Yet he is characterized quite specifically by the usual qualities of the genius of the Order. He has the bright, penetrating eyes, the ageless appearance, the foreign origins (indicated by his name), as well as the omnipotence and omnipresence of the traditional figure. In his hypostasis as Superior he is characterized by his ready willingness to serve others, but he is "humble like a devout pope or patriarch,"[8] clad in rich, gold-embroidered garments, and the epitome of dignity.

The journey to the East itself, finally, is the symbolic journey that H. H. undertakes in the service of the Order —a journey through space and time, embracing the themes of simultaneity and totality, but based structurally upon the journey taken by the hero of the traditional *Bundesroman* in the company of the emissary of the Order. The highpoints of the journey, the festivals of the Order, are again the counterpart of the celebrations to which the novice of the eighteenth-century orders was admitted. Like the Romantic adaptations of the *Bundesroman*, finally, Hesse's novel eschews any rationalistic solution to the mysteries of the Order; the story ends with a symbol, not with an analysis.

The parallels are so conspicuous that they cannot be

[8] GD, vi, 64.

considered merely accidental. Hesse consciously patterned his novel on the structure of the *Bundesroman* and its sublimation in the Romantic novel. It is equally clear that this tells us nothing about the meaning of the novel, for its significance lies elsewhere. The League Novel merely supplied the framework into which Hesse fitted the matters that concerned him most of all; at the same time he paid tribute, formally, to a period of literature that he loved above all. There is, indeed, more than a touch of irony to the conceit of employing a form adapted from the eighteenth-century novel as a vehicle by which to express an ideal that draws so heavily upon that same period for its substance. The Order, to use T. S. Eliot's overworked phrase, is the objective correlative of the realm of simultaneity and totality—the realm to which H. H. aspires. Its nature is underlined quite clearly by the references to the history of the Order scattered through the tale. Zoroaster, Lao Tse, Plato, Xenophon, Pythagoras, Albertus Magnus, Don Quixote, Tristram Shandy, Novalis, Baudelaire—outstanding representatives of the world of enduring spiritual values—are listed as founders or brothers of the Order.

Symbolic Autobiography

The Order symbolizes what Hesse calls the eternal element in the human spirit: But into this eternity is projected a totally different set of experiences—namely, Hesse's own symbolic autobiography. It is perfectly clear that H. H., besides representing Everyman generally, is also Hesse himself. The initials alone make this association indisputable. The autobiographical elements inserted into the story make it a *roman à clef* of sorts, much like *The Glass Bead Game*. The structure of the *Bundesroman* can be grasped immediately; the more obscure autobiographical references, however, are evident only to readers familiar with Hesse's other works, both fictional and essayistic.

On a grand scale the geographical movement of the novel takes us from South Germany and Swabia through Switzerland to Montagnola (called *Montags-Dorf* in the text)—the course of Hesse's own life. All of the specific localities mentioned, however tenuous the relationship may seem, refer to places that play a role in Hesse's own life: Bremgarten, Morbio Inferiore, Noah's Ark (the local name for the home of Hesse's patron Hans C. Bodmer in Zurich), the Chinese Temple (a reference to the home of the collector Georg Reinhart in Winterthur), and so forth. Especially the sequence "in Swabia, on Lake Constance, in Switzerland we met people who understood us"[9] refers to the progress of Hesse's own life from his childhood and youth in Württemberg, his first years of marriage in Gaienhofen, and his years of manhood in Bern and Montagnola. The route of the journey corresponds point for point to the migration of Hesse's own life.

More important, however, the cultural contacts represent the development of his literary interests from childhood on as well as a thumbnail sketch of his own writings. The "first miracles" that H. H. mentions, while he was "still a complete newcomer" (that is, a child), involve the giant Agramant, Mörike's *Hutzelmännlein*, and Saint Christopher[10]—adventure tales, fairy tales, and religious tales on the child's level. The journey "had not been long underway in Swabia," the narrator continues, when the influence of the *Kronenwächter* (from Achim von Arnim's historical novel of that title) made itself felt[11]—the adolescent enthusiasm for Romanticism. The lengthy passage

---

[9] GD, VI, 24.   [10] GD, VI, 16.   [11] GD, VI, 17.

in Chapter 1 recounting the "marvelously festive days" that the travelers experienced when they encountered other members of the Order is a symbolic catalogue of Hesse's own friendships during the twenties. He speaks of Jup the Magician (Hesse's name for his friend Joseph Englert); Louis the Terrible (the Swiss painter Louis Moilliet); Collofino the Smoke-Conjurer (Hesse's friend Feinhals, who is subsequently mentioned as one of the authors of the Latin motto to *The Glass Bead Game*); while Hermann Lauscher, Klingsor, and Anselm in search of the iris, are all heroes of Hesse's own tales, representing progressive stages of his development as a writer. Finally, "Ninon, known as 'the foreigner,' "[12] (*Ausländerin*, grammatically the feminine form of Ninon Hesse's maiden name) is a playful reference to his own wife. The climax of Chapter 1, the great celebration in Bremgarten, refers to the estate owned by Max and Tilli Wassmer, other friends of the author.

When H. H. visits his friend Lukas, the latter has already heard of "the desperate march through Upper Swabia, the triumph in Bremgarten, and the surrender of the Ticino Monday-Village"[13] and has wondered to himself whether these energies might not be deflected into the service of republican politics—an open reference to the attempts of some of Hesse's acquaintances to enlist his name and services for political causes. And when H. H. finds his own record in the archives, it is filed under the rubric:

> Chattorum r. gest. XC
> civ. Cav. infid. 49.

The numbers probably have a significance that eludes me. The remainder of the rubric is perfectly clear. *Chattorum*

---

[12] GD, VI, 22.   [13] GD, VI, 38.

res gestae refers to the deeds of the Hesses; in school at Göppingen the rector had called Hesse by the Latinized version of his name, Chattus; while *civis Calvensis* specifies our own Hermann Hesse, born in the Black Forest town of Calw, as the individual who became apostate (*infidelis*) to the Order (possibly in 1926 when Hesse was 49 years old?).

These autobiographical references make it clear that Hesse is attempting to depict not only his conception of an immanent eternal Third Kingdom of the spirit under the guise of the *Bundesroman* but also his own personal relation to the spiritual millennium and, most specifically, the high points in his life when he felt, through a sense of community, at one with his vision. At the same time Hesse indicates that his conception of the ideal has shifted, as we saw earlier, in the years since *Demian*. At one point, for instance, H. H. recalls that in the days immediately after the Great War, when he joined the Order, the country was susceptible to many illusory ideals, but at the same time capable of genuine spiritual commitment. Among the various laudable but spurious movements popular at the time he mentions "premonitions of the world-end or hopes for the coming of a Third Kingdom" (*Demian*), "bacchantic dancing groups" (*The Steppenwolf*), as well as "a turn to Indic, Ancient Persian and other eastern mysteries and cults" (*Siddhartha*).[14] Hesse's rejection of earlier formulations of the ideal does not imply that they were bad; they were the proper energies directed toward the wrong goal. Only in *The Journey to the East* has he formulated the final valid definition of the Third Kingdom: the timeless realm of the spirit into which the individual, by magical thinking, can enter as one joins an order: by swearing an oath of implicit fidelity to its principles.

[14] GD, VI, 13.

The Dilemma of the Narrator

The fiction of the story demonstrates that H. H., like Harry Haller, is unable to maintain permanently the perfect fusion of reality and the ideal. This determines the role of the narrator. In no other work of Hesse's is the act of narration so problematic, so much a part of the actual substance of the book, as here. One of the few episodes dealing with a minor figure who plays no symbolic role, relates the apostasy of another member of the Order during the journey to the East. The young man had been talked out of his commitment to the Order by a former teacher, whereupon he reproached the leaders of the journey and defected. When he is surprised to learn that he is also freed of the oath of silence, the leader explains the paradox. "Remember: You swore to keep silent regarding the secret of the Order in the presence of non-believers. Since, as we see, you have forgotten the secret, you will not be able to share it with anyone."[15] This scene, which exploits one of the central devices of the *Bundesroman* (the oath of secrecy), exposes the reader quite early to the problem of the narrator. Only someone who has forgotten the secret of the Order can become unfaithful to it and speak of it to outsiders. Hence anyone who becomes apostate has, unwittingly, forgotten the inner meaning; he can describe the form of the Order, but not its spirit. We see therefore why it was so imperative for Hesse to have a rigid form for his story: for the *form* of the Order is all that he can hope to render since his narrator, through his own apostasy, has forgotten the meaning. This irony, of which the reader becomes aware much sooner than the fictive narrator himself, is one of the central features of the story.

[15] GD, VI, 19.

When H. H. begins telling his story, some ten years after his last contact, he is still under the impression that the Order has dissolved, leaving him as its only faithful survivor. But precisely because he has spiritually deserted the Order, he is unable to tell his story. It bogs down at the most important points; he can render only the external events, but not their inner meaning. He is living in a "devalued world," as Hesse later wrote.[16] In a letter to a critic of this tale, Hesse conceded that it is impossible, even forbidden, to render the ideal;[17] this dilemma is part of the whole language crisis that we discussed earlier. Hence it is necessary to resort to surrogates, and the idea of an Order, patterned after the *Bundesroman*, suggested itself quite naturally.

From the first page on, the difficulties of narration are emphasized. Since the reader is admitted early into the secret, the story assumes the implications of subtle irony that Gide admired.

"Already here, as I see, I encounter one of the greatest obstacles in my report. If it were permissible to disclose to the reader the innermost secret of the Order, it would be relatively easy to make comprehensible to him the level at which our deeds took place, the spiritual plane of experience to which they belong."[18]

Since H. H. has unwittingly lost the spiritual center—the secret—of the Order, the difficulties of narration are further increased because of the great variety and apparent discongruity of events. There is no central theme to which he can attach his story. H. H. soon realizes that

[16] Letter of October/November, 1934; GS, VII, 578.
[17] Letter of September, 1932; GS, VII, 523.
[18] GD, VI, 11.

his narrative may seem "impoverished and silly" to anyone who did not experience the events of which he tells. It is necessary to stress the fact that we are confronted neither with the traditional topos of ineffability, so common in ancient and medieval literature, nor yet with the sheer incapacity of an author to deal adequately with his subject. The inability to tell the story is one of the major themes of the narrative precisely because the levels of reality involved lack any channel of communication. H. H. himself is the visible symbol of this breakdown of communication. Though he himself experienced the events in their full power, he has slipped back, as Hesse put it that same year in "A Bit of Theology," to the second level of despair. He is thus unable to communicate, with words of this level, the reality of a higher level. And more significant yet: without the words, the tools of communication, he is unable even to recall in full force his own experiences.

By the middle of the story H. H. has reached a nadir of despair. He would like above all, as the last survivor (he thinks) of that great expedition, to give an account of it, but even the beginning seems not to be accessible of narration, leading as it does into a boundless and incomprehensible chaos. "Everything becomes dubious as soon as I want to examine it closely; everything slips away and dissolves."[19] H. H. is left only with a "disintegrating mass of images, which were reflected in something, and this Something is my own self, and my Self, this mirror— whenever I want to question it—turns out to be nothing." The disintegration of reality reveals itself at this point of despair as the disintegration of the individual and leads H. H. beyond the question "Can your story be narrated?"

[19] GD, VI, 35.

to the most consuming doubt: "Could it even have been experienced?"[20]

In Chapter 1, H. H. describes the beginning of the journey to the East in the most superficial way. Chapter 2, in which he attempts to give an account of the disintegration of the Order, leads him to the realization that, perhaps, not the Order but *he* himself had disintegrated. At the beginning of Chapter 3 H. H. still has not found a solution: "I am still faced with chaos." The first two chapters, which comprise slightly less than half the story, are a narrative in retrospect of events that occurred some ten years earlier. The remaining three chapters take place in the narrative present. Whereas before there had been some semblance of narration of events, H. H. is now obsessed solely with the problem of narration, for which reason he consults his friend Lukas, who has had experience in writing. The shift is highly significant. It implies what so much modern literature states: the individual exists only existentially, that is, in his encounter with reality. H. H., unable to come to grips with his reality, is a mirror that does not reflect, a nothing, a chaos. From the simple urge to tell an important story the narrative has been intensified into a mode of existence: H. H. becomes desperate to tell his tale, for only by doing so can he prove to himself that he exists.

"The reality that I once experienced along with my comrades is no longer present, and although the memories of it are my most precious and lively possession, they seem so remote, are so much of another substance, as though they had occurred on other stars in other millennia, or as though they had been feverish dreams."[21]

[20] GD, VI, 36.   [21] GD, VI, 39.

In the frenzied attempt to recapture his own reality, H. H. gives up his pretense at narrating the story of the journey to the East. What he now does is to narrate his own *attempt to narrate* the journey to the East; the act of narration has become the subject of the story. When H. H. is later readmitted to the Order and, from the higher level of reality, permitted to examine his earlier efforts, the manuscript undergoes a symbolic transformation. H. H. sees that everything he had written is wrong and as he marks out one sentence after another, the words and letters disintegrate on the page, forming circles, flowers, stars—"a meaningless pattern of ornaments."[22] The impossibility of describing the ideal is fulfilled poetically. As H. H. penetrates more deeply into the secrets of the Order, he realizes that he can never finish telling his story, that his attempt is doomed to failure. This admission, of course, casts a different light retrospectively on the first two chapters, for the reader now realizes that what he has read is no more than the senseless ornamentation that dismayed H. H. The fictional situation is not unlike that of the "Tract" in *The Steppenwolf*; but there the "Tract" was rendered, for the reader's benefit, in its translation into the language of the third level.

As H. H. reads further in the archive, he comes across other reports of the ostensible disintegration of the Order by other well-meaning deserters, and at this point another central theme of modern fiction is brought home. Each report, dealing with precisely the same crucial event, differs radically from the others; while each author, like H. H., is convinced of the authenticity of his own version. Other novelists—Gide, Huxley, Faulkner—have made a structural principle of this relativism, building disparate points of view into their fiction. Hesse, for the purposes

[22] GD, vi, 59.

of his story, is satisfied with the implications. No matter how often the story may be told, it is only a part of the truth, for it is impossible to capture the higher reality, the essence that counts, in the language or through the fallible perceptions of everyday reality. At best one can hope, by shifting the focus constantly upon the object, to catch a distorted reflection of the object in an imperfect mirror.

The Apotheosis of Art

Despair finally drives H. H. to his friend Lukas in search of advice. As a result of Lukas' practical suggestion, H. H. is able to seek out and find Leo, and thus to pick up his lost contact with the Order. But a more significant aspect of the visit with Lukas lies in their conversation about writing. Lukas had written a celebrated book about the war. Like H. H., he had forgotten much of what he experienced; and he too realizes that even ten books, all of them more urgent than his own, could not possibly render the war vivid to anyone who had not himself experienced it. Just as in the case of H. H.'s present life and the journey to the East, the chasm between the two realities was too broad to be spanned by mere words. When H. H. asks him, after these admissions, how he had managed to write his book after all, Lukas replies: "I had either to write the book or to give in to despair; it was the only possibility of saving myself from nothingness, from chaos, from suicide."[23] This function of Lukas possibly explains his name. Luke, alone among the authors of the Gospels, finds it necessary to justify his undertaking, and he does so expressly in order to give an example to his friend Theophilus. Luke's foreword resembles Lukas' remarks in that both of them realize how little of the actuality *one* report can convey.

[23] GD, VI, 40.

This conversation, coming in the very middle of the book, explains one of the central riddles of the story: why H.H., despite his realization that his story could not be told, nevertheless persisted; why, in other words, Hesse wrote and published *The Journey to the East*. To say that the act of writing is salvation from chaos is not enough. We must ask why this is so. The answer is clear if we consider the two assumptions: higher reality cannot be portrayed, and art represents a defense against chaos. It is the apotheosis of art characteristic of Hesse's generation. The world of art, capable of being structured, harmonious and perfect, differs from the real world that Hesse (or H.H.) wishes to portray. But it differs only in substance. In principle the two worlds are alike: the aesthetic construct, by its own laws, is just as perfect as the world of the Order. They are different to the extent that art and nature differ, yet symbolically they are identical. The world of art is an autotelic entity that exists independent of reality and in accordance with its own laws. In this world aesthetic harmony is possible: the chaos can be resolved. Thus it is that H.H. decides to continue his writing despite the futility of attempting to describe what actually happened: "to save my life by giving it a meaning once more."[24]

Only this view of art can explain two of the most impressive passages in the book. During the celebration at Bremgarten H.H. experiences his most vivid encounter with the timeless realm of simultaneity and totality. There he meets not only figures from the historical past and from his own (that is, Hesse's own) personal circle of friends, he also sees poets and their created figures with equal intensity. "But even though these artists, or some of them, were very lively and lovable characters. the figures con-

[24] GD, VI, 43.

ceived by them were without exception much livelier, lovelier, happier and—to a certain extent—more right and more real than the poets and creators themselves."[25] As concrete examples, Pablo (from *The Steppenwolf*) is contrasted with his author (left nameless), who "crept along the shore like a shadow, half transparent in the moonlight." Even E. T. A. Hoffman, as vivacious and conspicuous as he seemed to be, was only "half real, half present, not completely genuine"; while Archivar Lindhorst (from *The Golden Jug*) is the very image of exuberant vitality. The world of art represents a vibrant totality as opposed to the listless chaos of everyday reality; consistently, the people of the aesthetic realm are, to use Hesse's characteristic comparative form, "more real" than their counterparts in the other world. This view is restated in an essay on "The Magical Quality of Books," written in 1930.[26] There Hesse explicitly links the phenomenon with the realm of timelessness. Poets live and die, he writes, often unknown or ignored. Then decades after their death, like Nietzsche or Hölderlin, they suddenly emerge "radiantly, as though there were no time." And in 1933 Hesse congratulated Thomas Mann on his novel *Jaakob*, claiming that the characters of the novel are "so much more real, more probable, more right, than the figures on the world-stage."[27]

Up to this point Hesse has represented in playful symbolism a view of art that has been common at least since Schiller. Art is not supposed to be mimetic in the naturalistic or realistic sense, but rather constitutes an independent world that is "real" in its own totality and according to its own laws. At the end of the story, how-

[25] GD, VI, 27.
[26] "Magie des Buches"; GS, VII, 343-54.
[27] GS, VII, 562.

ever, Hesse takes us one step further along this path of reasoning by cutting the last bond that links the two worlds. For in the traditional view the author himself serves as mediator between everyday reality—the world of his readers—and aesthetic reality—the world of his creation. In his person a contact is maintained between the two realms. In the last scene, however, Hesse destroys this contact, setting his aesthetic world adrift, as it were— an autotelic whole. When H.H.—the narrator and hence the link between the reader and the work of art—lifts the veil before the cubicle that contains his own records in the archive, he finds, instead of any written documents. a wooden or wax figurine. As he looks more closely he sees that the figurine consists actually of two figures, back to back—himself and Leo. Since the figurine is translucent, he is able to make out a vague flux inside, a constant melting or flow leading from his own image into that of Leo. With a conscious reference to the words of John the Baptist, H.H. thinks: "He must increase, I must decrease" (John 3:30).[28] In the same instant he recalls Leo's explanation of the phenomenon he had witnessed at Bremgarten: that figures from works of poetry are generally more vital and more real than the persons of their creators. The story ends as H.H., attacked by a sudden weariness, turns away and seeks a place to sleep. The hidden quotation from the Bible is, of course, no more accidental than was the case in *Demian*. Coming on the last page of the story, as it does, it heightens the significance of the symbolic ending. We realize that within the world of the Order Leo is to H.H. as Jesus is to John the Baptist: more real, more essential, more substantial. This difference is emphasized by the fact, simple though it may

[28] GD, VI, 76. This is one of the crucial passages mistranslated by Hilda Rosner, *The Journey to the East* (New York, 1957).

seem, that Andreas Leo is the only figure in the novel with a full name; while the narrator, the least substantial of all, is indicated only by his initials. Not until he has immortalized himself by an aesthetic creation will H.H. be entitled to a name—until then he lacks the substance of the other characters mentioned: both the creators and their "more real" creations.

The meaning of the symbolic ending is clear: H.H., the narrator, is absorbed by Leo, the creation of his own imagination. If this is the case, then the narrator is subsumed, as it were, into the very work of art. Losing all contact with everyday reality, he is swept up into the aesthetic world of his own creation, and the novel is left suspended—authorless—as an eternal world in itself. The novel becomes the symbol of its theme: the eternal nature of art. If this interpretation seems far-fetched, we might at this point recall the surprising ending to Hesse's "Conjectural Biography" from the year 1925. There, after a brief summary of his previous life, Hesse turns and looks into the future. He conjectures, reasoning consistently after the pattern of *In Sight of Chaos* and *The Nuremberg Journey*, that he will inevitably be arrested for his manner of thinking. He visualizes himself in his cell, where he is busy painting on the wall the picture of a train disappearing into a mountain tunnel. In the last paragraph he leaps onto the train and disappears with it out of the cell and into the aesthetic world that he has created by his art. By these radical symbols Hesse succeeds in rendering vividly and surprisingly the absolute nature of his Third Kingdom. His realm of simultaneity and totality is always there, independent of our world of everyday reality, ready to be entered by those who are willing to think "magically." Since thought processes do not lend themselves readily to concrete depiction, the author's sole recourse

is the world of symbols: the painted train and the translucent figurines. The final meaning of *The Journey to the
East* is expressed not by the relativism of point of view,
the impossibility of describing the mysteries of the Order—
but rather by the fact that the Order is so powerful that
it can absorb its creator.

Hesse is by no means unique in his attempt to create
an autonomous work of art. The *symbolistes* and their
followers in France, Germany, and England consciously
wrote poems that were hermetically self-contained and
autotelic—one thinks instantly of Stefan George, Georg
Trakl, Paul Valéry, or Ezra Pound. In modern fiction
Gide, Huxley, Joyce, and many others have sought by
one device or another to make the novel independent of
its writer. But the closest analogy that I know to Hesse's
effort to transpose the narrator from the realm of everyday reality into the aesthetic sphere of his own creation
is Hermann Broch's novel, *The Sleepwalkers* (1932),
written in the same years as *The Journey to the East*.
Superficially no two works could differ more radically
than these: Hesse's "romantic" tale and Broch's "poly-
historical" fictional monstrum. Yet in theme and execution
there are remarkable parallels. Throughout the first two
parts of Broch's trilogy and well into the third, the reader
is kept purposefully under the illusion that he is reading
a story written by an objective third-person narrator (to
be identified with Hermann Broch). In the middle of part
three, however, it becomes apparent that the narrator of
all three parts is in reality the author of the essay, "The
Disintegration of Values," that has been incapsulated into
the fiction; that is, the fictional stories of the novel become
a hermetic whole sealed off and embraced by the larger
framework of the theoretical essay. Yet at the close of the
book another shift has taken place: the author of the essay

turns out to be identical with the first-person narrator of one of the framework stories. The whole novel thus lives in a timeless state of suspension, an aesthetic whole with its own self-contained author and its own laws.

For Broch at that time the absolute nature of art has almost exactly the same meaning as for Hesse: a realm of perfection existing outside the chaos of our disintegrating everyday world that gives us an ideal to cherish. In both novels the same meaning emerges from the structure: even though the characters within the fiction are exposed to despair, conflict, and disintegration, they differ from their counterparts in real life inasmuch as their lives take place within an autotelic aesthetic whole that reveals a meaningful form not to be discerned in the chaos of everyday reality. There is an exquisite irony implicit here: it is impossible to portray the ideal, but the perfect rendition of despair balances out the despair within the work, thus raising it above the tangled chaos of the real world. This is what Hesse means by "sublimation." "Is art, from the artist's standpoint, anything but an attempt to replace the insufficiency of life?" he wrote in an essay "On Good and Bad Critics" (1930), ". . . in short: to sublimate in the spirit the indigestible aspects of reality?"[29] Hesse is not using the word "sublimate" loosely. In a letter to Jung in 1934 he defined his concept very clearly in order to distinguish it from the psychological sense of repression. "I use the word only when it seems fitting to speak of 'successful' repression, that is: the manifestation of an impulse in a realm that is, to be sure, unreal (*uneigentlich*), but culturally of a high order, for instance the realm of art."[30] Although sublimation is not permissible in

[29] "Über gute und schlechte Kritiker"; GS, VII, 364.
[30] GS, VII, 576.

psychoanalysis, he continues, it is highly desirable when it bears fruit in the form of a work of art.

The Ideal of Service

This leaves us with the identification of Leo, who has emerged as the central figure of the novel.[31] His fictional function is clear: he is at the same time the Superior of the Order and, as emissary, its most devoted servant. H.H. sees him, at first, only in the latter capacity and does not realize until the end that Leo is the supreme embodiment of the principle of the Order (as in the *Bundesroman*). It was Leo, as the guiding spirit, who held the Order together until the test at Morbio Inferiore; when he disappeared, the other members of the troop were not yet firm enough in their belief to go on alone, and so it seemed that the Order had disintegrated merely because the personification of its spirit had vanished. H.H. keeps returning to this point over and over in his attempted narrative, failing to realize that Leo was precisely the "center of the events, a common feature, something to which everything was related and which held everything together,"[32] lending it the causality that the events lacked in the chaos of H.H.'s memory.

Leo, as we have seen, has more than a fictional function as Superior of the Order: as the creation of H.H.'s imagination and longing, he is also the symbolic better half of H.H. He is everything that H.H. might be if he could shake off the dross of everyday reality and enter perma-

[31] R. H. Farquharson, "The Identity and Significance of Leo in Hesse's *Morgenlandfahrt*," *Monatshefte*, 55 (1963), 122-128, attempts—tongue in cheek, possibly—to identify Leo with Hesse's cat Löwe ("Lion"). While Hesse was certainly not above this sort of word-play, the figure of Leo in the story is definitely human—not feline.

[32] GD, VI, 35.

nently into the realm of simultaneity and totality: in other words, another of the frequent *Doppelgänger* in Hesse's fictional world, with the same relation to H.H. as Demian to Emil Sinclair or Mozart to Pablo. We have seen that most of Leo's physical characteristics are borrowed from the paraphernalia of the *Bundesroman*, but there is one important feature of his personality that is symbolically the most striking and which, possibly, accounts for his name. Leo is absolutely at peace with the world of nature. This is repeatedly stressed. When he is first mentioned, H.H. relates that all animals are fond of Leo, that he can tame birds and attract butterflies. In the celebration at Bremgarten Leo is described as playing with two white poodles. When H.H. finds him years later, Leo fondly pets a fierce dog that growls menacingly at H.H. He is "at one with the hour" and—here we come to the theme of totality and symbolic metamorphosis—he seems to be capable of infinite delimitation. Not obsessed with his own personality, he gives himself freely and seems to exist "in a perpetually flowing, undulating relationship and community with his surroundings."[33] In other words, he has, in sublimated form, the capacity for mutation characteristic of the emissary of the order in the *Bundesroman*. Leo symbolizes in his harmonious relation to the world the principle of totality that the Order represents. In view of Hesse's onomastic tricks—every name, as we have seen, is of significance—it does not seem unlikely to me that Leo, the most unleonine of characters, got his paradoxical name from Leo Pecorella, the favorite disciple of Saint Francis, who like his master, was also a friend of all birds and beasts. Hesse knew the legend of Saint Francis in great detail: in 1904 he published a study of his favorite saint, who also plays a role in the novel *Peter Camenzind*

[33] GD, VI, 51.

and who is mentioned frequently in other works, essays, and letters. In these connections Saint Francis serves as a symbol for attachment to nature. That Leo Pecorella was actually the inspiration for the figure of Leo is only a conjecture, yet it does not seem unlikely, especially since another rather recondite symbol has crept into his characterization—this time from Bachofen.

A further sign of Leo's oneness with nature, besides his open-air vegetarianism, is hinted at in his address: *Seilergraben 69a* (Ropemaker's Lane) and by the fact that Leo wears rope-soled shoes. Since this mention of rope-making occurs twice in such a symbol-laden book, we are justified in examining it more closely. One of the most brilliant chapters in Bachofen's *Grave Symbolism of the Ancients* (1859) is devoted to the symbol of the rope-maker Oknos. (Hesse reviewed a reprint of this chapter in 1923.) According to Bachofen, the rope-maker in his final form represents "the symbol of the highest level of human existence" and "the victorious power of the higher mysteries which overcome the terrors of death."[34] It symbolizes "the preservation of the eternal youth of the race by the eternal dying out of the individual" and "the transitoriness of all sublunary existence."[35] This interpretation fits perfectly into the significance of the Order as we have seen it and, specifically, of Leo as the Superior of the Order. In both his hypostases Leo represents complete harmony and unity of being as well as service to the eternal order that outlasts the death of individuals.

Leo's complete blissful harmony is expressed by the "pious obliging bishop's smile"[36] that he wears. Because he is totally at one with higher reality, he is able to regard

[34] J. J. Bachofen, *Mutterrecht und Urreligion. Eine Auswahl,* ed. Rudolf Marx (Stuttgart, 1954), p. 74.
[35] *Ibid.,* pp. 66, 69.
[36] GD, VI, 71.

life on earth, like Mozart in *The Steppenwolf*, as a game. "Naturally one can make all manner of other things of life—a duty or a war or a prison—but that doesn't make life any nicer," he tells H.H.[37] Hence he can smile at the apparent disharmonies of existence that torment H.H. and at the "inanities of his novitiate."[38] This conception of life as a game, however, is not a frivolous one, but rather one with the most profound implications. The "game" of which he speaks is the aesthetic game of creating a timeless realm in the work of art—a prefiguration of the Glass Bead Game. Only those who take everyday reality too seriously, like Harry Haller and H.H. after his defection, are doomed to despair and unable to participate in the aesthetic realm of eternal values. For the "awakened" members of the Order, however, life is nothing but a lovely game to be played as well as possible. Part of this game, the prerequisite, is to forsake the foolish claim for personalism, which is the source of all despair. The more one moves away from totality by individuation, the more one insists on one's individuality—the more one suffers. To yield to totality, to be reabsorbed in the whole, to subjugate personal desire to the order—in other words, to be willing to serve—is the key to bliss. Thus Leo, as the incarnation of the Order and its Superior, is at the same time its most devoted servant. His smile is the smile of ironic renunciation, for he knows that mastery in the everyday world is illusory while service to the timeless spirit is eternal. "It is the law of service," he tells H.H., explaining to him why the figures of literature are more lifelike than their creators. "That which wishes to live long must serve. That which desires to rule, does not survive for long."[39] Gradually the idea of community and solidarity has emerged in Hesse's works from the inchoate

[37] GD, vi, 49.   [38] GD, vi, 65.   [39] GD, vi, 28.

cravings for individualism expressed in the works during and immediately after the war. The *principium individuationis* has come full around to the will to merge again with the whole on a higher level of reality. The final irony of the book lies in the fact that H.H., as he permits himself to merge more and more with the figure of Leo, as he is drawn more and more into the realm of his aesthetic creation, assumes himself more and more reality. "He must increase, I must decrease." Indeed. But H.H. perpetuates himself in the aesthetic world of his own creation.

We are again confronted with a characteristic phenomenon of modern literature, anticipated by Rilke's *Notebooks of Malte Laurids Brigge*, where, as here, the narrative begins as total subjectivity and moves to absolute objectivity. Rilke's technique there resembles *The Journey to the East* in this connection. Like H.H., Malte is initially obsessed with his own individuality as the world around him breaks down into chaos. But the pervasive pronoun "I," used so conspicuously in the first half of the novel, gradually gives way to less subjective forms of narration until, at the end, the figure of Malte completely disappears behind the symbols, the "vocables of his anguish" as Rilke later called them, that represent him: the book begins with the isolated figure of Malte; it ends with the typological figure of the Prodigal Son. This same progression from egocentricity to symbolic generality has been noted in *The Journey to the East*, which begins stylistically with the repeatedly stressed first person, seeking desperately to locate itself in the face of chaos. The story ends, as we saw, when the "I" of H.H. is absorbed into the representative figure of Leo. Structurally the identity of the two is enforced by the progressive approximation of narrative time and narrated time. Chapters 1 and 2 take place ten or more years prior to the writing; Chapters 3 and 4 take place only a few days prior to the time of composition; while Chapter 5, in which the final identification is made, occurs on the day immediately preceding H.H.'s report of the action. Throughout the entire narrative there is a movement from "I" to "he," from individuality to community, from chaos to order; and the resolution takes place practically in the writer's present moment. Any further report would, of course, be impossible because once H.H. is fully assimilated into the figure of Leo, once he has reaffiliated himself with the Order, then he again exists on a level of reality that is impossible to communicate to us, the readers. The last sentence of the book is therefore the last utterance of H.H. before he leaves our plane for the realm of simultaneity. The book that began as symbolic autobiography ends with the apotheosis of art, which in turn represents supreme service to the eternal world of spiritual values. Hesse has reached Castalia.

12

The Glass Bead Game: Beyond Castalia

HESSE'S last novel forms a bridge from the aestheticism of his own generation to the existential engagement of the next. It not only contains one of the most striking symbols of man's faith in an eternal realm of art and the spirit; it also documents the author's struggle to free himself from this autonomous kingdom of *l'art pour l'art* for the sake of personal commitment to his fellow man. Because Hesse's attitude toward the aesthetic ideal (Castalia) changed during the eleven years of its genesis, the novel is not free of structural flaws. They are not, however, flaws of organization (as some critics have argued), but of point of view. We can approach the problem by comparing *The Glass Bead Game* with two other novels with which it has much in common.

Many critics have pointed out the similarities between Hesse's book and Thomas Mann's *Doctor Faustus* (1947). This is hardly surprising since both authors were struck by the resemblance.[1] Both books deal with the aesthetic sphere of music and offer, in addition to the action of the plot, a thumbnail history and theory of music in the text.

---

[1] Hesse in a letter to Thomas Mann on December 12, 1947; GS, VII, 669-70. Thomas Mann in *Die Entstehung des Doktor Faustus* (Berman-Fischer, 1949), p. 68. Among the numerous comparative studies see: Joseph Müller-Blattau, "Sinn und Sendung der Musik in Thomas Manns *Doktor Faustus* und Hermann Hesses *Glasperlenspiel*," *Geistige Welt*, 4 (1949), 29-34; Anni Carlsson, "Gingo Biloba," *Neue Schweizer Rundschau*, Neue Folge 15 (1947-48), 79-87; Karl Schmid, *Hermann Hesse und Thomas Mann: Zwei Möglichkeiten europäischer Humanität* (Olten, 1950).

Hesse's Tegularius, like Mann's Leverkühn (both of whom have traits borrowed from Nietzsche!), represents the hazards of excessive aestheticism and artistic despair. Both novels, in a certain sense, are *romans à clef*, referring to significant figures from the intellectual and cultural history of Germany; and both make use of a montage technique through which quotations and essayistic passages are built into the texture of the fiction. In both books, finally, a criticism of contemporary society is suspended in a network of tension between irony and seriousness. Many other points might be mentioned; the possibilities of comparison have by no means been exhausted by scholarship. Yet these points represent largely thematic similarities. Structurally the two novels are poles apart.

Doctor Faustus is a masterpiece of epic integration; like Joyce's *Ulysses*, which inspired it, the novel is constructed organically from within and forms a tightly knit artistic whole. *The Glass Bead Game*, while likewise highly organized, represents an entirely different structural principle; its balance, if the analogy be permitted, is less organic than architectonic—a fact that can be accounted for by the genesis of the novel. Hesse's structural ideas changed several times during the composition, while Thomas Mann had his general organization in mind from the outset.

Far closer to Hesse's novel, both in genesis and ultimate organization, is another work: the third volume of Hermann Broch's *The Sleepwalkers*, which Hesse read and reviewed shortly after its publication in 1932. In both of these works we find a range of technique that is lacking in *Doctor Faustus*: from the total objectivity of the abstract essay to the absolute subjectivity of lyric poetry. (In Mann's novel the essayistic passages are built organically into the fiction as conversations and reflections; the point of view of the narrator is consistent throughout.) Both eschew organic integration in order to broaden the horizons and implications of the central story by means of parallel plots and interpolated essays. Both revolve around a theoretical tract on the decline of values that culminates in the vision of an aesthetic ideal existing autonomously apart from reality. And both, finally, achieve their artistic integration through a narrator who—in contrast to the narrator of *Doctor Faustus*, who is unable to understand the full implications of his story and, at the same time, represents a dialectical antithesis to the hero—stands above his material, viewing it, so to speak, *sub specie aeternitatis*. This does not imply that Hesse was "influenced" by Broch's novel. Many of these devices were anticipated to a certain extent in *The Steppenwolf* and *The Journey to the East*. It merely demonstrates that Hesse and Broch were striving for integration of a different sort than Thomas Mann. *The Glass Bead Game*, structurally, must be judged according to different criteria from *Doctor Faustus*.

It is in this connection, I believe, that Hesse's novel can most fruitfully be compared with *Wilhelm Meister's Travels* (*Wanderjahre*). The innumerable scholarly discussions concerning the similarity of the two novels goes back, again, to Hesse's own hints. In the course of the book he explicitly refers, on several occasions, to Castalia as "the pedagogical province"—a term borrowed from Goethe's last novel; it has often been pointed out that his hero's name (*Knecht*, or "servant") is used in direct and conscious contrast to Goethe's Meister ("master"). Although a great deal has been written about these matters, in general the results have shown that the resemblances

are often superficial.[2] Goethe's conception of "Doing and
Thinking," for instance, turns out to be quite different
from Hesse's idea of "vita activa and vita contemplativa."[3]
Likewise, the more pragmatic goal of Goethe's pedagogical province is far removed from the aesthetic ideal of
Castalia. Moreover, in Goethe's novel the pedagogical
province is only one of the various areas of activity while
in Hesse's work it is the center of interest throughout. The
conception of Castalia as an aesthetic ideal emerged
organically, as we shall see, from ideas that Hesse had been
developing since *Narziss and Goldmund*. Goethe's pedagogical province unquestionably contributed certain motifs,
but it would be a mistake to assume that there exists any
close parallel in theme or intention.

Structurally, however, there are undeniable similarities.
Both Hesse and Broch have revealed an interest in
Goethe's late novel, in contrast to most writers who have
been concerned primarily with *Wilhelm Meister's Apprenticeship*. The *Apprenticeship* has long and rightfully been
regarded as the founder of a tradition of *Bildungsroman*
that reaches from the early Romantic novel right down
to contemporary works such as Thomas Mann's *The
Magic Mountain*. It can be argued with equal persuasive-
ness, however, that the *Travels* inaugurated a completely
different tradition—one that did not really make its impact
until the beginning of the experimental novel of the twenties and thirties. In the *Travels* we find anticipated many
of the features that strike us, in *The Sleepwalkers* and
The Glass Bead Game, as radical and modern: the depiction of a collective society with a corresponding reduction
in the role of the individual hero; an internalization of

[2] Discussed by Joseph Mileck, *Hermann Hesse and His Critics*,
pp. 97-100.
[3] Inge D. Halpert, "Vita activa and vita contemplativa," *Monatshefte*, 53 (1961), 159-66.

plot with emphasis not on the action itself, but rather on reflection about the action; interpolation of reflection into the novel as pure essay, which is not integrated by means of conversations; a questioning of the efficacy of language and traditional form with a corresponding breakdown of narrative structure in favor of a looser additive form; the development of an anonymous narrator who is sensitive to the problematic nature of his undertaking. These are but a few of the more conspicuous points of similarity, but they represent what I consider to be a more fruitful direction of inquiry into the influence of Goethe on Hesse's novel. An undue preoccupation with details of theme and plot only leads us further away from an understanding of *The Glass Bead Game* in its aims and implications.

For the same reason I should not like to insist too much on the novel's indebtedness to the tradition of the *Bildungsroman*. Although the central section—Knecht's life—has definite points in common with the *Bildungsroman*, the book as a whole has a different structure altogether; and even within the central section the emphasis is split between the hero and the institution to a degree that properly exceeds the limits of the traditional *Bildungsroman*. Although at a certain stage of the composition Hesse may have conceived of the work as a *Bildungsroman*, the shifting focus soon forced him, as we shall see, to shatter the limits of the conventional form.

The long novel—it was originally published in two volumes of 450 pages each—is ostensibly a historical study written around the year 2400 by an anonymous narrator, and it falls into three main sections. A lengthy introduction outlines the history, theory, and practice of the institution known as the Glass Bead Game. The central narrative relates the life of Joseph Knecht, a famous Magister Ludi (i.e. Master of the Glass Bead Game) who lived at about the time when the introduction discontinues, some years prior to the generation of the narrator. A full appendix contains the writings of Joseph Knecht: thirteen poems written surreptitiously while Knecht was in school, and three fictitious "Lives" composed by Knecht during his student years as exercises in history.

The twelve chapters of Knecht's biography proceed chronologically, relating the outstanding periods in his life from his selection, at age twelve or thirteen, into Castalia as a pupil, to his defection from the pedagogic province some thirty-five years later. We see Knecht progress smoothly through his studies at Eschholz and Waldzell (the school for students who wish to devote themselves specifically to the Glass Bead Game). We witness his friendship with Plinio Designori, the "auditor" who returns to the outside world when his studies are ended; with Fritz Tegularius, the hyperintellectual who caricatures, by exaggeration, the principles and values of Castalia; the old Magister Musicae, who represents beatific bliss and harmony achieved in life itself; the Older Brother, a Castalian who has devoted himself so one-sidedly to oriental studies that he has become almost Chinese himself; and Thomas von der Trave (a subtle tribute to Thomas Mann), the polished and urbane Magister Ludi. For two chapters we follow Knecht to the Benedictine monastery of Mariafels, where, as an official emissary of Castalia, he establishes diplomatic relations between the two orders and, from Pater Jacobus, learns basic lessons in history. For eight years, after the death of Thomas von der Trave, Knecht is in office as Magister Ludi, a position in which he attains great renown. After five or six years, however, grave doubts begin to assail him, and they are intensified by conversations with his old friend Plinio Designori. Knecht decides to defect from his position. He sends a

long letter of justification to the authorities and then goes
to Plinio's house, where he expects to take up a position
as tutor to Plinio's son, Tito. On the second day of his
liberty Knecht accompanies his pupil to a mountain lodge
where, unexpectedly, he drowns while following Tito in a
swim across the icy lake at sunrise.

An Exercise in Symbolic Logic

For an age in which electronic music has combined
music and physics, in which sculptures and paintings are
plotted according to the table of logarithms, in which
philosophy has fused with mathematics to create the new
language of symbolic logic, an age in which "literary" and
sociological research is carried on by IBM machines—for
such an age it is difficult to conceive of a more appropriate
symbol than the Glass Bead Game. The name itself,
Hesse's narrator assures us, is misleading. When it was
originally invented by a group of musicians shortly after
1900, the game was indeed played with beads arranged
on a device much like an abacus. By means of the abacus
the theme could be modified, transposed, set in counterpoint—in other words, manipulated completely without
the aid of musical sound itself. It permitted, in a still
primitive form, the total abstraction of the intellectual
elements of music. Very rapidly, however, two developments took place: the exercise outgrew the relatively naïve
form of the original abacus and developed a symbolic
sign system of its own; but it retained the original name
although it was no longer played with glass beads on an
abacus frame. The technique was gradually adopted by
other disciplines in which values could be expressed by a
set of mathematical notations: mathematics itself, classical
philology, logic, the visual arts, and so forth. For a time
the techniques of the Glass Bead Game were developed in-

dependently within the various disciplines, but finally it became apparent .that cross-references were possible. The
abstract notation of a musical theme, for instance, might
be identical with the abstracted formula of an architec-
tural edifice (one thinks in this connection of recent scholarship in medieval literature!), a process in physics, or an
astronomical configuration. The initiates gradually developed a set of symbols in which it was possible to express
graphically the interrelationship of all intellectual disciplines. When this new technique was combined with
meditation on the meaning of the symbols, the Glass Bead
Game in its supreme form was born.

We shall not make the mistake of some readers who
wrote to Hesse that they had invented the Glass Bead
Game long before he described it in his novel. (In Hesse's
letters one can read his amusing answers to some of these
humorless aficionados.) It is fruitless to attempt any
description of the rules and techniques of the game, for
nowhere is it outlined in detail. By way of analogy:
Thomas Mann never intended Adrian Leverkühn's compositions, which he describes with such professional detail
and precision in *Doctor Faustus*, to be performed. The
modern novelist is not satisfied to state merely that his
hero wrote a book, composed a symphony, constructed
a perfect game; he wants to depict the act of writing,
composing, constructing; and to do this he must describe
the work with persuasive realism. But it would be as futile
to attempt to set up a game as it would be to reconstruct
the score of Leverkühn's *Apocalipsis cum figuris*. As a
matter of fact, it would be a decided artistic flaw if the
game were described with such precision that a table of
rules could be drawn up. Though there are many examples,
the Glass Bead Game is intended purely as a symbol, and
any symbol must transcend its specific application or else

it degenerates into allegory. In the novel the Glass Bead Game symbolizes the universal longing for what Hesse calls the "unio mystica of all disparate elements of the Universitas Litterarum."[4] It is "a refined, symbolic form of the search for perfection, a sublime alchemy, an approach to the spirit that is unified in itself above all images and quantities, an approach to God."[5] Much space is devoted in the novel to descriptions of various games that are played and combinations that are achieved; but it is pedantic to regard these as more than symbolic. As we know from Hesse's poems and letters, he himself was fond of playing the Glass Bead Game. In his private life, however, it was not the elaborate ritual depicted in the novel, but rather the quiet reflection on permanent values that exist eternally in the works of art and intellectual life from different periods of history. The game as it is described in the novel is a successful symbol precisely because it can be identified with so many aspects of contemporary thought and art. It is a common denominator, as it were, for the many attempts in modern times to achieve a new unity, a unified field, from the disintegrated values of our civilization. One could do far worse than to imagine the game as an exercise in symbolic logic.

The mechanics of the game, however, is only one aspect of the problem. "For like every great idea," the narrator tells us, "it actually has no beginning but, as an idea, has always existed."[6] The game, in the terms of this novel, is another symbolic representation of the longing for simultaneity and totality that we have seen in every one of Hesse's later books, and as such it fits organically into the development of his thought following *The Journey to the East*. In his introduction the narrator reminds us that the basic idea can be found in Pythagoras, in late classical

[4] GD, VI, 109.   [5] GD, VI, 112.   [6] GD, VI, 85.

civilization, in Hellenistic-Gnostic circles, and among the ancient Chinese. Abelard, Leibniz, and Hegel were like-wise striving "to capture the spiritual universe in concentric systems and to unite the living beauty of the spiritual world and art with the magical power of formulization of the exact disciplines."[7] It was not until our own time—the era that Hesse disparagingly calls "the feuilletonistic age"—that the Glass Bead Game was actually precipitated.

Hesse's outline of the development of civilization lead-ing to the invention of the Glass Bead Game shortly after 1900 is remarkable in its similarity to Hermann Broch's essay on "The Disintegration of Values" in *The Sleep-walkers*. He notes two main tendencies in European intel-lectual life after the Middle Ages: "the freeing of thought and faith from any sort of authoritarian influence . . . and, on the other hand, the secret but passionate search for the legitimization of this freedom, for a new authority that, emerging from itself, would be adequate."[8] This can be very easily translated into the language that Broch em-ploys. After human intellect freed itself from the bonds of the Roman Catholic Church, it was no longer responsible to any central and authoritative set of values. As liberated intellect applied itself to various areas of activity, it de-veloped new, often conflicting sets of values. There eventually emerged from this chaos the longing for a com-mon center that would once again give meaning to life. During the "feuilletonistic age" the dilemma became par-ticularly acute. Technological developments had advanced at a rapid pace while moral consciousness had remained at a standstill: "they stood, almost defenseless, facing death, anxiety, pain, hunger, no longer consolable by the churches, uncounseled by the spirit." Hesse's narrator ex-plains the frenetic activity of the age—the many popular

---

[7] GD, VI, 85.   [8] GD, VI, 88.

lectures, card games, cross-word puzzles, as well as the consuming interest in light articles on cultural topics in the feuilleton—as the attempt of an entire generation "to flee in the face of unsolved problems and fearful premonitions of destruction into a harmless world of make-believe."[9]

It was at this time, among various groups determined to remain true to the values of the spirit (the narrator mentions the Eastern Wayfarers of *The Journey to the East* in this connection), that the Glass Bead Game tentatively emerged. As it developed, incorporating first all branches of learning and then the process of meditation, it was formalized into an institution of rigid hierarchical organization with a world commission to govern the archive of symbols, elite schools for the training of initiates, and—at the top—the Magister Ludi or Master Player. In his own mind Hesse clearly regarded this organization as another variation of the ideal as he had represented it in *Narziss and Goldmund* and *The Journey to the East*. "The creation of a purified atmosphere was necessary to me," he wrote in 1933. "This time I did not go into the past or into a fairy-tale timeless realm, but constructed the fiction of a dated future."[10]

The Shifting Focus

What we have outlined above is the theory of the Glass Bead Game as it appears in the introduction that was published, in fourth draft, as early as 1934. There, as in the final version of 1943, the introduction presents a utopian dream of synthesized totality that fits smoothly into the development of Hesse's thought as we know it from previous works. The introduction is dedicated to "The Eastern Wayfarers," and the motto—which Hesse

[9] GD, vi, 92.
[10] Letter of January 28, 1933; GS, vii, 541.

wrote himself and had translated into Latin by two friends[11]—indicates that he is concerned principally with representing an ideal vision of his aesthetic realm as persuasively as possible in order to further its realization (*enti nascendique facultati paululum appropinquant*).

It is primarily this introduction, along with the motto, that has given rise to the mistaken notion that *The Glass Bead Game* is a utopian novel. To be sure, the introduction of 1934 is utopian. We can detect there not a single hint of the problematic nature of Castalia as it is revealed in the text of the narrative itself. That is the most serious structural flaw of the book. After his own view of the Glass Bead Game changed, after his own defection from the aestheticism that it represents, Hesse did not adapt the introduction to correspond to the new tone of the later passages. Hesse himself was aware of this defect. "During the first three years my perspective was slightly altered several times. In the beginning I was concerned above all—almost exclusively—with rendering Castalia visible. . . . Then it became clear to me that the inner reality of Castalia could be rendered plausibly visible only in a dominating person . . . and so Knecht stepped into the center of the narrative."[12] In the introduction Knecht is briefly mentioned in passing, but the author's interest is focused above all on the game itself. Its importance is highlighted by the fact that the novel gets its title in the German version from the game—not from the man! At this early stage (1933) the theme of defection has not yet appeared. "I intend simply to write the story of a magister ludi," Hesse wrote to a friend. "His name is Knecht, and he lives ap-

[11] The motto was translated into monastic Latin by Hesse's former schoolmate Franz Schall and later revised by another friend, Feinhals. Hesse acknowledged the help in his whimsical textual note: *ed. Clangor et Collof[ino]*.

[12] Letter of 1949-50; GS, VII, 701-02.

proximately at the time when the preface ends. I know no more than that. . . . There will be a spiritual culture that is worth living in and serving—this is the wish-dream that I should like to depict."[13] At this time the Glass Bead Game and the institution of Castalia represent an ideal vision that, *mutatis mutandis*, corresponds to the League in *The Journey to the East* or the realm of the Immortals in *The Steppenwolf*. There is not the least indication that Joseph Knecht will ultimately question the value of the aesthetic realm. His whole function is merely that of a representative figure in whom the ideal realm can be exemplified.

For several years, however, nothing was done about Joseph Knecht. He is mentioned from time to time in letters and poems, but not until 1938 did Hesse actually begin writing the chapters of his biography. During the intervening years he was concerned with the poems and the "Lives," which were published separately in *Die neue Rundschau* as they were completed: in 1934 "The Rainmaker"; in 1936 "The Father Confessor"; and in 1937 "An Indian Life." In the final version of the novel these stories are introduced as fictitious autobiographies that Knecht wrote as part of his studies—exercises in projecting oneself into the historical past as were required of all students in Castalia. In the novel the narrator also speaks of a fourth "Life" that Knecht never wrote: one dealing with Pietism in eighteenth-century Swabia. There is some indication that Hesse wrote at least a preliminary version of that story, which he did not include in the final work.[14] In any event, the novel outlines the contents of this fourth "Life" and Hesse's letters in 1933 and 1934 demonstrate his extensive reading in the period.

[13] Letter of January 28, 1933; GS, VII, 540-41.
[14] Richard B. Matzig, *Hermann Hesse in Montagnola* (Basel, 1947), p. 7.

There is reason to believe, however, that these "Lives" were originally intended to fulfill a different function. Toward the end of 1933 Hesse reported to Thomas Mann on his work in progress, mentioning his wide background readings. "My plan of the past two years (concerning the mathematical-musical game) is growing into the conception of a multi-volume work—indeed, of an entire library—all the more lovely and complete in my imagination, the more remote it is from any possibility of realization."[15] Apart from Hesse's other remark to the effect that his perspective shifted several times in the course of composition, there is no documentary evidence to support my conjecture. But it does not seem unreasonable, in the light of textual evidence, to assume that Hesse at this time—from 1933 to 1937—was planning to write something like a history of the aesthetic realm by means of parallel representative lives from various periods, culminating in the figure of Joseph Knecht in Castalia. After all, if the course of Knecht's own life was still not clear to Hesse at this time, then how could he have foreseen that Knecht would be required to write the fictional "Lives" as part of his studies? It seems more logical to assume that the "Lives" were written independently according to a different structural conception: a series of parallel stories illustrating devotion to the spiritual ideal and the gradual emergence, especially in the fourth unwritten "Life," of the idea of a Glass Bead Game. This assumption would explain two problems. First, it would account for the lapse of time before Hesse began writing, in 1938, the central part of the novel; originally it was supposed to be not the *center*, but the *last* in a series. And, more important, it would justify the fact that the three published "Lives" portray a rejection of life and a devotion to the autono-

15 GS, VII, 562.

mous spiritual realm from which Joseph Knecht defects.

It is rather a surprise for the reader of the novel, when he comes to the three appended "Lives," to ascertain that they do not anticipate in any way the defection toward which the central part of the book builds so steadily.[16] Thematically they are related to Knecht's life by the ideal of service—a theme indicated by the variations on the names of the heroes, all of which mean "servant": Knecht, Famulus, Dasa. But it is service restricted exclusively to the spiritual ideal as we found in *The Journey to the East*.

This is particularly conspicuous in the earliest of the "Lives," which portrays the career of a rainmaker in a primitive matriarchal society. There are striking parallels in theme and vocabulary between this story and the theoretical introduction to the Glass Bead Game, both of which appeared in 1934. Briefly, the story tells of Knecht's apprenticeship to the rainmaker Turu, his own investiture as rainmaker and finally his self-immolation for the sake of his spiritual office. It must be stressed that his sacrifice is *not* for the sake of the tribe; the tribe, as Knecht knows, is in no further danger. He sacrifices himself in order to retain the faith of the tribe in the spiritual powers that he represents. His sacrifice represents, in other words, an act of allegiance to the realm of spirit and not of commitment to his fellow man. The rainmaker embodies, in this primitive society, the forces of spirit and intellect; society as a whole is regarded with the same feeling of distrust and hostility that characterizes the Introduction as well as Hesse's other writings up to this point. When he is first introduced to the mysteries of astrology, young Knecht "felt in the first shudder of premonition that everything was a whole and that he himself was ordered

[16] See Sidney M. Johnson, "The Autobiographies in Hermann Hesse's *Glasperlenspiel*," *German Quarterly*, 29 (1956), 160-71.

into and related to this totality."[17] He regards his tutelage
as "his reception into a League and Cult, into a subservient
yet honorable relationship to the Ineffable, to the mystery
of the world."[18] The magical signs that he learns represent
"a reduction of the infinite and the multiform into the
Simple, into a system, into a concept."[19] This entire conception of the role of the intellectual corresponds precisely to the definition of the Glass Bead Game and
Castalia in the Introduction: the striving for unification
and totality, the idea of a cult, and the symbolic function
of signs.

The second "Life" has fewer outstanding parallels. It
deals with two patristic fathers, Joseph Famulus and Dion
Pugil, both of whom have devoted their lives to service
of the spirit as personified—in the context of the story—
by the Christian God. At an advanced age, however, both
of them are overtaken by doubts as to the validity of their
function as confessors. The story relates how each, by his
example, comforts the other and leads him back into service of the spiritual ideal. In both cases we have a temporary impulsive doubt, but it leads back to a renewed and
intensified devotion to the spirit—not, like Joseph Knecht's
defection, out of the spiritual realm and into the world.

"An Indian Life," finally, focuses even more sharply on
the life of the spirit than the other two. Although Dasa
undergoes what appear to be highly sensual adventures in
the world of the flesh—a logical inconsistency, by the way,
when the inexperienced and unworldly scholar Knecht is
later purported to be the author of these "Lives"—these
events are subsequently revealed to have been nothing but
an illusion, the veil of Maya. Dasa ends his days in the
forests in the company of an aged yogin, forsaking the
temptations of the world. Again: the ideal of service is

---

[17] GD, VI, 569.   [18] GD, VI, 571.   [19] GD, VI, 583.

a theme, but it is service specifically isolated from the realm of life and consecrated to the eternal spirit.

The most interesting of the "Lives" is the fourth, unwritten one. According to the narrator, the school authorities urged Knecht to turn his attention to a period that offered more documentary evidence and to concern himself more with historical detail—a subtle indication that Hesse was not unaware of criticisms made of *Siddhartha* and *Narziss and Goldmund*. So he turned to the eighteenth century. "He intended to appear there as a Swabian theologian who later gave up the church for music, who was a pupil of Johann Albrecht Bengel, a friend of Oetinger, and for a time a guest of the Zinzendorf congregation."[20] All of these names occur frequently in Hesse's letters and essays; they belong to the cultural period in which, as we have seen, he felt most at home: the Swabian eighteenth century. In the present connection, however, it is the theologian Bengel who concerns us most. Later in the novel he is mentioned again, specifically as a precursor of the Glass Bead Game. "In his early years, before the great Bible work took up his time, Bengel once told his friends of his plan to encompass all the knowledge of his day in an encyclopedic work organized symmetrically and synoptically around a central idea. That is exactly what the Glass Bead Game does. . . . Bengel was striving not only for a parallelism of the areas of knowledge and research, but for an interrelationship, an organic order; he was searching for the common denominator. And that is one of the basic concepts of the Glass Bead Game."[21] It is impossible to determine why Hesse never completed this "Life," which in many respects should have meant most to him. But it should be pointed out that he was working on it most intensively in the years 1933 and 1934,

[20] GD, VI, 192-93.   [21] GD, VI, 249.

precisely at the time when he wrote the theoretical introduction to the novel. It requires no great insight to ascertain the striking parallels between the two projects. The
"Life" of the Swabian theologian, had it been written,
would have represented a pre-stage of the Glass Bead
Game. Even in the few hints we can see the main principles: the idea of unification of all knowledge, the element of music, and the religious impulse. Like the other
"Lives," this one glorifies the aesthetic and spiritual ideal
at the expense of life itself.

Although Hesse wrote these "Lives" before the theme
of Knecht's defection had emerged in his mind—and
probably, as I have suggested, in accordance with an
originally different structural plan—they still fit organically into the work as it was finally published. For the
narrator carefully points out that they were written at a
time in Knecht's life when his doubts concerning the
validity of a purely aesthetic realm like Castalia had not
yet assailed him. Secondly, they were written as official
studies, and so Knecht would have been careful to sup-
press any doubts that he may have had from the authorities. As they appear in the work now, they represent
young Knecht's faith in the realm of the spirit and in the
ideal of service to the hierarchy, in which the personality
of the individual is effaced and subjugated to the needs
of the whole. This ideal of selflessness conforms, in turn,
to the biographical principles of the narrator, who tells
us in his introduction that the Castalian conception of
biography differs from that of the "feuilletonistic age,"
which was fascinated less by the typical than by the
aberrant characteristics of individuals. "For us only those
men are heroes and worthy of special interest, who by
nature and training are put into a position in which their
persons are subsumed almost totally in their hierarchic

function."[22] Joseph Knecht of the early chapters fulfills this ideal almost completely.

Three Castalias

Hesse himself has pointed out that Knecht in his early years "represents the inner meaning and value of this world, whereas the older Knecht, who has been trained in history, embodies the thought of the relativity and transitoriness of even the most ideal world."[23] This ambivalency must be stressed. Up to now we have discussed those parts of the novel (introduction and the "Lives") in which all concerned—Hesse, the fictitious narrator, and Knecht—are convinced of the utopian value of the spiritual realm represented by Castalia. In the central text of the novel, however—the twelve chapters of the biography—the perspective has shifted considerably: Castalia is no longer a utopian ideal, but rather a dialectical antithesis to the forces of life that Knecht encounters in the course of his career. Knecht himself, as we shall see, becomes aware of the problematic nature of Castalia only gradually. The fictitious narrator, however, who is in a position to survey Knecht's life from beginning to end, perceives the dangers inherent in a purely aesthetic realm even while Knecht is still basking in the euphorious bliss of the Glass Bead Game. We must not forget that the narrator, who according to Hesse's fiction is living some years after Knecht's death, has profited from Knecht's experience. His Castalia has benefited from Knecht's defection and death.

Some readers have tended to interpret the ending of the novel solely from the viewpoint of Tito, the young boy whose tutor Knecht becomes after his departure from Castalia. The narrator repeatedly makes it clear, however,

[22] GD, VI, 82.
[23] Letter of November 1, 1943; GS, VII, 637.

that Knecht's sacrifice had profound implications for
Castalia itself, which underwent a revaluation of its principles after the abrupt defection of the renowned Magister
Ludi. At one point the narrator interjects a personal remark to condone Knecht, who recognized "long before the
rest of us that the complicated and sensitive apparatus of
our republic was an aging organism that was in need of
rejuvenation in certain respects."[24] Later, after relating
that Castalia was temporarily split into two factions over
the validity of Knecht's criticism, the narrator points out
that it is no longer necessary to take sides in the argument,
for "the synthesis from that conflict of verdicts and opin-
ions concerning Joseph Knecht's person and life has long
since been in process of formation."[25] Finally, the changed
attitude of the authorities is evidenced by the very fact
that the narrator, a Castalian himself, is allowed to undertake a biography of the great renegade Knecht; that he
has at his disposal not only more or less public documents
like the "Legend" relating Knecht's last days but also
letters by Knecht as well as many addressed to him, conversations jotted down by friends both in Castalia and in
the world outside, copies of Knecht's own lectures, and—
finally—official reports from the archives of Castalia.
Without belaboring the textual details we can state that
the fiction of the narrator is maintained consistently
throughout the novel; he reports only those incidents,
conversations, and thoughts for which he has an acknowledged and legitimate source. Far more important is
the mere fact that the biography was written. To state the
case most radically: the true beneficiary of Knecht's sacrifice is neither Knecht nor Tito, but the narrator himself,
who represents a Castalia tempered by the criticisms made
by Knecht during his lifetime. The novel actually depicts,

[24] GD, vi, 374.   [25] GD, vi, 386.

implicitly or explicitly, *three* visions of Castalia: the utopian spiritual realm portrayed in the introduction and *only* there; the Alexandrine republic of aestheticism, sharply attacked by Knecht and the narrator alike in the text of the novel; and finally a more balanced synthesis of life and spirit represented by the narrator himself. It is necessary to make sharp distinctions between these three stages.

Now what Hesse and most of his critics mean when they speak of Castalia is the realm portrayed in the central section of the novel—the "pedagogical province" from which Knecht defects. It is obvious that this Castalia is no utopia except in the etymological sense of the word. Hesse has carefully denied its idealistically utopian nature. The only time he used the word "utopia" without any qualifying restrictions to apply to his novel was in the explanatory note accompanying the publication of the introduction in *Die neue Rundschau* in 1934: "This treatise is the preface to a utopian work; one should think of it as having been written approximately around 2400." As we have seen, only that introduction is genuinely utopian in the sense, say, of *The Journey to the East*. All of Hesse's later remarks qualify the expression "utopia" when it is used. "I am glad that you recognized so correctly the structure of my utopia and formulated it so well: it shows merely one possibility of spiritual life, a Platonic dream—not an ideal that should be considered eternally valid, but a potential world that is conscious of its own relativity."[26]

A more fruitful approach, and one that permits us to fit the novel into the tendencies of modern literature in general, is to regard Castalia not as a utopia, but rather as what might be called—to borrow a term from art criti-

[26] Letter of November 1, 1943; GS, vii, 637.

cism—a realistic abstraction.[27] It is necessary, in order to discuss this novel, to be able to distinguish between the abstractionism of the game itself and the abstract nature of the structure. The rejection of aesthetic abstractionism is the principal theme of the novel, culminating in Knecht's defection. Yet the structure remains abstract throughout. To indicate a similar dilemma in painting, Piet Mondrian spoke of neo-plasticism and "peinture abstraite réelle." In 1930 Theo van Doesburg introduced a new name for the same concept in the title of his journal *Art concret*. All of these terms were an attempt to avoid the implications popularly associated with the word "abstract" as it was used after 1910 by Kandinsky and others in order to designate a wholly non-objective art. The new art of the twenties marked a return to real and concrete objects, even though the objects were portrayed in their ideal essence rather than in their naturalistic manifestation.[28] Now precisely this distinction can be useful to us. The Glass Bead Game is wholly abstract, as we have seen; it operates with symbols abstracted from the original object or thing. The novel as a structure, on the other hand, is a realistic or concrete abstraction.

Utopias, along with their negative counterpart, the apocalyptic novel, are by no means absent from recent

[27] Oskar Seidlin, "Hermann Hesses *Glasperlenspiel*," *Germanic Review*, 23 (1948), 263-73, has most articulately opposed the utopian interpretation: "Aber um eine Utopie, d.h. eine Zukunfts- vision einer höheren individuellen oder gesellschaftlichen Existenz, handelt es sich durchaus nicht. Kastalien ist nicht Utopie, sondern Mythos: d.h. Konkretisierung eines Ewigen, eines Etwas, das war, das ist und das sein wird" (p. 264). Although I agree completely with Seidlin's analysis and definition, I prefer the term "realistic abstraction" for two reasons: it serves more easily to link Hesse with other modern artists; and it avoids certain ambiguities asso- ciated with the term "myth." One might say that a realistic abstrac- tion can in time, if it is accepted as valid, become a myth.

[28] See Werner Haftmann, *Malerei im 20. Jahrhundert, Textband*, p. 279.

literature. In postwar German literature one thinks—to take only the most conspicuous examples—of Franz Werfel's *Star of the Unborn* (1946), Hermann Kasack's *City beyond the River* (1947), and Ernst Jünger's *Heliopolis* (1949). It is noteworthy, however, that most utopias are conceived by writers of the older aesthetic generation. The authors of the postwar era no longer have the faith implicit in any utopia, whether it be aesthetic, social, political, or otherwise. The general tendency in their writings has been toward the realistic abstraction. Superficially this type of abstraction has certain features in common with the utopia—specifically the qualities of timelessness and placelessness. The utopia traditionally and typically represents the envisaged realm as an ideal to be achieved; it has no time or place because it has not been realized here and now. The realistic abstraction, on the other hand, exploits the techniques of utopism and uchronism for diametrically opposed reasons. The abstraction assumes that the situation it renders is so typical and so omnipresent that it would be misleading to pin it down to a specific time or place. These writers are dealing with problems—say, the question of human guilt or freedom—that are equally valid whether the scene be France, Germany, or America, whether the time be the present, the future, or the remote past. This is conspicuously the case in many contemporary dramas; one thinks of Thornton Wilder, Max Frisch, and various young German playwrights such as Tankred Dorst or Richard Hey. The German *Hörspiel* (radio drama), whenever it has attained the status of a genuine and unique art form, has exploited precisely this built-in placelessness of its medium. Although the novel tends to cling more closely to its roots in realism, the realistic abstraction has a distinguished forerunner in the fiction of Franz Kafka, and it has found contemporary exponents in writers such as Albert Camus, Alfred Andersch, or William Golding. None of their works could be called utopias; none, on the other hand, could be termed realistic depictions. What they have in common is a concern with immediate and recognizable human problems, abstracted to the extent that the situations transcend the specific and become general or universal; yet they maintain a freedom of characterization that distinguishes them in turn from simple allegory.

A definition of this sort seems to be implicit in all the utterances in which Hesse seeks to explain the implications of his novel. "Actually, in the book I was thinking neither of a utopia (in the sense of a dogmatic program) nor of a prophecy; rather, I tried to portray something that I consider to be one of the genuine and legitimate ideas, the realization of which one can sense at many points of world history."[29] In another letter he emphasizes the fact that Castalia is merely the representation of a mode of life that already exists. "In connection with Castalia one must consider that it is not only—not even primarily—a utopia, a dream, and a future, but also reality. For orders, Platonic academies, yoga schools—all of these have existed often and for a long time."[30] In a letter to Thomas Mann, Hesse praises in *Doctor Faustus* precisely the qualities that he had striven to achieve in his own novel: ". . . the way in which this set of problems is transferred into the realm of music and analyzed there with the calmness and objectivity that are possible only in the abstract. What I find most astonishing and surprising is the fact that you do not allow this pure extract, this ideal abstraction to soar out into an ideal realm, but that you locate it in the midst of

[29] Letter of January, 1944; GS, VII, 637.
[30] Letter of February 22, 1944; GS, VII, 640.

a realistically visualized world and time. . . ."[31] This analysis amounts to a definition of the realistic abstraction and might well be the structural principle underlying Hesse's own book.

Hesse was not trying to represent an ideal or utopian society. Instead, after his devastating satire of the "feuilletonistic age" in the introduction, he goes on to lay bare the dangers of its antithesis: a purely intellectually or aesthetically oriented existence that lives without commitment to the world around it. This exposé is accomplished in an abstracted vision of society, but it is no less a plea for engagement and commitment than other more naturalistic works of our own generation. The reasons for Knecht's defection are made quite clear in the course of the novel; it is more difficult to account for Hesse's own swing from the aestheticism attained in *The Journey to the East* to the commitment to life and to fellow man symbolized by the ending of *The Glass Bead Game*. However, in 1932 it was far easier to maintain an attitude of detached aestheticism than was the case during the succeeding decade of world history. The first signs of disenchantment with the aesthetic ideal can be detected in the poems that Hesse wrote in the middle thirties, a selection of which was later included in the novel as Knecht's own work.

The Untenable Ideal

The "Lives," as we saw, were written from a positive attitude toward Castalia and their inclusion was subsequently justified on the grounds that they represented official studies of Knecht as a student. Hesse obviously realized the self-contradiction implicit in the poems, which, for the most part, reject that same ideal. As a result, they

[31] Letter of December 12, 1947; GS, VII, 669.

are explained by the narrator as being surreptitious products of Knecht's first doubts—poems written expressly in opposition to the rules of the institution and preserved secretly in manuscript form. The narrator is aware of the crisis manifested in the poems. "In certain lines there resounds a deep sense of disquiet, a basic doubt in himself and in the meaning of his existence, until in the poem 'The Glass Bead Game' the devout submission seems to have been achieved."[32] From the vantage point of our knowledge concerning the genesis of the novel, this explanation is not lacking in a certain irony. The poem that the narrator mentions as expressing the resolution of Knecht's conflicts—the one printed last in the collection—was actually written in 1934 *before* all the other poems. "The Glass Bead Game," which does indeed reveal full approval of the aesthetic ideal, dates from the same year as the introduction. The other more skeptical poems were written later—mainly in 1935 and 1936, during the crucial transitional period—but in order to satisfy the fiction of the novel the early poem was arranged as the final one. According to the plot Knecht's early doubts had to be resolved for a time! This is another example of the careful structuring through which Hesse sought to integrate the diverse materials of his novel as it changed in conception and perspective. By and large, I believe that the attempt was successful, for few readers, without a knowledge of the genesis, would guess the true order of composition.

To return to the earlier question: other poems, written at a later date, reveal Hesse's own doubts regarding the validity of his original ideal. "The Last Magister Ludi," written in 1938, is typical in this connection, for it shows that the imminent war in Europe was making a travesty of his aesthetic realm. The poem depicts the last magister, an old man, sitting alone in a land devastated by battle. At one time he had been a famous man, surrounded by eager hordes of students and admirers. Now he is antiquated, useless in a changed world:

> Jetzt blieb er übrig, alt, verbraucht, allein,
> Es wirbt kein Jünger mehr um seinen Segen,
> Es lädt ihn kein Magister zum Disput;
> Sie sind dahin, und auch die Tempel, Büchereien,
> Schulen Kastaliens sind nicht mehr. . . .

> (Now he was left, old, exhausted, alone.
> No longer do disciples seek his blessing,
> No magister invites him to debate.
> They are gone, and also the temples, libraries,
> Schools of Castalia are no longer. . . .)

Even the beads, which once symbolized the total synthesis of knowledge in his aesthetic realm, have lost their meaning and roll noiselessly into the sand.

It does not require much imagination to realize that the vision of an aesthetic kingdom had to pale before the harsh reality of the war that threatened, in 1938, to engulf and destroy Europe. Hesse realized that his ideal, which had sufficed for a time, must give way to another view of reality. Castalia was but one transitory stage in his own development and not the permanent utopia that he had conceived in 1933 and 1934. The latest poem in the group, "Steps" (1941), best expresses the idea that constant progress—Gide's *disponibilité*—is necessary, that every ideal must be transcended:

> Wir sollen heiter Raum um Raum durchschreiten,
> An keinem wie an einer Heimat hängen,
> Der Weltgeist will nicht fesseln uns und engen,
> Er will uns Stuf' um Stufe heben, weiten.

(We must cheerfully pass through one area
after the other,
Clinging to none as though it were home;
The world spirit does not wish to fetter and hem
us in;
It wishes to raise and enlarge us, step by step.)

The last lines, finally, imply the new commitment to life
that ultimately motivates Knecht's defection:

Des Lebens Ruf an uns wird niemals enden . . .
Wohlan denn, Herz, nimm Abschied und gesunde!

(Life's call to us will never end . . .
Very well, then, heart—take leave and recover!)

The structure of Castalia can most easily be grasped
as a realistic abstraction based upon other hierarchical
organizations of world history—most notably the Roman
Catholic Church. Castalia is a concept that emerged only
after the introduction was written. In the introduction the
word "Castalia" does not occur; the narrator speaks of
"the order," "the hierarchy," "the academy"; but it is
described in only the most general terms. The description,
moreover, does not correspond in every detail to the elaborate hierarchy developed in the body of the book. Like
the idealized conception of the Glass Bead Game, this is
a structural inconsistency that was not obviated in the
final version. In the introduction the (nameless) institution is centered exclusively on the game itself, and the
Magister Ludi is the supreme head of the order. In Hesse's
subsequent relativized conception the Magister Ludi is
only one member of a commission that embraces all areas
of intellectual endeavor. It is methodologically false to consider remarks on these two different stages of the Castalian
idea as though they represented the same institution.

Castalia is a rigidly hierarchical institution that branches down from the directorate of twenty members to the elite schools in which the members of the order are trained. In this hierarchy more than the Glass Bead Game is represented; there are altogether thirteen disciplines in the College of Masters. In addition to the Magister Ludi we hear of a Magister Musicae, Magister Philologiae, as well as masters of meditation, mathematics, philosophy, physics, pedagogy, astronomy, and other fields. In this system the Magister Ludi is substantially reduced in importance, and he distinguishes himself principally by the fact that his discipline is most remote from the world of everyday life. Physics, mathematics, and the other subjects have a useful function in the world outside. The Glass Bead Game, practiced only within the province, is the most endangered area of Castalia since it will be the first to disappear if once the purely aesthetic values represented by the province should be questioned and outside support withdrawn. The other disciplines could conceivably justify and support themselves—not the game.

More significant than the details of the organization is the fact that it is consciously patterned after the Roman Catholic Church. (In the chapter on *Narziss and Goldmund* we considered Hesse's attitude toward the Church as an institution.) Superficially the hierarchy from the elite schools upward to the College of Masters resembles the ladder from the Catholic seminaries up to the College of Cardinals. The rules of the order stipulate poverty and celibacy. The narrator employs phrases like *ad maiorem gloriam Castaliae*, which are overtly based upon the liturgy. And the annual *ludus sollennis* is described in terms that might equally well be applied to the Pope's Easter message. Hesse has not, of course, written a Catholic novel any more than he copied Goethe's pedagogical province. It is stated repeatedly in the course of the book that the Church maintained an attitude of hostility or reserve toward Castalia and its principles. Yet in constructing his spiritual realm, Hesse turned to the hierarchical institution whose organization he most admired.

It belongs to the nature of the realistic abstraction that it enriches the texture of its abstract construct with details instantly identifiable as realistic. The Church, in this sense, contributes texturally rather than structurally or contextually to the novel. The same may be said of the various Chinese elements that give the novel its unique tone.[33] To take a specific example: on several occasions Knecht consults the book of wisdom *I Ging* in order to confirm his decisions or to plan his course. These prophetic utterances fit so naturally into the development of plot and theme that they seem almost, like the motto, to have been written by Hesse himself. Actually, they are taken verbatim from Richard Wilhelm's translation of the Chinese classic and thus contribute richly to the realistic texture of the fiction. This is but another example of the careful montage technique that Hesse, like Thomas Mann in *Doctor Faustus*, uses here with such virtuosity. But montage is not essentially a structural principle, but rather a device used, as we observed, to give a realistic texture to the basically abstract structure.

Pater Jacobus Burckhardt

Knecht's rejection of the aesthetic realm is the result of a gradual process that he calls "awakening," but it is precipitated consciously by his conversations with the brilliant Benedictine historian, Pater Jacobus. Like so many of the names in the novel, Pater Jacobus is a hidden tribute to a figure from real life. Thomas von der Trave has been identified as a reference to Thomas Mann, born in Lübeck on the Trave; Carlo Ferromonte is a Latinization of the name of Hesse's nephew Karl Isenberg; and practically every other name has some association—more or less private—in Hesse's own life.[34] In the case of the Benedictine father, Hesse has made an explicit reference: ". . . for my ability to see Castalia, my utopia, in its relativity, I am indebted to the Jacobus from whom the Pater got his name: Jacob Burckhardt."[35] Burckhardt belongs, along with Nietzsche and Bachofen, to the triumvirate of Swiss thinkers who decisively affected Hesse's ideas, and his interest in the Basel historian is well documented. In 1951 Hesse published a newspaper account of his early years in Basel (1899-1903), while he was still a young bookdealer: "Here everything was saturated by the spirit, the influence and the example of the man who for several decades had served intellectual Basel as a teacher and, in cultural affairs, as *arbiter elegantiarum*. His name was Jacob Burckhardt, and he had died only a few years earlier. Even at that time I read him, of course. In Tübingen I had read *The Culture of the Renaissance* and, in Basel, *Constantine*. But I was still too deeply enchanted by Nietzsche to be completely susceptible to his direct influence. The indirect influence was all the more powerful. I lived, a receptive young man eager to learn, in the midst of a circle of people whose knowledge and interests, whose reading and travels, whose way of thinking, conception of history and conversation were influenced and shaped by no one so much as Jacob Burckhardt."[36] In

[34] See Joseph Mileck, "Names and the Creative Process," *Monatshefte*, 53 (1961), 167-80.

[35] Letter of November 1, 1943; GS, VII, 637.

[36] "Ein paar Basler Erinnerungen"; quoted in *Hermann Hesse: Eine Chronik in Bildern*, ed. Bernard Zeller (Suhrkamp, 1960), p. 36.

1946, in the preface to his essays on *War and Peace*, Hesse mentions three great influences that shaped his thinking: the Christian and non-nationalistic spirit of his parental home, the great Chinese writers, and "the only historian to whom I was ever devoted in trust, reverence and grateful discipleship: Jacob Burckhardt."[37] This last testimonial must be read with a grain of salt: it was written in 1946 by a man no longer young, who chose to forget the immense impact that more romantic spirits such as Nietzsche and Jung, Dostoevsky and Bachofen had exerted upon him at crucial stages in his career. Yet in the present connection the date is relevant, for the remark was written shortly after the completion of *The Glass Bead Game*. In general, the references to Burckhardt are far more frequent in the letters and essays of the thirties and forties than was the case earlier, and the influence of Burckhardt on the novel is unmistakable.

In addition to his name Pater Jacobus owes at least one of his remarks, literally, to Burckhardt. Knecht closes his circular letter to the officials at Castalia with a quotation from the Pater: "Times of terror and of deepest misery may come. If, however, there is to be any happiness in the midst of the misery, it can be only a spiritual happiness: facing backward for the preservation of the achievements of the past and facing forward toward the serene and undismayed representation of the spirit in a time that might otherwise capitulate wholly to material concerns."[38] With the exception of the first sentence, this paragraph is taken word for word from Burckhardt's study of "The Revolutionary Age"[39] and built into the texture of the

[37] "Geleitwort zur Ausgabe *Krieg und Frieden* 1946"; GS, VII, 435.

[38] GD, VI, 472.

[39] "Das Revolutionszeitalter," in Jacob Burckhardt, *Historische Fragmente aus dem Nachlass. Gesamtausgabe* (Berlin & Leipzig,

novel like other passages from *I Ging*, Novalis, and Nietzsche—a use of the quotation strikingly similar to that of Thomas Mann in *Doctor Faustus*.

We are concerned here, however, with the deeper implications of Burckhardt's thought for Hesse's novel, and in this connection the series of lectures published posthumously as *Observations on World History* are of central importance. Here Burckhardt expressed the principles according to which his great historical studies were carried out. Three main ideas seem to have made the most profound impression on Hesse. The first is Burckhardt's categorical rejection of all philosophy of history, which he called "a centaur, a *contradictio in adjecto*."[40] According to Burckhardt the study of history is the coordination of facts, not the subordination of facts to a system, as is the goal of all philosophy. He refused to view history as a dialectical process, but sought in the past the constant and typical elements: in a word, the exemplary facts that repeat themselves unceasingly. Hand in hand with this goes the second point, namely Burckhardt's insistence on the relativity of human institutions. He sees permanency in the human spirit and regards history as a "spiritual continuum."[41] But the temporal manifestation of this spirit in institutions is highly relative: "The spirit is mutable, but not transitory."[42] Finally, Burckhardt regards civilization and history as the interaction of three powers or forces upon one another: the state, religion, and culture. We shall take up the third of these points in a later section. The first two belong together as the basis for Knecht's

---

1929), VII, 426. The passage was originally identified by G. F. Hering, "Burckhardts Worte im Glasperlenspiel," *Die Zeit*, Nr. 28 (July 10, 1947), p. 6.

[40] *Weltgeschichtliche Betrachtungen*, ed. Rudolf Marx (7th ed Stuttgart, 1949), p. 4.

[41] *Ibid.*, p. 9.   [42] *Ibid.*, p. 7.

defection from Castalia, for they summarize, in brief, his rejection of the aesthetic abstraction of the Glass Bead Game and his realization that Castalia, as an institution, can claim no eternal validity.

Although Hesse, by his own acknowledgment, derived his thoughts largely from Burckhardt, Joseph Knecht's process of "awakening" is portrayed as a gradual one that simply was precipitated in his conversations with Pater Jacobus. "Awakening" is the name that Knecht applies to the existential experience of reality in contrast to the abstract view of life that is practiced in Castalia; it is a form of the epiphany that Siddhartha experienced in his development. This "awakening" impels Knecht ultimately to forsake the exclusive *vita contemplativa* of Castalia for a tentative *vita activa* of commitment in the world. "In the state of awakening one did not penetrate more closely to the core of things, to the truth; one grasped, carried out or suffered only the relationship of one's own Self to the momentary state of affairs. One did not discover laws, but made decisions."[43] Instead of standing at a distance and analyzing a situation intellectually, one felt involved and committed to the moment.

One result of this "awakening" is the serene bliss characterized by the smile and gaze of certain Castalians, a serenity that the narrator defines as "the affirmation of all reality, the state of awakeness on the brink of all depths and abysses."[44] Another implication is the phenomenon of ineffability that we have observed earlier in connection with such epiphany-like awakenings. On several occasions Knecht relates that the experience of these moments is essentially inexpressible, that it is impossible "to make rational what is obviously extra-rational."[45] These moments take him into an area beyond the periphery of

[43] GD, vi, 490-91.   [44] GD, vi, 419.   [45] GD, vi, 508.

experience that can be reduced to the abstractions current in Castalia. "Communication from this realm of life seemed not to be among the functions of language"[46]— that is, rational expression as it is known to the Castalians. It is worth noting that even the vocabulary of these passages—though not technically existentialist—would not be unfamiliar to philosophers such as Karl Jaspers or Sartre. The almost overwhelming sensation of the reality of things, the necessity for decision and action, the *Grenzsituation* on the brink of despair—these belong to the lingua franca of existentialism in its various forms. This existential attitude, of course, implies a criticism of the very foundations of the Glass Bead Game, which is based upon the assumption that a situation or process can be grasped in its abstracted essence, which can in turn be compared with other abstractions so as to construct an elaborate aesthetic structure.

Knecht's inner doubts are first stirred during his years at the school in Waldzell, when he engages regularly in debates with Plinio Designori. (It was these early misgivings that ostensibly produced the poems appended to the biography.) In these debates Plinio advocates the role of Life as opposed to pure, disengaged intellect. "I have to remind you again and again," he argues, "how daring, dangerous and, in the last analysis, unfruitful a life is if it is directed exclusively toward the mind."[47] Though Knecht distinguishes himself by a skillful justification of Castalia and its form of existence, he is persuaded inwardly that his own realm does not embrace all life, as he had supposed before. "The whole of life, physical as well as mental, is a dynamic phenomenon, of which the Glass Bead Game encompasses only the aesthetic aspect."[48] Already here the keynote is sounded: the Glass Bead

[46] GD, vi, 491.   [47] GD, vi, 184.   [48] GD, vi, 186.

Game and Castalia are identified as aesthetic views of life rather than as points of view that can be totally satisfying and all-embracing.

The most conspicuous personification of the dangers inherent in pure aestheticism is Knecht's friend Fritz Tegularius, who has been persuasively identified by Joseph Mileck as a characterization of Friedrich Nietzsche.[49] Tegularius, like Nietzsche a classical philologist, is a brilliant adept at the Glass Bead Game. He is unequalled in his capacity for sharp analysis, but his physical frailty and emotional lability make him unfit for any position of authority or responsibility. Characteristically, Pater Jacobus reacts against Tegularius just as Burckhardt recoiled from Nietzsche. Like Nietzsche, Tegularius has a strong aversion to the study of history as such, conceding only that the *philosophy* of history can be an amusing pastime. In one of his conversations with Tegularius, Knecht objects to the excessive abstractionism represented by his friend's attitude. "Not everybody can breathe, eat and drink abstractions exclusively for a whole lifetime. History has one advantage over those things that a tutor at Waldzell deems worthy of his attention: it deals with reality. Abstractions are delightful, but I support the view that one must also breathe air and eat bread."[50] In the novel Tegularius embodies the extremes that pure aestheticism can attain, and he serves as a living warning to Knecht, who understands him so well. At the same time, he represents a stage in Hesse's own development—an attitude of anti-historism expressed most forcefully in an essay on "World History" (1918) written during the period when Hesse was most directly under the influence of Nietzsche. In that essay Hesse polemicizes specifically against the historical op-

[49] "Names and the Creative Process," p. 175.
[50] GD, VI, 377.

portunism of intellectuals and others who adapt their view of history to the political exigencies of the moment. But he lets himself be carried away, maintaining that true poets and religious thinkers can never succeed in thinking historically. He anticipates reproaches of the sort to be made twenty years later by Pater Jacobus: "I hear the voices of those who see in our unhistorical and apolitical thinking nothing but the blasé indifference of 'intellectuals.' "[51] Probably no quotation better illustrates Hesse's remark that, in those early days, he was too much under the influence of Nietzsche to be responsive to Burckhardt's ideas.

Most Castalians live in complete ignorance of the dangers inherent in the system and of the threat from an outside world that might one day weary of supporting an institution that was becoming more and more autonomous in its disengagement from reality. Only a few political officials are alert to these dangers, and it is Dubois, the chief of the political bureau, who indoctrinates Knecht before his mission to Mariafels. Dubois points out that Castalia, contrary to the widespread fancy of most Castalians, is indeed dependent upon the world outside and not an autotelic aesthetic realm that can exist indefinitely by itself.

Despite all earlier premonitions, however, it is Pater Jacobus who articulates the suspicions that had up to now remained more or less inchoate in Knecht's mind. Knecht's reaction to Plinio Designori was instinctive. Dubois' comments dealt with practical matters. Pater Jacobus is the first person who appeals to Knecht's mind. He criticizes the illusory nature of an "intellectual-aesthetic spirituality" that exists without any real foundation in life. "You treat world history as a mathematician treats mathematics,

[51] "Weltgeschichte"; GS, VII, 121-26.

where there are only laws and formulas, but no reality, no good and evil, no time, no yesterday, no tomorrow—only an eternal, flat, mathematical present."[52] Pater Jacobus intensifies Knecht's reservations about a purely aesthetic culture and then adds to this the new ingredient of historism. The Castalians, he says, are great scholars and aestheticians, but their total concern is only a game. "Your supreme mystery and symbol is nothing but a game—the Glass Bead Game."[53] He makes no attempt to convert Knecht, remarking disparagingly that Castalia is too remote from life even to comprehend theological questions. He is concerned above all because Castalia has cut itself off from the world. "You don't know what men are like, their bestiality and their likeness unto God. You know only the Castalian—a specialty, a caste, a rare experiment in breeding."[54] Gradually, through his conversations with the Pater, Knecht comes to realize that the greatest deficiency in his own education and the greatest threat to Castalia is the total lack of political awareness in the broad sense of the word: a knowledge of human relations. He was even, to his own dismay, uninformed about the historical circumstances that had attended the establishment of Castalia. From this time on the conversations between the two revolve more and more about contemporary political issues, dealing specifically with Knecht's own potential role in history. Knecht begins to think of himself no longer as an aesthete dwelling apart in an absolute and timeless realm, but as a man engaged in life and swept along by the tide of history.

The Symbols of Resolution

Shortly after Knecht's return from Mariafels he is elected to the position of Magister Ludi, an office that he

[52] GD, VI, 251.   [53] GD, VI, 273.   [54] GD, VI, 274.

fills with honor and devotion for eight years. Up to the
very day of his defection he carries out his duties so
meticulously that of his closest associates only Tegularius
is aware of his inner turmoil. The theme of inner conflict
is paralleled by the motif of outer representation (a motif
often strong in the works of Thomas Mann). This produces the frequently incongruous situation that Knecht,
after performing a brilliant public Glass Bead Game, is
able in the next instant to warn his students of the dangers
that lie in store for Castalia. The years spent with Pater
Jacobus produce two practical effects in Knecht's life
during his tenure as Magister Ludi. First, he begins to
concern himself deeply with the history of Castalia and
the Glass Bead Game, seeking to determine its function
and position in the history of the world. Secondly, he
begins to think of his office—as Magister Ludi—less in an
abstract sense and more in literal terms: that is, as a
schoolmaster engaged in practical teaching, rather than as
a mandarin of the aesthetic game. Since he recognizes now
the dangers of excessive abstraction, he hopes to eradicate
these evils at a basic level by giving a proper introduction to pupils in the most elementary principles. If it is
too late to heal types like Tegularius, at least—he hopes—
he can prevent the growth of others. Both of the teachings
of Pater Jacobus have left their mark on Knecht. At the
same time, he is aware of his own limitations. He does
not urge an abrupt turn from aesthetics into the world of
politics and action—there is too much of Castalia in him.
"We should not flee from the *vita activa* into a *vita contemplativa*, nor vice-versa; rather, we should be alternately
in both, at home in both, participating in both."[55]

By the end of his eighth year in office Knecht is still
dissatisfied. His efforts to reconstruct Castalia from within

[55] GD, VI, 329.

have had some success, but only relatively so. In the first place, he realizes that the institution is too vast to be changed in the lifetime of one man, no matter how strenuous his efforts may be. Secondly, all his action has been within the aesthetic province, with no effect whatsoever on the wide world outside. His failure is brought home to him vividly when he sees Plinio Designori again after many years. Plinio had left the province originally with the intention of bridging the gap between Castalia and the world, of injecting the spirit of Castalia into his functions as a statesman in the world outside. But he failed, and his failure has embittered him toward Castalia. His struggles have left their mark upon him, for his face shows lines of character unaccustomed among Castalians, whose lives are spent in a serene, unabrasive atmosphere. When Knecht sees Plinio, he realizes how futile his own attempts at reform had been. Confined as he was to Castalia, he had been spared all contact with the world of life. Knecht resolves, after careful deliberation, to give up his position in Castalia and to fulfill his function—that of a teacher, not a man of affairs—in the world outside. He outlines his reasons in detail in a letter to the authorities of Castalia, but basically they are variations on the two themes that we have been considering: the dangers of isolated aestheticism and the historical relativity of Castalia.

Knecht's "awakening," a gradual process that takes place over a period of some thirty years, is the central theme of the novel. The ultimate resolution of Knecht's inner doubts in the synthesis of *vita activa* and *vita contemplativa*, however, is anticipated throughout the novel in the symbol of music. In *The Glass Bead Game* music does not have the structural function that it had in *The Steppenwolf*, but it is equally important in other respects. It supplies much of the texture of the story and forms the substance of many essayistic passages in which the history and theory of music are discussed. Most of all, music as a symbol provides the counterpole to the game itself. If aestheticism as exemplified by the game marks the outset of the novel, a synthesis of life and spirit as manifested in music anticipates the finish. Music, as we have seen, provided the original basis for the game and has remained, throughout its history, a central discipline in Castalia— a branch represented by Knecht's friend Carlo Ferromonte. Symbolically, however, music embodies the synthesis of aesthetics and actions that Knecht finds at the end of the book. This chord is struck in the introduction when the narrator quotes a passage from *Spring and Fall* by the Chinese philosopher Lu Bu We, to the effect that music arises from the harmony of Yin and Yang, the two poles of life. If either pole—intellectuality or sensuality—prevails, then music degenerates, marking a decline in the civilization that produces it. Precisely this conception of music is advanced by the most harmonious figure in the novel, the man who more than anyone else embodies an ideal vision of Castalia: the old Magister Musicae. Even before Knecht's admission to Waldzell, the master warns him of the dangers inherent in the game, which tends to deal only with the cerebral aspects of music, ignoring its sensual elements. The Magister Musicae is the only figure in the novel, apart from Knecht himself, who experiences life existentially rather than abstractly, and his warning to Knecht early in the novel anticipates the ending. "Divinity is in you, not in concepts and books. Truth is lived, not taught."[56] In his own lectures as Magister Ludi, after his awakening through Pater Jacobus, Knecht repeats this message. He warns his students that music is made with the hands and the fingers, the mouth and the lungs—not

[56] GD, VI, 157.

with the brain alone. A man who can read music but not play an instrument cannot claim to be a competent musician, for music more than all other arts demands a synthesis of the abstract and the concrete. This view determines Knecht's attitude toward the history of music. He regards the music of the nineteenth and twentieth centuries as degenerate since there the sensuous elements outweigh the intellectual. In the Glass Bead Game, on the other hand, the opposite danger prevails: too often the purely intellectual is abstracted from the full substance. For Knecht perfection in music is achieved in the period 1500-1800 (specifically by Bach), in which a delicate balance of the intellectual and the sensual is maintained. Just as the Glass Bead Game is an adequate symbol of pure aestheticism, this conception of music as the synthesis of the poles of life corresponds admirably to the theme that it symbolizes.[57]

The Three Powers

Joseph Knecht's life differs markedly from that of almost all other Castalians—whether they are typical members, extremists like Tegularius, representative like Thomas von der Trave, or idealized like the old Magister Musicae—because their lives are spent within the confines of Castalia while his carries him, on the one hand, into the monastery of Mariafels and, on the other, into the world and the home of Plinio Designori. If we ask why Hesse chose to deal specifically with these areas of life—after all, it is a step beyond the customary duality of nature and spirit that we have encountered in the earlier

---

[57] This conception of music as resolution is identical with the function of music in Hermann Broch's novels (especially *Der Versucher*), but quite different from the more Romantic and demonic conception of Thomas Mann in *Doctor Faustus* and earlier works, in which music is regarded as a symbol of irrationality.

works—it seems reasonable to assume that the influence of Burckhardt has again made itself felt. Here the influence is not restricted as in the preceding considerations to questions of theme, but it actually determines the structure of the work.

Burckhardt devotes the two central chapters of his *Observations on World History* to a definition of the three powers—state, religion, culture—and to a discussion of their interaction.[58] State and religion are expressions of the political and metaphysical needs of mankind that he regards as universal. Culture, on the other hand, is the sum of mankind's intellectual achievements—technical, artistic, poetic, scientific—and varies or adapts itself from age to age. In these areas he sees an expression of three basic needs of mankind, and he insists that the most fruitful approach to history is through the study of these areas in their interaction.

The Glass Bead Game deals with the three powers that Burckhardt outlines. They may constitute an arbitrary division of human activity—Burckhardt anticipates the objection. Yet they are the three areas that he chooses to define and that Hesse employs in his novel. This is especially striking in view of Hesse's earlier novels in which theme played an important structural role. In *Siddhartha*, for instance, we found theme projected into landscape: the two sides of the river, symbolizing nature and spirit. The same polarity was exploited, in a different way, in *Narziss and Goldmund*, where the monastery and the world outside again represented life and spirit, where actual geographical location could express thematic tension. Beyond these two works, what we have seen in every case—the "two worlds" of *Demian* as well as the

[58] *Weltgeschichtliche Betrachtungen*: Chapter 2, "Von den drei Potenzen"; Chapter 3, "Die Betrachtung der sechs Bedingtheiten."

contrast between Haller's library and Pablo's jazz den in *The Steppenwolf*—is a basic *duality*. So it is instantly striking to find in the last novel *three* symbolic areas of activity. Pater Jacobus is explicitly a representative of the Church and the authority of religion. Plinio Designori is a statesman involved deeply in the political affairs of the world. And Castalia can almost be described by Burckhardt's definition of culture: "We call culture the entire sum of those developments of the mind that occur spontaneously and make no claim upon universal or compulsory validity. . . . Furthermore, it is that multiform process by means of which naïve and impulsive action is transformed into reflective ability—yes, in its last and highest stage (science and especially philosophy) into pure reflection."[59] The last phrase even expands the definition to embrace an implicit criticism of the hyperintellectual abstractionism of Castalia.

The narrative chapters of the novel constitute an architectonically structured work. In the first three chapters— "The Call," "Waldzell," "Years of Study"—the development of incidents is determined almost programmatically by the hierarchic organization of Castalia. Knecht's early life, and, to outside observers, even his later years are in many respects exemplary. "Undisturbed by sudden disclosures and indiscretions the noble process took place— the typical boyhood and early history of every noble mind. Harmoniously and evenly inner world and outer world worked and grew toward each other."[60] In no other work of German literature besides Adalbert Stifter's *Indian Summer* (*Der Nachsommer*) and Novalis' *Heinrich von Ofterdingen* (both of which Hesse admired immensely) is the development of a young man depicted with such classical evenness and with such a total absence

[59] *Ibid.*, p. 57.   [60] GD, VI, 130-31.

of abrasive conflict as in these early chapters. In this world even death has lost its sting. The few deaths mentioned are so tranquil and ethereal that they fit unobtrusively into the pattern of Castalian existence, providing no shock for those concerned. Characteristic of this invalidation of death is the portrayal of the last days of the old Magister Musicae. "He was not sick, and his death was not actually an act of dying; it was a progressive dematerialization, a disappearance of the bodily substance and the bodily functions."[61] The old man vanishes, almost like the Cheshire Cat, behind the glow of his serene smile. In the absolute aesthetic realm of Castalia—the timeless, mathematical present that Pater Jacobus decried—the threat of death has been annulled. To this extent the novel, as a *Bildungsroman,* differs from traditional representatives of the genre from Goethe's *Wilhelm Meister's Apprenticeship* or Gottfried Keller's *Green Henry* down to Thomas Mann's *The Magic Mountain,* in all of which death—and in general the abrasive conflict between the hero and reality—plays an important role. As Hesse has pointed out, young Knecht was intended to symbolize the inner meaning of Castalia in its loftiest manifestation, and in these three opening chapters theory and practice of Castalia merge into a smooth, flowing development.

These chapters are followed by two that describe Knecht's mission to Mariafels and his conversations with Pater Jacobus. From this point on the tension between theory and actuality provides the narrative impulse. After Mariafels, another group of three chapters depicts Knecht's return to Castalia and his years as Magister Ludi. On the surface the harmony of the early years is maintained by Knecht's sense of responsibility and his conception of his representative function. The two chapters defining the

[61] GD, VI, 377.

area of religion are paralleled by two that introduce the area of the state: Plinio's return for a visit in Castalia and Knecht's conversations with him as well as his visit to Plinio's home in the world outside. These four groups of parallel chapters—idealized culture, religion, relativized culture, state—complete the development of the novel. In the last two the logical conclusions are drawn. In "The Circular Letter," Knecht outlines to the authorities the reasons for his defection, but no new arguments are advanced; the chapter is a summation of what has preceded. "The Legend" relates the story of Knecht's brief excursion into the world and his death. The rigid structuring of the chapters indicates beyond a doubt that Hesse, whether he consciously followed Burckhardt or not, was interested in defining precisely the same three areas of human activity with which the historian was concerned. In view of his own acknowledgment of indebtedness to the Swiss historian, we are probably justified in assuming that this structure is consciously patterned after Burckhardt's three powers.

The question of the interaction of these areas is far more interesting and, I believe, equally plausible. Here lies the key to the meaning of the novel. The much discussed relationship Knecht-Tito, namely, represents merely one of the four possibilities of interaction that concerned Hesse in the novel. As we anticipated in our discussion of the narrator, the true beneficiary of Knecht's sacrifice is neither Knecht nor Tito nor Plinio nor any of the other figures of the novel; but rather, the later generation represented by the anonymous narrator. Some critics have asserted that the narrator lives in an age of decline, that he is an epigonal figure. This claim cannot be documented by the text. From the point of view of the introduction, to be sure, some such interpretation might be made. But the narrator of Knecht's life is not writing from the same

point of view—an inconsistency that we have already
noted. This narrator represents the Castalia of which
Knecht dreamed. The game is no longer played so bril-
liantly, but from the standpoint of the mature Knecht, that
is an improvement rather than a decline. As the narrator
points out, "there exists in recent times in the directorate
of the order a tendency to discard certain specialties in
the pursuit of knowledge, which were felt to be over-
refined, and to compensate for this by an intensification in
the practice of meditation."[62] The abstract aestheticism
symbolized by the game has given way to a Castalia more
fully attuned to the other two areas of life: religion and
the state. Knecht was dismayed, for instance, by the historical ignorance and political naïveté of Castalia when he
returned from his mission to Mariafels. The narrator is
fully aware of the historical circumstances surrounding the
origins of Castalia and of the position that Castalia occupies with relation to the other powers. Knecht dies before
he is able to see any of his hopes realized; Plinio is already
an old and weary man; Knecht's contemporaries in Castalia are unmoved by his eloquent pleas for reform; and
Tito, though the ending of the novel suggests that his life
will be changed by Knecht's death, is just one person.
Only the processes of history, directed by the actions of
Knecht's life, can bring about the changes for which he
hoped—no single individual. The nameless narrator, writing years after Knecht's death, is the living voice of a
Castalia that has achieved what Knecht was striving to
bring about. The processes that made possible this new
and ideal Castalia were catalyzed by Knecht's symbolic
interaction with Pater Jacobus and Plinio. His death is a
moving symbol of his commitment to life and fellow man,
of his rejection of Castalian aestheticism and abstraction.

[62] GD, VI, 374.

But it would be romantic to interpret the entire long novel simply from the standpoint of Knecht's death, which comes so suddenly in the last few pages of the book—so suddenly, indeed, that it has struck some critics as an arbitrary ending.[63] His life, which was devoted to an instigation of the interactions of which Burckhardt spoke, is vastly more meaningful than his death. Hesse himself has indicated something of the sort in a remark of Pater Jacobus that Knecht passes on to his friends. "Great men are, for youth, the raisins in the pastry of world history."[64] But the Pater (and by implication Hesse) goes on to say that the mature mind is interested, rather, in the history and development of great institutions. This observation, applied to the novel, means that the significance of Knecht's life in any but an exemplary sense must not be overstressed; it is the development of Castalia and its relations with the other two powers that are of true significance— even *after* Knecht's spectacular death, which is so dramatic that it threatens to overshadow the meaning of his life!

We have seen how Knecht's development was affected by Pater Jacobus. It has not so frequently been observed what an impact Knecht, in turn, made upon the Pater and what vast implications their friendship had for the future of Castalia. Knecht is sent to Mariafels ostensibly to give instruction in the art of the Glass Bead Game to a few interested monks. He soon observes, however, that he has been sent as much to learn as to teach. After two years his stay in the monastery is given a more specific direction. At the time of the story there exists an attitude of cool suspicion on the part of the Church toward Castalia. The Castalian authorities hope that Knecht, by capitalizing on the favorable impression that he had made on Pater

[63] See Curt von Faber du Faur, "Zu Hermann Hesses *Glasperlenspiel*," *Monatshefte*, 40 (1948), 177-194.
[64] GD, VI, 252.

Jacobus, can persuade that influential personage to give his approval to an official diplomatic exchange between the two powers. The Pater, who begins with vociferous criticism of Castalia's aestheticism and anti-historism, gradually begins to perceive the merits of a pedagogical province that could produce a man like Knecht. He agrees to the proposed establishment of diplomatic relations. One of the narrator's remarks indicates that a strong bond of interaction did actually develop as a result of the friendship between Knecht and the Pater. "How attentively the Pater followed Knecht's elucidations and how extensively, through them, he came to know and to acknowledge Castalia, is revealed by his subsequent attitude. To these two men we owe the understanding between Rome and Castalia that reaches down to the present day. It began with benevolent neutrality and occasional scholarly exchange and has developed with each subsequent contact into true collaboration and confederation."[65] As this statement proves, the major effect of the friendship and initial interaction took place later—that is, only after Knecht's death, as a historical process.

We observed, on the other hand, how Knecht's friendship with Plinio Designori, from the date of their early disputes at Waldzell, made Knecht aware of the claims of life and the state upon Castalia. Plinio's own ambitions, in turn, reveal how anxious he is to bring about a synthesis of Castalia and the state—an attempt in which he failed. In his debates with Plinio as well as the Pater, the narrator reminds us, Knecht "succeeded in compelling them to acknowledge honorably his person as well as the principle and ideal that he represented."[66] Previously the relationship between these foreign areas had been marked by an almost total inability to communicate. In one of his discussions

[65] GD, VI, 281.   [66] GD, VI, 364.

with Plinio, Knecht concedes that absolute communication among men is probably impossible. "Yet if we are of good will, then we can still communicate very much to each other and can guess or surmise much that transcends what is exactly communicable."[67] The alienation between Castalia and the state is another problem that, implicitly, is solved by the time of the narrator of the biography. In contrast to the perspective in the introduction, he is able to assume that his readers are well informed about circumstances in Castalia. The very fact that Castalia still exists, despite its perilous state during Knecht's lifetime, is proof in itself that a fruitful interaction took place in that area as well.

All of these factors—the historism of Pater Jacobus and its impact on Knecht's thinking, the three areas of activity and the careful structuring of the novel, the repeated implication that the Castalia of the narrator represents an advance beyond the endangered Castalia of Knecht's lifetime—convince me that the meaning of Knecht's life and defection must be sought in his life, not in his death. To put it most radically, what happens to Knecht after his defection is totally irrelevant as far as the central theme is concerned: the role of spirit in the modern world. That question is answered by the narrator, not by Knecht's death. It is necessary for the area of intellect and spirit to interact fruitfully with the realms of state and religion. In other words, spirit must be given meaning by religion; and it must be given direction by the state (practical life). As far as the fiction of the novel is concerned, the historical processes that bring about this interaction are set in motion before Knecht's death, and their action is inevitable regardless of his own fate. When he departs from Castalia, Knecht has completed his function as an exemplary figure.

[67] GD, VI, 394.

Since his mission to Mariafels and his circular letter to the authorities have activated the gears of history, nothing that he now does will affect Castalia one way or the other. His representative life is over. He is now free to live or to die as an individual.

The Existential Act

Knecht's death is his only act in the entire novel which has no exemplary significance, but a purely personal and existential meaning for him as an individual. It is motivated by his sense of commitment and responsibility: commitment not in a narrow political sense, but with the broader meaning of involvement in the general human condition; and responsibility (Hesse uses the two expressions *mitverantwortlich* and *mitschuldig*) as the explicit opposite of the disengagement traditionally characteristic of Castalia. In his circular letter he singles out this lack of responsibility as one of his principal objections to the aestheticism of Castalia. "The average Castalian may regard the man of the world, the non-scholar, without contempt, without envy, without animosity; but he does not regard him as a brother, he does not see in him his employer; nor does he feel in the least responsible for what happens in the world outside."[68] Knecht's own defection stems from his feeling of responsibility to the world at large. But more specifically: he feels that Castalia failed in its education of Plinio Designori because it did not prepare him adequately to cope with the problems arising from his efforts to bring about an interpenetration of the ideals of Castalia and the world. Instead of dismissing as too impersonal and abstract this responsibility of the entire province to Designori, Knecht decides to take it upon himself. He discards the disengagement of abstrac-

[68] GD, vi, 455.

tion for the responsibility of action. As in the process of awakening, he feels unable to keep himself sufficiently remote from the problem to analyze it intellectually. Instead he plunges in to rectify it by deed.[69]

It is useful to make a distinction between the ideal of service, which has so often been discussed in connection with the novel, and the sense of commitment and responsibility as defined above. Service (*Dienst*) is, of course, an important theme in the novel. But one should keep in mind that service emerged as a theme in *The Journey to the East* and that it is most meaningful within the framework of the aesthetic realm defined in that book and in the early parts of *The Glass Bead Game* before the ideal of Castalia is questioned. As the possibility of interaction between the three powers becomes more and more evident, the narrator uses words for "commitment" and "responsibility" more frequently. Service to the ideal and to the hierarchy is one of the cardinal principles of life in Castalia. While Knecht never forsakes the ideal of spirit consecrated to life, he does, by his defection, reject the tenet of service to the hierarchy. I believe that the shift from "service" to "commitment" characterizes in diction the shift of emphasis that takes place in the course of the novel from detached aestheticism to engagement. It can be easily ascertained that the ideal of "service" occurs more regularly in the introduction, the "Lives," and the first three chapters than it does later as increasing doubts cause Knecht to reexamine his values. During the crucial

[69] In connection with the ending see especially Oskar Seidlin, "Hermann Hesse's *Glasperlenspiel*," *Germanic Review*, 23 (1948), 263-273; Hilde Cohn, "The Symbolic End of Hermann Hesse's *Glasperlenspiel*," *Modern Language Quarterly*, 11 (1950), 347-57; and Kenneth Negus, "On the Death of Joseph Knecht in Hermann Hesse's *Glasperlenspiel*," *Monatshefte*, 53 (1961), 181-89.

years as Magister Ludi when Knecht must serve the very hierarchy whose meaning he seriously questions, the theme of representation, significantly, begins to replace the ideal of absolute service. From service through representation to rejection—that is the development of Knecht's attitude toward the hierarchy of aestheticism. The counterpoint is supplied by his progression from disengagement through interest to commitment to life.

As a sign of his sense of commitment he undertakes the tutelage of Plinio's son Tito. Ironically, this same impulsive sense of "awakening" leads him, on the third morning of his freedom, to his death. For had Knecht, instead of plunging suddenly into the icy lake, paused to consider the situation coolly and rationally, he would never have drowned. Having once committed himself to a course of action instead of reflection, he has no choice. To renege at this point, to disappoint his pupil in this first crucial trial, this first plea for commitment, would mean total failure and would travesty his defection. So Knecht plunges to his death. His unhesitating willingness to commit himself summons up a new sense of responsibility in Tito. "Oh, he thought in horror, now I'm responsible for his death. . . . And as he felt, despite all objections, a sense of guilt in the master's death, he was overcome in a solemn tremor by the premonition that this responsibility would reshape him and his life, requiring far greater things of him than he had previously ever demanded of himself."[70] Hesse himself has interpreted the ending of the novel in a similar way.

"He could have refrained, finely and intelligently, from leaping into the mountain water despite his illness. Yet he does it all the same, because there is in him something

[70] GD, VI, 543.

stronger than intelligence, because he cannot disappoint this boy who is so difficult to win over. And he leaves behind a Tito for whom this sacrificial death of a man vastly superior to him will remain forever an admonition and example, which will teach him more than all the preachments of the wise."[71]

This is almost a recapitulation of the words of the old Magister Musicae that we quoted earlier: "Truth is lived, not taught."

The concluding words of the novel seem clearly to imply a symbolic commitment of the world and state to Castalia, for Tito assumes his responsibility for Knecht's death just as unhesitatingly as Knecht took upon himself the duty of Castalia toward Plinio and the world. Structurally and thematically the novel is closed. It would be pointless for Knecht's life to go on; he could hope to accomplish no more than has been accomplished. By his deeds he has succeeded in bringing about the interaction of Castalia with religion and the state, and he dies at peace with himself. Knecht's defection, of course, does not imply a repudiation of the realm of culture. It is only a rejection of the stage of ineffectual aestheticism to which Castalia had degenerated in the course of its historical development. The Castalia represented by the narrator, as I have argued, is the spiritual realm that Hesse and Knecht envisage: not a realm of abstract aestheticism, but of spirit and intellect committed to the service of mankind.

Hesse has not, of course, written an existentialistic novel in any programmatic sense. Yet I do suggest, at the risk of exaggerating the parallels, that the changes in the theme of the novel during the long years of composition

---

[71] Letter of November, 1947; "Ein Briefwechsel," *Die Neue Rundschau* (1948), 244-45.

mirror in no small measure contemporary developments in the world and in literature. The differences between the beginning and the end of the novel seem to reflect what R. W. B. Lewis has in mind when, distinguishing between the concerns of Proust, Mann, Joyce, and those of the generation that followed, he speaks of an "aesthetic" and of a "human" world.[72] Knecht starts out in an aesthetic world, but he dies because of his commitment to a human world and because of his new sense of an almost existential intersubjectivity.

This shift in emphasis left its mark on the structure of the novel, for despite the external integration of the parts, there remains, as we have noted, a certain internal inconsistency in the role of the narrator and the conception of Castalia. But if we esteem personal integrity more than artistic virtuosity, then we can only conclude that the value of the novel, at least as a human document, is enhanced by these flaws. It is perhaps the final irony of the work that its shift of allegiance away from aestheticism to human commitment is reflected by artistic shortcomings in the form. Because of his intense sensitivity to changes in the world Hesse was able, in his last novel, to achieve a rejuvenation similar to that which produced *Demian*. Here again he has succeeded in anticipating the feelings of a new era, which has little patience with the aesthetic— "calligraphic" is the pejorative expression favored by many postwar writers—literature of the twenties and thirties, and in bridging, in one work, the chasm between generations. To this extent there exists, despite all differences, a remarkable similarity between the first and the last of the major novels—a parallel that lends to Hesse's later career a pattern of consistency and unity. Through the

[72] *The Picaresque Saint*, p. 9.

evolution of themes and the variety of structures there emerges one constant factor in Hesse's work that we must value above all: absolute honesty to himself and to the world, even at the expense of treasured ideals that must be transcended.

PART III. EPILOGUE

Today we all live in despair, all awakened people, and are thus cast between God and Nothingness. Between these poles we breathe, sway, and pendulate. Each day we are tempted to throw away our lives, but we are sustained by that within us which is suprapersonal and supratemporal. So our weakness—without our being heroes for that reason—becomes bravery, and we preserve a little of the faith that has been handed down from the past for those who will come after us.

(Hesse, Letter of 1948)

❧❧❧❧❧❧❧❧❧❧❧❧❧❧❧❧❧❧❧❧❧❧❧❧❧❧❧❧❧❧❧

13

Between Romanticism and Existentialism

THE AMBIGUITY implied in the title of this section is calculated. No one, today, would call Hesse a romantic writer without qualifying the term rigorously.[1] At the same time, while several critics have pointed to existential tendencies in Hesse's work,[2] he is obviously no existentialist in any systematic sense of the word. The only "ism" really applicable to Hesse, as Franz Baumer argued, is individualism or non-conformism. This epilogue is not an attempt to categorize Hesse. It only raises a few questions. Another book would be necessary to answer them.

1

Let us first consider the basic distinction between typological romanticism and historical Romanticism. This is an easy distinction that ordinarily causes no confusion. Typological romanticism, as the term implies, refers to an intrinsic attitude toward life that can be found among certain individuals of every era; only this romanticism, of course, can be compared or contrasted with existentialism. Historical Romanticism designates the general outburst of the romantic temper in Europe between roughly 1770 and 1830, and it includes a whole syndrome

[1] See especially Franz Baumer, *Hermann Hesse* (Berlin, 1959), pp. 76-94; and Eva J. Engel, "Hermann Hesse," in *German Men of Letters*, ed. Alex Natan, vol. II (London, 1963), pp. 249-274.

[2] See Franz Baumer, *Hesse*; Oskar Seidlin, "Hermann Hesse: The Exorcism of the Demon," *Symposium*, 4 (1950), 325-348; and Hans Jaeger, "Heidegger's Existential Philosophy and Modern German Literature," *PMLA*, 67 (1952), esp. pp. 676ff.

of secondary phenomena: a preference for certain literary forms (e.g. the *Märchen*), an interest in "Romantic" times and places (e.g. the Middle Ages, the Orient), and so forth. When Novalis is called a romantic poet, it is true in both senses: historically and typologically. If someone says that Thomas Mann is a romantic writer, then we infer that this is meant only in the typological sense since the secondary phenomena are not pronounced in his novels.

But what do critics imply when they say that Hesse is a romantic writer? I am not convinced that they always have a clear distinction in mind. Hugo Ball, who created the fashion when he called Hesse "the last knight in the glorious cavalcade of Romanticism,"[3] was obviously referring to historical Romanticism: "He is the last in an unbroken line extending from Jean Paul. . . ." Ball is concerned mainly with the secondary characteristics of theme and form that Hesse shares with the poets of Romanticism. Ball, who died in 1927 and thus never read the novels after *The Steppenwolf*, devoted over half of his book to the works preceding *Demian*. He tended quite naturally to see Hesse in the light of historical Romanticism because the earliest collections—*Romantic Songs* (1899), *An Hour beyond Midnight* (1899), *Hermann Lauscher* (1901)—were unabashedly Romantic in nature, setting the tone for most of the works of the next decade. And in his major novels Hesse continued to exploit structures that go back to historical Romanticism, transforming them more or less radically to suit his own purposes. This process was evident in his use of the *Bildungsroman*, the *Bundesroman*, the *Doppelroman*, and the *Märchen*. Ralph Freedman has persuasively demonstrated that Hesse's

[3] Hugo Ball, *Hermann Hesse. Sein Leben und sein Werk*. New edition with supplement by Anni Carlsson (Suhrkamp Verlag, 1947), p. 26.

whole conception of fiction as lyrical is ultimately Romantic.[4] And as far as setting is concerned, Hesse's fondness for the Orient (*Siddhartha*), the Middle Ages (*Narziss and Goldmund*), and the timeless present (*The Journey to the East*) can be called Romantic. Moreover, in his language Hesse remained for the most part a conservative. Even when he discusses problems that are characteristically modern, he does so in the vocabulary of Novalis and Goethe. There is no abrupt break with tradition, but rather an attempt to shape Romantic convention in such a way as to make it an adequate vehicle for the expression of contemporary reality.

To this extent we can surely agree with Hugo Ball. As an advocate of historical Romantic forms in the broadest sense, Hesse is a romantic writer; and precisely this distinguishes him sharply from most major writers of the twentieth century, who rejected the older forms for more experimentally new ones. But this proclivity for the trappings of Romanticism is misleading and has perpetuated, I think, a mistaken conception of Hesse's intent. As André Gide shrewdly remarked, in Hesse's works only the expression is tempered—not the thought.[5] And as soon as we turn from expression to thought, or from structure to theme, we move into the area of typological romanticism, where it is much more questionable to call Hesse romantic. For the rearguard of romanticism tends at many points to blur almost imperceptibly into the vanguard of existentialism.

2

Typologically, romanticism has a place in the genealogy of existential thought that reaches back through the

[4] *The Lyrical Novel* (Princeton, 1963), pp. 42-118.
[5] "Préface au Voyage en Orient de Hermann Hesse," in *Préfaces* (Paris, 1948), p. 184.

nineteenth century to Pascal and St. Augustine. It is thus part of a historical development leading up to the existentialism of our own century, and for this reason scholars have been able to detect certain parallels between the two attitudes. The philosopher Schelling has attracted the attention of modern thinkers because of his existential analysis of human consciousness. Since World War Two Heinrich von Kleist's *Prince of Homburg* has been hailed in France as an existential drama. Similarities have been uncovered between the poet Eichendorff, long regarded as the incarnation of the Romantic spirit, and Kierkegaard, the prophet of existentialism. And sooner or later existentialistic ethics will note an affinity with the doctrines of the Romantic theologian Schleiermacher. There is much in Romanticism that cries for comparison with existentialism. Conversely, critics of existentialism must inevitably take into account various romantic tendencies in their subjects. Thus Iris Murdoch's study of Jean-Paul Sartre (2nd edition, New Haven, 1959) appeared with the subtitle "Romantic Rationalist." Students of Camus must come to terms with his romantic "nostalgia for unity."[6] William Barrett, in his attempt to determine *What is Existentialism* (New York, 1964), even goes so far as to suggest that "Heidegger's philosophy represents the scholasticism, the final anatomy, of the Romantic individual" (page 104).

And immediately we find ourselves stumbling in the academic minefield of definitions. Many years ago Arthur O. Lovejoy despaired of any possibility of discriminating

[6] See Michel Benamou, "Romantic Counterpoint: Nature and Style," *Yale French Studies*, 25 (Spring, 1960; issue devoted to Albert Camus), 44-51. Hazel E. Barnes, *The Literature of Possibility: A Study in Humanistic Existentialism* (Lincoln, Nebraska, 1959), finds it necessary to justify this troublesome aspect of Camus's thought: "We must not classify Camus as pantheist or romantic. There is in his work neither deification nor personalization of nature" (p. 190).

between romanticisms.[7] More recently, in the second edition of *Classic, Romantic and Modern* (New York, 1961), Jacques Barzun showed that the debate is far from settled and assembled an amusing catalogue of contradictory meanings regularly assigned to the term "romantic" both popularly and in scholarly usage. This is worth noting, for whether we like it or not, "romantic" is often used disparagingly by Hesse's detractors. It is not a safe word to use without precise definition. William Barrett, on the other hand, admits candidly that "we become a little embarrassed at the word 'existential' altogether" (page 20). A brief glance at the disputes between Camus and Sartre, between Jaspers and Heidegger, between Christian and Humanistic existentialism, between existentialism and the philosophy of existence, merely verifies the suspicion that existentialism defies definition at least as much as does romanticism. In fact, Maurice Friedman devotes his valuable "critical reader" on *The Worlds of Existentialism* (New York, 1964) to the proposition that existentialism "is not a philosophy but a mood embracing a number of disparate philosophies; the differences among them are more basic than the temper which unites them" (page 3).

Yet without committing ourselves to an absolute definition, we can determine certain typological similarities between Hesse and other writers of the past and present who seem, by common agreement, to represent one or the other attitude. Let us visualize the problem in terms of a sliding scale. Close to one end there is a poet like Novalis, in whom we clearly recognize what might be called the romantic temper. Near the other end stands a writer like Albert Camus, who strikes us, despite his nostalgia for

[7] Arthur O. Lovejoy, "On the Discrimination of Romanticisms," *PMLA*, 39 (1924), 229-53 (reprinted in *Essays in the History of Ideas*, Baltimore, 1948, pp. 228-53).

unity, as representative of something that can be identified
as the existential mood. In the middle, with fingers of
relationship extending in both directions, we find Hesse.
What needs to be determined is this. Which elements of
his thought lean more toward the romantic pole; which
move toward the existential pole; and which remain in
the border area that is common to romanticism and
existentialism alike?

Hesse is largely responsible for confusing the issue.
Whereas he repeatedly documented his love of German
Romanticism and, by implication, of typological romanticism, his utterances on existentialism and existentialistic
writers are negligible. He wrote many essays on Romantic
poets, edited their works, mentioned them often in his
letters and his fiction, and acknowledged his indebtedness
to them gratefully. (It should be noted, however, that
Hesse avoided calling himself a Romantic in any but an
ironic sense.)[8] As far as his attitude toward existentialism
is concerned, we know only that he was acquainted with
Heidegger's system and rejected it at least in part.[9] At
the same time, he was a long-standing admirer of the
existentially oriented philosophy of Martin Buber, whom
he recommended repeatedly for the Nobel Prize. But
Hesse's attitude regarding systems of thought, whether

[8] E.g. *The Nuremberg Journey* (GD, IV, 128-29), in which
Hesse wonders ironically why anyone would attend his lectures:
"No, it can be of no importance whatsoever what such a Romantic
has to say about a trip, and anybody who still might listen to the
clown must do it at the risk that the clown, after the manner of
humorists, will constantly lose sight of his ostensible theme and
must laboriously seek it."

[9] Joseph Mileck, *Hermann Hesse and His Critics*, p. 305, recounts: "When, upon occasion of a visit in Montagnola in the
summer of 1954, conversation turned to Heidegger, Hesse could
only shake his head slowly in an obvious expression of antipathy."
And Franz Baumer, p. 66, cites Hesse's rejection of Heidegger's
"Geworfensein" as a principle of existence.

romantic or existentialistic, is irrelevant for our purposes. We are not trying to prove that Hesse is an existentialist; he isn't. We merely want to determine where he stands in the development from romanticism toward existentialism as literary expression. Most of this must be done by analysis since Hesse has not documented his attitude toward existentialism. But it is worth stressing at the outset that his intellectual background is largely identical with that of modern literary existentialists. Like them, he emerges from the tradition of late nineteenth-century thought in which Nietzsche and Dostoevsky figure so prominently.

Hitherto most critics, following Hesse's own lead, have investigated his position with an eye to the past. Apart from the customary nod in the direction of Thomas Mann, almost no attention has been paid to Hesse's location with regard to his contemporaries and to succeeding generations. But this is precisely what needs to be done. As valuable as it is to ascertain the Romantic elements in Hesse's style, the comparison with writers of the past leads us sometimes to confuse Romanticism with romanticism, to mistake form for content. Although Hesse remained closely linked to historical Romanticism in style, it is only when we compare his thought with that of other contemporaries that we realize how far he is from typological romanticism. To put it in another way: most critics have used the method of intrinsic typification, describing Hesse's thought in his own terms. Now since his terminology stems from Romanticism, this intrinsic typification forces his thought into a preestablished pattern of romanticism. The following discussion will point out a few examples of extrinsic typification: for it is possible to describe Hesse's themes with great precision in the jargon of existentialism. But that is a parlor-game rather than serious criticism. Ultimately extrinsic typification is just as misleading as intrinsic typification. In dealing with a writer who stands between romanticism and existentialism, we can obtain the best results through neutral typification, choosing terms that reveal the similarities and differences between the two attitudes.

I am convinced that it is important to make these distinctions for two reasons. First, it will give us a fairer idea of Hesse's own achievement, which cannot be circumscribed by the word "romantic" alone. Second, it will reveal Hesse's position as a literary mediator. This is important. Despite the conventionally accepted brackets of literary history and despite the fond delusions of youthful literary rebels, literature, like nature, has a way of avoiding leaps. This principle is clearly recognized with regard to literary form. It has been demonstrated over and over again that works which seemed suddenly to spring out of nowhere were in reality the precipitation of a long and slow process of historical maturation. We know this of Joyce's *Ulysses*; we know it of Kafka's novels. No matter how radically new the latest product of the avant-garde may seem to be, we can trace its provenience through a series of less radical forms back to an often surprisingly traditional and familiar source. Thus the absolute poetry of an arch anti-romantic such as Gottfried Benn—if we examine its genealogy back through French symbolism to Baudelaire, Poe, and Novalis—can be seen to have its roots ultimately in the very Romanticism that Benn so vociferously repudiated. But stylistic boldness is no guarantee of radicality of thought. James Joyce was a rather conventional thinker. And Gottfried Benn's blurred and unrealistic notions permitted him to accept many Nazi doctrines more gullibly than those writers he decried as "romantic."[10] Hesse, though more conventional and Romantic in form, was bolder and more realistic in his thinking than many stylistic innovators. It is in a complex development of this sort that we must locate him typologically. No longer romantic and not yet an existentialist, he occupies a transitional position between the two attitudes. This is not, perhaps, a profound conclusion, but it is one often overlooked by critics who tend to confuse form with content or to forget that history has a Janushead, looking not only into the past but also to the future. If Hesse looks to writers of the past like E. T. A. Hoffmann in the form of his works, he faces the future in his thought, anticipating existential thinkers such as Albert Camus.

3

We can begin by singling out several basic experiences that constitute the starting point of existentialism and romanticism alike. When all accepted systems of order break down—religious, political, social, philosophical—reality presents itself to the individual as a fragmented chaos. This is as true of Friedrich Schlegel and Novalis, in whose vocabulary the word "chaos" plays such an important role, as it is of Camus and Sartre, who see life as irrational and meaningless. In the face of this chaos the individual experiences doubt and uncertainty when he attempts to find meaning. Ludwig Tieck, Clemens Brentano, and E. T. A. Hoffmann describe this state of doubt as *Zerrissenheit*; modern existentialists would call it anguish or despair. In his attempt to find meaning, the individual is hurled back upon himself as his sole authority.

[10] I have borrowed this relevant comparison, with which I fully agree, from Franz Baumer, *Hesse*, p. 81.

The search for meaning thus becomes ultimately a quest for identity, whether we call it "the inward way" with Novalis or "ontic transcendence to authentic selfhood" with Karl Jaspers. Finally, this basic subjectivity implies the freedom of the individual to determine his own world. Let us not be misled by terminology. Whether expressed in early nineteenth- or mid-twentieth-century vocabulary, the basic experience of chaos, doubt, subjectivity, and freedom is typologically common to romanticism and existentialism alike.

Thus the characteristic hero of Hesse's novels from *Demian* to *The Glass Bead Game*—the tormented self-seeker—is in himself neither particularly romantic nor existentialistic, for introspection, doubt, and alienation alone are not, as some critics have maintained, romantic qualities *per se*. The determining factor is the response to the basic typological experience. Whereas the romantic temper, in general, proposes a resolution of conflict in the transcendent ideal of organic unity of being,[11] the existential attitude rejects the consolation of any such transcendent belief and concentrates, instead, on the possibility of existence in a meaningless world. We might say, generally, that any novel culminating in the achievement of transcendent harmony is primarily romantic: *Siddhartha* and *Narziss and Goldmund*. Yet precisely these two novels, as we noted, are problematic among Hesse's works. *Siddhartha* required an unusually long period of composition, with frequent interruptions, because Hesse had not himself experienced the inner harmony that he wished to

[11] Students of romanticism will note that I accept, as the most successful and most useful working definition of romanticism, the one advanced in various articles by René Wellek. See, for instance, Wellek's survey of "The Concept of 'Romanticism' in Literary History," *Comparative Literature*, 1 (1949), 1-23 and 147-72.

represent at the end of the book. And *Narziss and Gold-mund*, as a novel, falls apart because the resolution is forced onto a structure that will not bear it.

None of the other novels, however, ends with such clear symbols of transcendent resolution. As a novelist Hesse preferred to deal with the second level in his scale of individuation, and on that level the existential confrontation with reality is more important than ultimate resolution. This is perfectly clear in the case of Harry Haller, who is condemned by his vision of the Immortals to live in this world, and in the case of Joseph Knecht, who rejects the aesthetic ideal in favor of existential commitment to his fellow man. But sometimes the difference is a matter of emphasis rather than a clear-cut distinction. To illustrate what I mean let us reconsider Hesse's conception of magical thinking in the light of romanticism and existentialism.

4

Magical thinking is one of Hesse's themes most frequently singled out as romantic—and for apparently good reasons. In his "Conjectural Biography" of 1924 Hesse specifically mentioned Novalis in connection with his own "magical conception of life." This passage, along with others, suggests the parallel between "magical thinking" and the "magical idealism" that plays a central role in Novalis' thought. The name and the definition are strikingly similar. Hesse defines magical thinking as the ability to exchange inner and outer reality, as the acceptance of the reversibility of nature and spirit. This is precisely the vocabulary and intent of Novalis, for whom "Magic is = the art of using the world of the senses at will." He elaborates: We have two systems of senses that are seemingly quite different but in actuality most closely related. One is the body; the other is the soul or spirit. The former is dependent upon external stimuli: nature or the outer world; while the latter is dependent upon internal stimuli: the spirit or the spirit world. The two systems are connected, usually in such a way that the soul responds to the stimulation of the body. But there is evidence, Novalis continues, that the reverse relationship also obtains, and one soon perceives that the two systems should operate in a reciprocal tension. They should sound together as a chord, and not individually as two separate tones. "In short: both worlds, just like both systems, should constitute a free harmony, not a disharmony or monotony. The transition from monotony to harmony, to be sure, will go through the stage of disharmony—and only at the end will a harmony arise. In the period of magic the body serves the soul or the world of spirits."[12] In still another place Novalis writes: "If you cannot make external objects of your thoughts, then make thoughts of external objects. . . . Both operations are idealistic. He who has both completely in his power is the magical idealist."[13]

In Hesse as in Novalis we note a progression from chaos to a harmony of nature and spirit through a process that is called magical. What would be simpler, in view of Hesse's often professed love for Novalis, than to identify magical thinking with magical idealism? Yet that would be the fallacy of intrinsic typification. Any such direct equation of the two attitudes is misleading because a subtle shift has taken place. In Hesse's thought, though he speaks of nature and spirit, magical thinking is primarily an ethical conception. The definition was developed in the essays of *In Sight of Chaos*, where Hesse was concerned with the reversibility of assumptions concern-

[12] Novalis, *Schriften*, ed. Paul Kluckhohn and Richard Samuel (Leipzig, 1929), II, 336.
[13] *Ibid.*, III, 110.

ing good and evil. Emil Sinclair, Siddhartha, and Harry Haller have this in common: they all learn through symbolic experience that they are capable of affirming wholeheartedly certain areas of life that they had previously rejected because of their source in nature, or the sensual impulses.

When Novalis speaks of nature and spirit he uses the words in the technical sense of Romantic *Naturphilosophie*—that is, ontologically and not ethically. According to Schelling, whom Novalis closely followed, mind is an invisible form of matter while nature is a visible manifestation of spirit. Novalis believed, for instance, that "the physical magus" should be able, through an act of mind, to restore a withered limb, to change the shape of his body, and—eventually—to bring life to the dead. For the theory of the organic unity of being that underlies magical idealism presumes that mind can transform matter in a very literal sense. Novalis intended to symbolize this organic unity in a grand vision at the end of *Heinrich von Ofterdingen*; "People, animals, plants, stones and constellations, flames, sounds, colors must, at the conclusion, act and speak together like One Family or Group, like One Clan." This theme of ontological reunification can be detected at the basis of a simple Romantic fairy tale like Fouqué's *Undine*, in which the water nymph who marries a mortal in order to acquire a soul represents nature striving to be reunited with spirit.

It is not necessary to specify to what extent Hesse shares this belief in the identity of nature and spirit. In some passages (e.g. *At the Spa*) he writes as though he accepted it quite literally. And in any case he uses frequent symbols of ontological unification: in fairy tales like *Pictor's Metamorphoses* and in the visions at the end of *Siddhartha*. But the problem of unity is not at issue here. Modern science and philosophy are predicated to a great extent on the belief in the organic unity of being. One thinks of Einstein's Unified Field Theory, of the inter- action of subject and object in Werner Heisenberg's Principle of Indeterminacy, or of Alfred North White- head's theory of organism (in *Science and the Modern World*). Romantic *Naturphilosophie* was a protest against the materialistic concepts of orthodox scientific theory in the eighteenth and nineteenth century. Unity, which repre- sented the ultimate goal in Romantic philosophy and in Novalis' magical idealism, is accepted as a fact in much modern philosophy and in magical thinking. The emphasis has shifted. Hesse's magical thinking is not primarily ontological, but ethical. The belief in the unity of being, in other words, does not represent a solution to the prob- lems of existence in the world.

In the autobiographical sketch entitled "Childhood of the Magician" this shift in emphasis is made explicit. As a child, Hesse writes, it was his fervent wish to trans- form reality magically; that is, he literally wanted to change the physical reality of objects and, like Novalis, to make thoughts into things. In adult life, however, the magic has been internalized: it is no longer the external world that he desires to transform, but his own inner world. This corresponds to the theory in his essays and to the practice in his novels, where there is no magical transformation of external reality. What Emil Sinclair learns is to reject, in his own mind, the established ethical patterns that govern the outside world. In his thinking he breaks down the barrier between traditional notions of good and evil, determining instead to create a free new ethical code of his own. What we have in Hesse's magical thinking is a Romantic structure of thought, but the elements of the formula have been modified. Magical idealism, on the way to magical thinking, has become immanent and ethical rather than transcendent and ontological. This does not mean, of course, that Novalis was not interested in ethics or that Hesse has no ontological ideas. It does imply, however, that Novalis' magical idealism is primarily ontological, focusing on the achievement of a transcendent unity, while Hesse's magical thinking is primarily ethical, concerned with present reality—a distinct shift in emphasis that signals a difference between the two attitudes.

5

Hesse doubtlessly took over the term "magic" from Novalis. But he outlined his theme of magical thinking in his essays on Dostoevsky. It is symptomatic that both Sartre and Camus use the Russian novelist as the *terminus ab quo* for their ethical considerations. Sartre stated that existentialism began at the moment when Dostoevsky said that God does not exist. And in *The Myth of Sisyphus* Camus elaborates:

" 'Everything is permitted,' exclaims Ivan Karamazov. That, too, smacks of the absurd. But on condition that it not be taken in the vulgar sense. I don't know whether or not it has been sufficiently pointed out that it is not an outburst of relief or of joy, but rather a bitter acknowledgment of a fact. The certainty of a God giving a meaning to life far surpasses in attractiveness the ability to behave badly with impunity. The choice would not be hard to make. But there is no choice, and that is where the bitterness comes in. The absurd does not liberate; it binds."[14]

[14] Quoted from *The Myth of Sisyphus and Other Essays*, trans. from the French by Justin O'Brien (New York, 1959), p. 50.

Confronted with a world in which all established standards have collapsed, existential man realizes with a sudden
surge of despair that he no longer has recourse to any
higher appeal. This means that he is totally free, but it
is what Camus and Sartre call a "dreadful freedom" because man must now assume the responsibility for all of
his actions with no appeal to a supreme authority. There
are no longer guilty men, says Camus, but only responsible
ones. In existential thinking this has several implications.
Unable to stand the anguish of uncertainty, a man may
lapse back into some ready-made pattern of behavior.
Sartre calls it *mauvaise foi* when the individual does not
accept the freedom to become himself, letting himself fall
instead into a stereotype (religious, political, philosophical,
or otherwise) that affords the consolation of ethical justification; and Camus calls it philosophical suicide. Or man
may make a "leap into faith" by creating for himself a
new deity as a transcendent source of appeal.

In the essays of *In Sight of Chaos* Hesse uses a different
vocabulary, but his implications are identical with those
of Sartre and Camus. Like them, he is interested in the
ethical responsibility of the individual who peers into
chaos and assumes "the new, perilous, terrible sanctity"
implied by "the turn away from all established ethics and
morality." In *Demian* he depicts the practice of this
theory. Emil Sinclair's development is characterized by
anguish and doubt. His pendulation, his frantic returns to
the accepted standards of the family and society, his willingness to assume the role of the Prodigal Son, represent
his lapses into a Sartrean "bad faith." His subsequent
attempt to create an external god like Abraxas is an effort
to establish a transcendent authority to whom he can
address his appeal. Abraxas can almost be defined in the
words with which Camus criticizes Karl Jaspers' existen-

tialism. "The absurd becomes god (in the broadest meaning of this word) and the inability to understand becomes the existence that illuminates everything." This is Abraxas —a god conceived to embrace the poles of nature and spirit, good and evil, God and Satan. Ultimately Sinclair rejects the consolation of Abraxas just as he had rejected the "bad faith" of established creeds. When Demian dies and Sinclair is finally strong enough to look into his own heart to find the sole justification of his actions with no recourse to conventional standards or to a deified chaos, he has fully accepted the "dreadful freedom" of the existentialists.

It should be perfectly apparent that magical thinking, though it retains the vocabulary of Novalis, goes far beyond romanticism in any precise sense of the word, approaching in a very significant way the meaning of some existential thinkers. It is not, in other words, an attempt to establish an ontological resolution in the sense of magical idealism; but rather the acceptance of freedom and ethical responsibility in the existential encounter with reality. It can certainly prepare the way, as it does in *Siddhartha*, for symbols of ultimate resolution. But as an attitude it is primarily existential, not romantic. And precisely this shift in thematic emphasis necessitated the transformations of Romantic form that we have noted. We no longer have the unilinear development of the Romantic *Bildungsroman* toward a transcendent ideal of unity, but rather the frantic pendulation arising from the tension between existential freedom and the security of "bad faith" and the "leap into faith."

To analyze Hesse's themes in the light of romanticism reveals their structure and places them in the intellectual tradition of the nineteenth century from which Hesse emerged. But it does violence to the substance of his thought: the analysis of man's existence in the modern world. As existential analysis the works mark an important step forward from romanticism toward—but not necessarily to!—existentialism. And we see in retrospect that the rejection of the aesthetic ideal in *The Glass Bead Game* was actually subtly anticipated by this shift in Hesse's thinking that began as early as 1917.

6

This epilogue is, in part at least, a methodological justification of the preceding chapters. It was our aim to consider Hesse's works inductively, observing how his themes emerged directly from his encounter with reality and how the structures were shaped to express his own unique vision. Avoiding any categorization that might distort the substance of Hesse's thought by putting it into a ready-made framework—which would be a sort of critical *mauvaise foi*—we noted relevant parallels as they suggested themselves. In connection with the structures, examples from historical Romanticism seemed to be most conspicuous and to explain the forms within which Hesse chose to operate. As far as the themes were concerned, the most compelling parallels pointed to other modern writers obsessed, like Hesse, with the existence of man in this world. The example of magical thinking demonstrates how misleading it is to accept Romantic nomenclature as an invitation to label Hesse as a typological romantic.

Hesse's ties to historical Romanticism are much clearer than his position with regard to typological romanticism and existentialism. Whereas the former have been investigated extensively,[15] the latter is still virtually unexplored.

[15] E.g. Kurt Weibel, *Hermann Hesse und die deutsche Romantik* (Winterthur, 1954), which notes scores of superficial parallels without examining the transformation of Romantic elements in Hesse's works. For a critique of Weibel's dissertation as well as

The problems of composition in novels like *Siddhartha* even suggest that we have in Hesse the rather anomalous case of historical Romantic form superimposed upon a substance that is anything but romantic: the form requires a resolution that the author, existentially, is not prepared to achieve. Future studies of Hesse, in any case, should distinguish rigorously between the two meanings of romanticism and avoid the fallacy of intrinsic typification. And account must be taken of Hesse's own pendulation, in his novels, between romantic resolution and existential acceptance of freedom and responsibility in a meaningless world. Ultimately the very rhythm of Hesse's composition reveals his transitional position. Torn between romanticism and existentialism, he strives—in *Siddhartha, Narziss and Goldmund*, and *The Journey to the East*—to create the transcendent ideal of resolution that he rejects in *Demian, The Steppenwolf*, and *The Glass Bead Game*.

Until the relationship between romanticism and existentialism has been more precisely determined, it will be impossible to assign to Hesse a firm place in the development. (And the peculiar ambivalence that we have noted is characteristic, of course, of many other writers of his generation: e.g. Rilke and Hermann Broch.) If we can agree that Hesse is not primarily a "romantic" writer, but located somewhere between the two typological attitudes, then we have made at least a step in the right direction. It is by no means only in magical thinking that this ambiguity is evident. We have already pointed to the structural similarities between *The Steppenwolf* and E. T. A. Hoffmann's *Märchen*-form. Analysis and comparison will show, however, that the novel is equally close in theme

---

further titles of (mostly unpublished) studies see Joseph Mileck, *Hermann Hesse and His Critics*, pp. 100-03 and p. 72.

to Camus' *The Myth of Sisyphus*. In that connection it can be seen that Hesse's conception of humor lies somewhere between Romantic irony, which for Novalis and Friedrich Schlegel is an objective aesthetic attitude, and the more subjective existential awareness of the absurd. We can observe over and over again in Hesse's major themes a reduction of transcendence to immanence, of the ontological to the ethical, of the speculative to the existential. With romantic tools he seeks to analyze the existential encounter with reality. It would detract from the plausibility of the similarities we have noted to press the parallels too far. Hesse has little in common with the elaborate ontology of systematic existentialism. And his novels are by no means "situational" in the sense of the fiction of Sartre and Camus. But the shift in emphasis from romantic resolution to problems of existence in this world is a step in the development of existential thought. And only by taking this existential shift into account can we properly evaluate Hesse's position as a writer.

Is Hesse a typological existentialist with an orientation toward historical Romanticism in vocabulary and form? A romantic existentialist with a proclivity for the past and a nostalgia for unity? Or an existential romantic whose thought has become secularized with the age? If one had asked Hesse these questions, he might have exclaimed, paraphrasing his painter-hero Klingsor, that critics who try to pin down the individual within such rigid categories ought to perish under the wheels of a locomotive—a rather existential attitude toward typification. Or he might have retreated behind the beatific smile of the old Magister Musicae in *The Glass Bead Game*, who is beyond such futile dialectics—which, I suppose, is a romantic gesture.

A writer must ultimately be judged by the totality of his work: by the success with which he achieves the rendition of meaning through form. It makes little difference how we label the meaning and the form as long as the structure is an adequate vehicle for the theme. To determine this aesthetic integration is an act of criticism that must be exercised anew with each writer and with each work. In the analyses of Hesse's major novels, therefore, I indicated my own assessment with no appeal to categorization. I like to think that Hesse would have approved.

Index of Works by Hesse

General Index

Abelard, Peter, 292
Abraxas, as symbol, 26, 109-11, 122, 142, 356-57
Acta Sanctorum, 155
acte gratuit, 21. See also Gide, André.
action-novel, 224, 227
Adorno, Theodor, 191
aestheticism, 48, 50, 83, 271, 275-76, 283, 294, 303, 318; dangers of, 307-08, 322, 333
Agramant, 262
Aktionsroman, see action-novel
Albérès, R.-M., *L'Aventure intellectuelle du XXe siècle*, 16n
Albertus Magnus, 261
allegory, 306; allegorical structure of *Narziss and Goldmund*, 232
Andersch, Alfred, 306
anima, 134-35, 138. See also Jung, Carl Gustav.
apocalyptic novel, 304-05
Aquinas, Thomas, 173, 233, 234
archetypal images, 77, 118, 120; Frau Eva as archetype, 132-38
Arnim, Achim von, *Die Kronenwächter*, 262
art, as mediator between nature and spirit, 246-51; epistemological function of, 248
artist, role of, 249-52
Auerbach, Erich, "Figura," 119
Ausländer, Ninon, *see* Hesse, Ninon
autobiography, in *Steppenwolf*, 178-79; in *Journey to the East*, 261-64
"awakening," 312, 316-17, 322

Bach, J. S., 191, 324
Bachofen, Johann Jakob, 89, 110n, 117, 313, 314; Hesse's attitude toward, 111-13; and symbol of egg, 114-15; *Oknos the Rope-maker*, 112, 279; *Matriarchy*, 112; *Grave Symbolism of the Ancients*, 112
Bahr, Hermann, 18
Ball, Hugo, *Hermann Hesse: Sein Leben und sein Werk*, 125n, 126, 342, 343
Barnes, Hazel E., *The Literature of Possibility*, 344n
Barrett, William, *What is Existentialism*, 344, 345
Barzun, Jacques, *Classic, Romantic and Modern*, 345
Basilius, H. A., 193n
Baudelaire, Charles, 205, 261, 348
Baumer, Franz, *Hermann Hesse*, 341, 346n, 349n
Beissner, Friedrich, *Der Erzähler Franz Kafka*, 79n
Benamou, Michel, 344n
Bengel, Johann Albrecht, 299
Benn, Gottfried, 41, 348
Bernoulli, Carl Albrecht, 110n, 112
Bible, Hesse's use of, *see* Cain, Christ, Jacob, John, Luke, Prodigal Son, Revelations, unrepentant thief, Zion, Daughter of.
Biblical images in *Demian*, 105-06, 126-27
Bildungsroman, 89-91, 94, 200, 286, 287, 327, 342, 357
bird and egg as symbol, *see* egg
Boccaccio, Giovanni, 234
Böcklin, Arnold, 102
Bodmer, Johann Jakob, 258
Bodkin, Maud, *Archetypal Patterns in Poetry*, 118
Bodmer, Hans C., 262